VINO, I LOVE YOU

OSCAR FARINETTI

SHIGERU HAYASHI

VINO,
I LOVE
YOU

The founder of Eataly, Oscar Farinetti,
meets the great Italian wine producers:
Gaja, Antinori, Incisa della Rocchetta,
Gravner, Charrère, Rinaldi, Massa, Allegrini,
Lungarotti, Bucci, Planeta, Rallo

MONDADORI

Translation
Sylvia Adrian Notini

www.librimondadori.it

Printed and bound by Elcograf S.p.A., Cles (Trento), in August 2014
Printed in Italy

To my father, Commander Paolo
of the 21st Matteotti Brigade.
A lot is said about fathers in this
book.
My own passed away in 2009.

To my mother, Bianca.
Not enough is said about mothers
in this book, and that's not right.
My own mother is present in every
page, in every line!

Oscar Farinetti

The Cast

Oscar Farinetti. I Write the Way I Speak
Being from Piedmont is always at my side, so I'll write the way
I speak. In the end that's what I've decided to do. I don't have what
it takes to be a writer, at most I can try to play at being the narrator,
but without expecting to amaze you with an art I don't possess.
There's no point in aping some of my friends who really know how
to write and quite rightly do so for a living. So keep your eye
on the contents because that's what really deserves your attention.
I've met some special people who've said some pretty special things.
I've written them down the way I would have told them. I've asked
Simona to help me, and to do the same. Happy reading.

Shigeru Hayashi. A World Issue
I've been studying Italian wine for the past thirty years. It's a passion
that began when I was living in Italy and that has never left me.
I'm the same age as Oscar, and our parents were born in the same
years. I was born in the country, too, in a small town on the slopes
of Mount Fuji. My father was a farmer. In this book I describe sixty
wines or beers and I talk about them with the producers. I wrote the
things that my eyes, my nose, my palate, my mind and my heart saw
and felt. The eyes, nose, palate, mind and heart of a Japanese person,
for, however much I am familiar with and have studied Italy, I will
always be the son of my land, my culture, my traditions. But Oscar,
who has always loved Japan and our cuisine, wanted just this:
Italian wine told by a Japanese person. After all, Italian wine is
and is destined to increasingly become a world issue.

Simona Milvo. I Came Back Rich
I spent an amazing week traveling around Italy with Oscar
and Shigeru. I had the pleasure of meeting men and women
who have made Italian wine great in the world. Oscar asked me
to help him write their stories. He asked me to use a simple,
dry writing style, which is what I did. He was free to remove some
parts and maybe add other parts later.
After this trip I came back enriched and more aware.
If you feel the same way after you read this book, that will
make me very happy!

Contents

Essential Foreword on Courage

Courage isn't just overcoming your fears, being determined
in the way you do things, willpower. As I see it, courage, unless
it's accompanied by the ability to be analytical, to undertake
a careful study of the scenario and possess a good deal
of stubbornness, then that just isn't courage. Courage, of the
healthy, fruitful kind, has to be accompanied by a predisposition
for doubt. For some time now I've upheld the supremacy of the
importance of doubt over certainty. Nurturing doubts doesn't
mean being insecure, rather, it means being curious, willing
to listen, to understand other people's reasons, to change your
mind if need be. Our courage would be inconclusive without this
kind of sensibility.
Courage requires respect, that is, a sense of civic consciousness,
meaning the willingness to live in harmony with nature and people.
Self-esteem and a sense of respect can, actually they must, coexist.
Courage requires a sense of responsibility: to do and to comply
with what you do. How many times do we hear the words: "I don't
want to take the responsibility…" What an awful thing to say!
A community of people who refuse to be responsible is destined
to failure.
Courage requires friendship. It's easier to find the courage to face
a project when your true friends are there with you.
Courage requires the ability to simplify. To simplify problems,
to prioritize is essential to making sure our courage is headed
in the right direction.

Courage requires goodness: being good means being fair. Because there's what's fair and what's unfair. Wickedness is always unfair. Wickedness, coupled with courage, is the most destructive combination possible in the life of an individual or a community.
Courage requires math: knowing numbers is of fundamental importance. Numbers are absolutely the most accurate indicator of the state of things. It's a good idea to always have numbers in your head that are as correct as possible, to remember them, and to be able to do some simple mental arithmetic.
Courage requires a balanced combination of honesty and cleverness. These two things can coexist, actually, they must coexist.
Courage requires pride: be careful not to confuse pride with self-esteem. Which is important, but without going overboard. I'm talking about taking pride in what you represent, pride for the land, the factory, your job, even if it's humble, your family, homeland, history.
Courage requires optimism: mind you, this doesn't mean thinking that everything's always fine, but that there's a solution to everything. This proactive optimism has to be accompanied by a primordial one, which consists in enjoying what you have.
Courage doesn't necessarily mean growing in quantity. Sometimes you need courage not to grow. But when it comes down to quality, then I have no doubt at all: with quality you always have to grow.
Lastly, courage requires a conscience: the music of the soul that enables you to tell good from bad, that shows you the way forward.

Rules are important, of course, but without a conscience you can't do courageous things.

So courage may seem to be something complicated in that it has to go hand in hand, in my opinion, with all the values I've listed here. But that's not the way it is.

It's easy to learn how to be courageous. The best way to do that is to look at the stories about the courage of ordinary people who became special because they were courageous. As is often the case, experience, that is, observing life, can be of more use than studying. And when it comes to courage this is definitely so. Do you know why? Because courage is infectious.

Don't expect amazing stories and awesome feats. Don't expect grit alone. There's lightness and harmony in the winemakers I've interviewed. There's family, commitment, future, but also the past, love, Italy, the world, politics, and there's hope.

But above all there's courage, trust me.

Let yourself be infected with it and then become infectious yourself.

What our Italy needs is courage.

Vino, I Love You

I hadn't had my fourth birthday yet when my grandfather on my mother's side, Mario, would dip my pacifier into the glass of Barbera that was always sitting before him on the table. Amid my grandmother's cries of protest, he would pop it back into my mouth, curious to see how I would react. My grandmother, many years later, said that my expression was anything but one of disgust.

This was my first encounter with wine.

I was born on September 24, right in the middle of the harvest, in Alba, the capital of the Langhe. It was 1954, an excellent vintage. My father Paolo was from Barbaresco, my mother Bianca from Barolo. My fate was sealed from the day of my birth.

Stories about wine accompanied my teenage years. Magical stories about farmers who struggled against the inclement weather of the postwar years and the infamous diseases that decimated the vines. Stories about producers who were starting to travel around the world, arguments, while holding a drink, about the vocation of the land.

Diano d'Alba is the best for Dolcetto, no it isn't, that part of Como, toward Mango, is better. For Barbera the very best is Govone, you're out of your mind, there's nothing better than Monferrato. The best wines are the ones on the right bank of the Tanaro River, not true, they're not bad on the left bank either. And where do they make the best Barolo? Our elders have always said Serralunga, right, but you should try the one from Monforte. You people don't understand anything, Barolo has to be from Barolo.

I'm not sure when I started drinking wine regularly. When I turned sixteen, every end of summer I'd go and do the grape harvest in Fontanafredda, at 500 lire an hour. In the evenings I'd work bottling and labeling in a small wine cellar in Alba that exported its wine to United Kingdom, which meant another 500 lire for me. I used that money to pay for my dinners with friends who, starting from when I was eighteen, began to mark the most beautiful evenings of my life.

I would have liked to study at Wine Academy, seeing that we have one of the finest right here in Alba. But at the time it seemed too limited, so I chose a classical lyceum instead. Luckily, some of my friends who did go to the Academy were at those dinners, too. Wine was the main subject of discussion, of course after the one that's typical of twenty-year-old males with their hormones out of control. It was the early 1970s and a lot of bad wine was being made at the time. Luckily, there were a few good producers, too. My friends, young wine experts, knew how to make the distinction, and they even taught me, someone who'd studied Greek and Latin.

Che piombe! "Piomba" is a word in Piedmontese dialect that means intoxicated, plastered. But I discovered that the same expression is used in Veneto and Trentino, places where people like to drink. It probably has ancient roots, probably comes from the Romans, who unwittingly contaminated wine with lead, thus leading to the side effects that some say went so far as to cause the Fall of the Empire. Luckily, mine were intoxications brought on by good wine and I survived.

Even back then I wanted to work in the world of wine. Unfortunately, my parents had no land and then chance had it that I ended up in an altogether different place. First the university (never finished) and then off to work with my father, who produced and sold food, but wasn't into wine. He drank very little, hardly anything at all. Lastly, my love for electrical appliances, Unieuro and Trony, a whole different ballgame.

But I never stopped having those dinners with my friends. Always the same friends as before, and always good wine. Actually, as our budgets got larger, the wines we chose improved. Along with Fulvio, Luciano, Michele and Paolo, my childhood friends, came Bruno Fieno, my partner at Unieuro, and Sergio Capaldo, membership card no. 5 at Slowfood, who much more than us had traveled around Italy and the world. We would often go to a different region. There are lots of different vine species in Italy, and lots of good wine, even though each one of us was ready to swear that nothing could beat the Piedmont, although in our hearts we knew that ours was purely the spirit of being tied to our roots.

And beyond Italy there's France and after that the world. That's how we discovered those magnificent Rieslings, not just from France, the Pinot Noirs from Burgundy, those great Spanish red wines. We'd talk about apellations, vocations, traditions. We weren't getting drunk anymore, but we would certainly get up from the table feeling merry. I've always loved wine for this too. It makes me feel happy.

Toward the late 1990s I was already thinking about leaving electronics. I thought I'd given it all I could; I wasn't having fun anymore. I became a partner in my first wine cellar, "Cantine del Castello di Santa Vittoria," Arneis, Barbera and Nebbiolo. That was when I started expressing my own opinion about wine, as a producer.

But it was mostly rubbish. I still hadn't understood that it takes a long time for things to change in wine, that you need harvest after harvest to understand that marvelous and magical balance between the hand of man, the land, the sun, the winds and the seasons. Angelo, the farmer, and Beppe, the wine expert, put up with my ramblings purely out of respect for what I had managed to do in other areas up until then. But the expressions on their faces showed their compassion. When faced with my assertions "next year I want it fresher," "too alcoholic, make it lighter," "make it less sulfurous," and so on, they tried to explain to me that good wine is made in the country, that the processes are slow, that if we really wanted to change the style of our wines we were going to have to start from the work in the vineyard.

But I was in a hurry, like I had been all my life, and I behaved with them the way I would have with my washing machine suppliers, whom I would ask to change the knobs and increase the number of functions.

The Beppe I mentioned before, a wine expert, was Beppe Caviola, a special guy, excellent at whatever he did, whom I was farsighted enough to hire as a consultant from the very start, and who even today takes care of most of my wine cellars. Patiently, he took me by the hand and explained what the world of wine was all about. It was a slower, much slower world.

In 2003 I sold Unieuro and decided that when I grew up (I was a fifty-year-old child) I'd work in the food and wine sector. That was when the Eataly phase of my life began.

In 2004 I bought 50% of Serafini & Vidotto, a cellar with 20 hectares of outstanding Cabernet Sauvignon, Cabernet Franc and Merlot, in Montello, Nervesa della Battaglia, right there, where the Piave River mumured.

Francesco Serafini is an unbelievable person, and not just because he's a fabulous enologist. There aren't many people in the world who know more about vineyards and cellars than he does, and he knows how to put poetry into everything he does. He's taught me a whole bunch of beautiful things about wine. For more than 180 years phylloxera had degenerated the rootstocks on his land, whereas the French ones had found an ideal environment. His wines hold up just fine when compared to great Bordeaux wines, and for the past fifteen years his Rosso dell'Abazia had won all the most cherished prizes. Of course he fines all his wines in barriques.

I'll never forget that day around Easter 2005 when I took Francesco to Langa to meet Bartolo Mascarello in Barolo. Bartolo, who I regret to say is no longer with us, had been a Partisan fighter, and a great friend of my father. He had always made wine in the most traditional way possible in Langa, meaning by this that he fined it in large Slavonian oak barrels. He couldn't understand some of the young producers from Langa who had begun to fine their wines in barriques. That woody taste made him cringe, to the point that he'd even designed a label for his Barolo that read "No Barrique, No Berlusconi," combining his political ideas, which he was always expressing, with his ideas on wine.

You can just imagine Francesco Serafini who, besides the fact that he came from a region sympathetic to the Northern League, also used barriques. He was, to say the least, concerned about how Bartolo would receive him. For the whole trip, along the bends on the way to Barolo, I calmed him down, reassuring him that yes, I was going to introduce him as a producer of great wines, and that in no way would I ever have revealed his "barrique" origins. Naturally, no sooner had I entered the small office where Bartolo received his guests, amid a multitude of books, than I said: "Bartolo, let me introduce you to Francesco Serafini. He makes great wine on the banks of the Piave River, and he only uses barriques!"

Francesco's cheeks turned as red as one of his wines, he shot a glance at me, looked like he was about to faint, but Bartolo, who was instead unshaken, declared: "It's OK to do that there. It's here in Langa that barriques have nothing to do with it. Now we'll get him to taste some real Barolo."

In late 2006 I bought San Romano in Dogliani. A small cellar of Dolcetto. Ten hectares, including something that's really gorgeous: the Vigna del Pilone, the whole crest of a hill, a sort of "panettone" that tops the vineyards of Dogliani with a turret at its very peak. The steeple of a church that's no longer there. Just that tower, called Pilone unsurprisingly, which unmistakably distinguishes the hillside. It was well worth the trip just to see them, those vineyards swaying in the four winds. And when the trip was taken in late August so that you could taste the Dolcetto grapes on the four slopes, and therefore understand the sun's role in how a bunch of grapes ripens, everything had an even fuller meaning.

My friend Giulio Napoli had invited me to Dogliani in the right season. I didn't need much convincing to buy the winery that owned that hill. Giulio is a top-notch industrialist. He'd started making wine out of passion, but by then he'd grown tired of being a farmer. I wondered if that might happen to me, too, but I answered myself no. No, winemaking would be one of the main reasons for living for the rest of my days.

But the Barolo was still missing, the king of wines around here, the wine I liked the most, the wine of the world. The one Pavese had written about: "Barolo is the wine you drink when you want to make love in the winter days, but only women understand such things." I wouldn't have known how to add Pavese's poetry to it, but seeing that I had decided to turn wine into my *raison d'être*, this wasn't going to happen without Barolo.

In October 2007 my mother called: "Your father wants to talk to you." When my father had my mother call me it meant it was something very important, it was a way of saying, "come right away, it's serious." Of course I hurried right over. He was holding a copy of *La Stampa*. "Read here, Monte dei Paschi is buying Antonveneta. It's decided to sell all its non-strategic properties. One of these is Fontanafredda. Don't let it slip away."

Don't let it slip away, don't let it slip away: those words kept buzzing in my brain all night long. When my father said I should do something, that something had to be done. He was Commander Paolo, ever since the years of Partisan struggle he was accustomed to giving orders, although he always did so kindly.

The fact of the matter is that I was busy at the time making a deal to buy Borgogno, in Barolo. A historic wine cellar, dated to 1761. A sort of monument to Barolo, with 22 hectares spread across hillsides with legendary names like Cannubi and Liste, a cellar measuring more than 5,000 square meters, built in 1761, as I said before, in the heart of the town. Reposing in the dark, tenuous moistness of its bowels were more than 50,000 bottles of historic Barolo from the harvests between 1961 and 1990.

In comparison, Fontanafredda, dated to 1858, was like a young girl. And what a girl at that! One hundred twenty-two hectares arranged like a natural amphitheater unequaled in the world. A whole village built by Victor Emmanuel II, three years before the Unification of Italy, to consecrate a great love story.

Fontanafredda is the child born from a love story. Between the king who united Italy and the real woman of his life, his lover, known as "la Bella Rosina." Rosa Vercellana had come to live there one summer with her two children, Emanuele Alberto and Maria Vittoria, the children of a king, who would never become prince and princess, however, at the very most counts, the Counts of Mirafiore.

As he was growing up, Emanuele Alberto had fallen in love with wine, and in 1878, after traveling to Bordeaux, Reims and Burgundy to learn how to make good wine, he turned Fontanafredda into a winery. His father, the king, had died that very year. His wines, labeled "Casa Emanuele di Mirafiore," soon become famous across the world. Nowadays we can safely say that Emanuele Alberto played a key role in the birth of Barolo and its worldwide popularity. He was a good man, he loved his farmers, he founded the Cral, a children's nursery, and he built both a church and school. In those days there were 250 people living in Fontanafredda, a happy oasis in the heart of the Langhe where everything fit together like clockwork. Good wine, country life without too many trials and tribulations, good salaries, children playing, women cooking and the everyday life of a peaceful community.

But sometimes good things are short-lived. In 1894, at the age of forty-three, Emanuele Alberto died of an unknown disease. He was succeeded by his son Gastone, who was as generous as his father, but evidently not as talented, and also less fortunate. In the early part of the twentieth century phylloxera attacked the grapevines and ravaged them all. In 1929 the Great Depression swept across all the markets. Gastone went to the wall, the legendary Casa di Emanuele di Mirafiore, founded by the King of Italy Victor Emmanuel II, in the hamlet of Fontanafredda di Serralunga d'Alba, was bankrupt.

Along came Monte dei Paschi, the most powerful bank at the time, and in 1931 it bought it up. The entire property, 140,000 square meters of cellars, royal palaces and houses. One hundred twenty-two hectares, including the legendary Vigna La Rosa and Vigna Lazzarito, in Serralunga d'Alba, plus four in Barolo, on the hill called Paiagallo, the natural continuation of the Cannubi. It bought up everything except for the label.

That label, Mirafiore, was much too important for Gancia, the richest sparkling-wine family of Canelli, to let it slip away. They also wanted to sell their still wines, and that label was the strongest one around. At the bankruptcy auction, the Gancias went beyond every reasonable expectation, and for 600,000 lire, an exorbitant figure for those days, they bought the Mirafiore label. Monte dei Paschi invented the Fontanafredda label, based on the geographical indication for the site, but for the next seventy-six years it tried to buy the historic label back from the Gancias, without ever succeeding in doing so.

In December 2007, along with my partner at Eataly, Luca Baffigo, I started negotiating with Monte dei Paschi. In my mind I kept hearing my father's words, "Don't let it slip away." After a few months of shilly-shallying we finally reached a conclusion. Incredible, there I was, the chief executive officer of Fontanafredda, the same cellar where thirty-eight years before, as a working student, I would harvest grapes for 500 lire an hour. But this time the pay was zero, we needed to save, deal with the debts we'd had to make to be able to buy it. Soon after we also bought the Mirafiore label, having finally convinced the Gancias to sell it to us.

But I refused to give up on Borgogno. I knew it meant making sacrifices, but when was I ever going to have another opportunity like this one in Langa? Around here no one ever sells anything.

Practically at the same time as Fontanafredda I also bought the Giacomo Borgogno and sons' Barolo wine cellar. Hoping all the time that I hadn't bitten off more than I could chew. I asked Piero Bagnasco, who's been working with me for more than thirty years, to take care of it. That way I wouldn't lose any sleep over it.

You might say that 2008 was the year of my first complete harvest as a wine producer.

In Barolo, the Boschis family, formerly the owners of Borgogno, promised me they'd continue to work there for the harvests of 2008 and 2009. My son Andrea, the youngest of the three, had just finished Wine Academy and went to work with them, a very useful experience for his future.

At least I'd managed to convince him to go to Wine Academy. And Graziella, my wife, had given me a hand. For the other two kids instead it had been nothing doing. Francesco, our eldest, studied at a classical lyceum, followed by a degree in Media Studies. Nicola studied at a scientific lyceum and then majored in Political Science. Now both of them are CEOs at Eataly, along with Luca Baffigo, our young partner right from the outset. Andrea instead makes wine, thanks to those two blessed harvests.

In Fontanafredda I found an old high school friend, Gian Minetti, doing a fine job as the general manager, and three great guys managing three key departments: Alberto Grasso head of agriculture, Danilo Drocco head of the cellar, and Roberto Bruno head of sales. And then I found another 120 people between the country, cellar, plant and offices, all of whom were really attached to the company. I confirmed all of them in one fell swoop and we got down to work.

Keeping in mind all the stupid things that were said and sometimes done in my first cellars, this time I did a lot of listening, limiting myself to describing to them, as poetically as I could, what I imagined the future of wine to be. I had recently reread *The Little Prince*, "If I need to tell you how to build a ship I'm not going to tell you where to get the planks and how to bend them, I'm going to tell you how beautiful and exciting it is to sail." Those may not have been the exact words, but that was more or less the meaning and it got the idea across.

Fontanafredda was already producing good, really good wine. It couldn't have been any other way with those vineyards. But it still seemed like we were the only ones who knew the wine was that good. To my mind, the previous management, which had lasted about seventy-six years, had simply forgotten to say so.

Roberto and I would take care of that.

Alberto and Danilo were supposed to work on creating a specific identity for the style of Fontanafredda wine. There was only one area which we had to insist on: cleanliness. We were lucky enough to own this closed-off amphitheater of vineyards which could count on the fact that it would stay uncontaminated. Our job was to get rid of chemical fertilizers and weed killers, and place sex dissuading agents for the parasites in between the rows. We were going to stop using industrial yeast and start producing endogenous yeast from our Vigna Lazzarito. We were going to put a phenomenal stop, in the cellar, to the use of sulfites. In other words, we were going to make clean wine, the way it used to be, but good, the way it is now, actually better. In short, more genuine.

I can still remember that day in 2008 when we gave our project a name: "Riserva Bionaturale di Fontanafredda." Together we decided that once we had achieved our goal we would call our wine "Vino Libero," i.e. Free Wine.

Being the son of a Partisan can come in handy sometimes. Freedom is the key value my father fought for. Freedom is the absolute value of life. Why not seek it out in every field, including the products that we create over the course of our lives?

Freedom from chemical fertilizers, freedom from weed killers, freedom from sulfites. Our wine was going to be free. And the value of freedom didn't end there. Freedom from polluting packaging, freedom from medieval distribution systems, freedom from fads, exorbitant prices, excessive sensory testing. The future for me was and still is Free Wine.

We thought that five years was the right amount of time to complete the project. It meant five years of hard work up ahead, but the goals were so beautiful we never felt weary.

It was also a way for me to speed things up and in some ways rebel against this atmosphere of slowness that, albeit indispensable, is sometimes excessive in the world of wine.

I had just finished reading the Baroness de Rothschild's book: "Winemaking is really quite a simple business... only the first 200 years are difficult." I had in the past few days received the blessing of an important winemaker from Langa: "I've had fifty-six harvests, you'll see that after the twenty-fifth you'll start to get it right." What encouragement! I was fifty-four years old at the time! Words like that make you want to quit right there on the spot or else rebel. The idea of Free Wine was my first way of rebelling. As I said before, having a Partisan for a father helps.

Five years have gone by since then, five harvests. The Riserva Bionaturale di Fontanafredda sparkles in the sun, just as it does in the fog, of Serralunga. Each week thousands of people visit the vineyards and the Bosco dei Pensieri. The Free Wine project is in full swing. We've given it our all and the results are plain for all to see. We also have two new CEOs, Roberto Bruno, forty-six years of age, twenty-two of which at Fontanafredda (continuity), and Andrea Macchione, thirty-eight, a new graft of energy (innovation). I just love apparent contradictions. I'm the company president, having the time of my life sailing in between continuity and innovation. The less I talk the better it is.

In 2009, along with my partners and friends at Eataly, we bought 33.3% of Monterossa in Franciacorta, and in 2010, 50% of Le Vigne di Zamò on the eastern hillsides of Friuli. Great wines, but it was worth it just to get to know Emanuele Rabotti and Pierluigi Zamò. Now we all go on vacation together in August, to the Côte d'Azur. Beautiful people make beautiful wine.

Nor did we let a small cellar in La Morra get away in those years either: 9 hectares of Nebbiolo for Barolo, Dolcetto and Barbera grown organically. Together with Piero Bagnasco we bought 80%, with 20% held onto by the founder, Carlo Cavagnero, who's still managing, being the farsighted farmer that he is, the Agricola Brandini with an iron-clad organic regime and excellent results.

And here we are today. Included in the whole property and stakeholdings, we have eight cellars, which are entirely independent as concerns the cultivation, production and the style of the wines, but with all the right synergies in terms of the search for "clean" quality and commercialization. I'm not going to give you all the numbers, except one, the one that's closest to my heart. There are three hundred people at work here, and they all seem happy to be doing so.

In 2010, for the opening of Eataly in New York, I sold my whole stakeholding in Eataly to my sons. I also stepped down as CEO, leaving the running of Eataly to Francesco and Nicola. I decided to deal exclusively with the wine. That way I'm also complying with the U.S. law that prohibits someone who sells wine in the United States from also owning it.

In April 2013 *Wine Spectator* dedicated its cover to me. Angelo Gaja wrote to me to say: "Congratulations. It took me fifty years to end up on that cover." He will always be a legend to me. I will never stop thanking him for having welcomed me into the world of wine with a smile and a frank "break a leg," without ever throwing his multitude of harvests in my face.

The truth of the matter is that they published that cover more for Eataly than for my wines. However, if you look through the magazine you can read that Vigna La Rosa 2008 Fontanafredda (my first year of full harvest) earned ninety-five points and cost less than 100 dollars, an unquestionably low price in America for a great Barolo. A great satisfaction, and you have no idea what Cannubi 2008 from Borgogno is going to be like, which is still in the cellar and will be on the market in 2014. My son Andrea produced it, and without me having to breathe down his neck too much of the time.

"There's something that joins the earth and the sky, fear and hope, victory and defeat. There's something that joins man to his life, science with conscience, trust with goodness. There's something that joins pride with irony, authority with informality, honesty with shrewdness. It's wine. Wine is vine, vine is life. Getting up early in the morning, throwing the window wide open, gazing at the sky and wondering what your wine will be like. I love wine."

I wrote these words on December 8, 2012, while I was sipping some Già 2012. Già, which means "already" in Italy, is a wine that was born right inside my head three years ago. I wanted a wine that was already a wine a few months after the harvest, but not a new wine. This was the only name for it. Già is the synthesis of the three main vinestocks that make up the Piedmont region: Dolcetto, Barbera and Nebbiolo. A fresh wine, with a low alcohol content. You can smell the fragrance of the must, the cellar during harvest-time, and you can taste an explosion of fresh fruit, at the peak of its youthful flavor.

After three years of attempts that weren't too bad, but that didn't meet my expectations, finally, the 2012 vintage was perfect, exactly as I had imagined it to be. On top of that, Danilo Drocco had made it for me without added sulfites. Zero, that's right, none at all. Unbelievable.

I started thinking about the magical relationship between expectations and the end results. I thought about people who are far more important than me in the world of wine, about all the years they spent living between their expectations and the final results, doing everything they possibly needed to so that they could strike this balance. I thought about all the harvests that marked their lives and how much they had learned from their harvests. I thought about how the experiences they had had in the multitude of their harvests had affected them, turning them into masters of life, as well as masters of wine. I thought about the values that these people put into their wines. I thought about how they were great sophisticators, marvelous sophisticators, after all, because they knew how to put so much more, besides the grapes, into their wine. They put themselves into it.

I thought about how in this rather bedraggled Italy, these people's values could help us if we wanted to try to get it back into shape.

So I took a piece of paper and wrote down twelve names. I would go and see them and ask them to tell me about certain things. And I was going to write these things down, and turn them into a book. And that's how I got the idea for *Vino, I Love You.*

In my forty years as a wine drinker and thirteen as a producer I have had the opportunity to meet lots of beautiful people in the world of wine. To be honest, there were lots more people who deserved a visit and an interview. But I couldn't have met more than I did. I was given a week to travel up and down Italy. Twelve visits were all I could manage.

So that's when I got the idea of taking with us four wines made by other "sophisticator" producers, that way we'd be able to talk about them, too, as we tasted their gems. In the end we would have drunk five wines together, the fifth one chosen by the interviewee and taken directly from the cellar.

At this point, I needed a formidable palate that, unfortunately, despite my decades of training, I do not possess. This is something that really pisses me off. I study, give it my all, force myself get the taste buds ready, widen my nostrils, but nothing doing. My capacity for tasting is fairly good, but no way near great.

A great palate is something you're born with. And the greatest palate I know was born on the slopes of Mount Fuji, in Japan, right smack in the middle of the countryside, 150 kilometers from Tokyo, the same year I was born, 1954.

His name is Shigeru Hayashi, and he is a connoisseur of Italian wine like few Italians are. Shigeru is now the president of Eataly Japan; obviously I would never have let him get away. I met him nine years ago when he was an Italian wine consultant in Japan, and I asked him to help me sell more. Over these nine years we've become friends, and he's helped me to understand Japan.

To me he *is* Japan. He's a combination of everything I love about Japan: civic consciousness, a good education, he's always on time, he's precise, he has a sense of duty, respect for others, respect for raw materials, he's curious, he wants to learn and develop. But also of Japan's faults, which I'm not going to list here because they're so few in comparison. I'll just mention one, the most obvious: not much of a sense of irony. But I have to admit that, now that he's spending so much time with me, Shigeru is bashfully beginning to make some witty remarks.

So in April 2013, I, Shigeru and Simona Milvo, my trusted and excellent press agent, set off to travel around Italy, from Valle d'Aosta to Sicily. Twelve amazing encounters, the unforgettable experience of a lifetime, that made us come back richer and braver. That's why we chose to call the project *Stories about Courage* as well. Shigeru tasted the wines along with the interviewee, while I interrupted their dialogues on wine with questions and comments that apparently had nothing to do with it. Family, love, politics, hopes, visions, Italy, world, in other words, life. Simona recorded everything and wrote. She even took the pictures.

In Valle d'Aosta Costantino Charrère, a gently rigorous man, much like the mountains there, took us to heaven so that we could taste the wine and chat at the same time. In Piedmont Angelo Gaja, a man who stands for quality, charmed us by telling us about the relationship with his father and his daughters. With Beppe Rinaldi, whom everybody calls Citrico, we talked about tradition and politics, conservation and revolution. Walter Massa called his friends over to cook for us and accompanied us in "balancing point above the madness." In Veneto Marilisa Allegrini, who spends six months a year selling wine abroad, told us about the loves of her life, which of course all come after Amarone. In Friuli, on the border with Slovenia, Josko Gravner took us by the hand to the essence of truth: real wines and real people. In Tuscany Piero Antinori, in his gorgeous new cellar, told us about how can you go from 50 to 2,000 hectares while still having fun and thinking about what you want to be when you grow up. His cousin Niccolò Incisa della Rocchetta moved us with his stories, with tears in his eyes, about Ribot, the horse of all horses... and we thought we were going to talk about Sassicaia. In Umbria, Teresa Severini and Chiara Lungarotti, two sisters, made us understand just how important complementariness is to success. In the Marches Professor Ampelio Bucci magically proved to be as soft as the hillsides of his landscapes. In Sicily José Rallo sang inside her *barricaia*, giving us goose bumps. While Francesca and Alessio Planeta, however young they may be, showed us how you can have your ancestors' harvests in your blood.

We start out on the next pages, in geographical order, starting from the northwest.

We hope you have fun too. Happy reading and... make sure you have a good glass, of wine, of course, sitting in front of you.

We're off
From Wednesday, April 10, to Tuesday, April 16, 2013

"It's always the three of us, three outlaws and three donkeys," were the words Domenico Modugno sang, and there are three of us this time, too. Outlaws for sure: lighthearted, ironic, cheerful and optimistic (where I come from, we use the word "brigante," which means "outlaw," to describe a child who is rambunctious), but "donkeys" too, that is, three people who don't know anything about the worlds we're about to observe from close up. And I'm also talking about Shigeru, who may know everything about Italian wines, but certainly can't imagine just how complicated and exciting the little big world of Italian family-run businesses is. He's going to be dumbfounded for sure. Later on he'll use the word "lightningstruck." I had to explain to him that the word he was probably looking for was "thunderstruck." The first encounter is about to start, and it will be music, a symphony. I, a thoroughbred native of the Langhe on both my mother's and father's side, invented Eataly and am taking it all around the world. I'm also, literally this time, taking my two companions on this adventure around the world. We've got 2,000 kilometers to travel. I'm driving the car we're using to get around and do our interview tour. Simona Milvo, 50% a native of the Langhe on her father's side, at my side from the day Eataly opened, is my press agent, but also the playful reference for all the schoolchildren who come to Eataly Lingotto to learn about food. Two jobs is par for the course with us. She has big blue eyes that always have a look poised somewhere between irony and wonder. Shigeru Hayashi wards off any accusations of our being provincial, he's 100% Japanese. I want to talk to you about him with great fondness and admiration. These days he'll always be there along with the winemakers, but you'll never hear him say anything except to comment on the wines. Imagine him busy, totally focused, sniffing, one nostril at a time, tasting, taking notes without ever slurping the wine. He swishes it around inside his mouth with his eyes closed and making sinister noises, and then he spits it out. Sheer torture for me! He's my age, but he looks ten years younger, damn the Japanese, they never seem to get old! He's small and his hair is a bit disheveled, with very attentive dark eyes, a slight frown, and always very focused. He keeps his lips closed tight, and you keep expecting him to stick his tongue out between his teeth, they way children do. Simona and I poke fun at his pronunciation, but we're really just envious, because we only wish we knew Japanese the way he knows Italian. Shigeru has a real command of Italian, even if he never uses possessive pronouns, "I like you wine!" Simona, Oscar, Shigeru: SOS! Could this be a tell-tale sign for our hosts?

Les Crêtes: Costantino Charrère
The "Rich" Son of a Poor Culture

Interview in Heaven

Just past Aosta, heading toward Mont Blanc, we reach Aymavilles. With a population of just 2,000 the town is located right at the entrance to Val di Cogne. It's like being in the mountains, but the altitude is 640 meters a.s.l., no more, no less than that of Belvedere Langa and Paroldo, in Alta Langa. The landscape is different here. If you look up, on three sides you can see Italy's tallest mountains, snow-capped all year round. To the right the Monte Rosa massif, which I am especially fond of, and before you to the left that of Mont Blanc. There's a hint of spring in the air, the sky is bright blue and I feel so lucky to be here!

Oscar "Shigeru, don't tell me Mount Fuji's better than this!"

Actually, I only say this to tease him, to hear what he has to say because I know he might even amaze me.

Shigeru "Yes, Mount Fuji isn't as tall, but it's a volcano, it has fire inside. Within fifty years we'll be drawing from it all the energy we need to become powerful again."

Touché, sweet utopia is always welcome.

We meet Costantino Charrère in the town center and the first thing he says is: "Do you want to come with me? I'm going to take you to a tasting in heaven!"

Oscar "Yes, go for it! Wow, this is a good way to start!"

Costantino turns out to be very determined, like the mountains that have surrounded him all his life. He has sharp features, a hook nose, a feisty chin, a deep look in his eyes and he's lanky. He'll tell us how he's always been very athletic, but now his body unquestionably also reflects his moral rectitude and his inner strength. These are my first impressions and I'll soon find out how right I am.

The first thing we do is go over to the winery because he's eager to introduce us to his daughters. He's enthusiastic and spontaneous as he talks to us, wasting no time, in the car, up the stairs, as we go into the offices. And he's never breathless.

Costantino "I live in the hamlet of Moulin, where my family settled in the nineteenth century when it came here from Alta Savoia. The house I'm still living in today is the place where our first walnut oil mill was located, and after that where wheat and rye were ground."

He introduces us to Elena and Eleonora right away. Elena was born in 1977, she has a Law degree and takes care of sales, while Eleonora, who was born in 1980, is an agronomist and sees to the wine cellar. She's five months pregnant and will make Costantino a grandfather for the first time.

Oscar "Do you already know if it's going to be a boy?"

Elena, future aunt, who's always the quickest to answer, says: "Yes, and his grandfather is on top of the world about it."

Costantino "That's right, because until now I've been blessed among women."

Elena "Not true, you always say you're resigned to being among women."

Oscar "Are both of you married?"

Elena "No, neither of us is married. We're both engaged."

Costantino "Eleonora is the first to set an example but Elena promised me she'll do the same."

Oscar "And will she have a boy, too?"

Costantino "Well, of course! After all the trouble I've gone to putting this thing together."

Oscar "Do you like their fiancés? Are they *muntagnin*, mountain folk, too?"

Costantino "One of them is Valdostano. The other one is Calabrese, but he was born and raised here."

Costantino's last words make everyone laugh. The tone here is one of irony and amiable joking all around. Two well-mannered, sensitive women like Elena and Eleonora could never be disrespectful to their father. The feeling I have is of finding myself in a family where everyone loves everyone else. I'll have a chance to see that I'm right. To me, this is already worth the trip, just like—I realize I'm not being modest here—the reading that will follow will be worth your while. After all, the value of this book lies first of all in learning some true stories about all sorts of humanity, and to be inspired by them so that we can improve ourselves. To rouse courage.

Oscar "Is your wife Valdostana, too?"

Costantino "No, she's from San Marzano Oliveto, in the province of Asti. Ours was an 'Isefino' love, meaning that we met at ISEF. We're both former phys ed teachers."

Oscar "Ladies, how are things going in the business? How are sales?" Elena is always the more exuberant of the two, but Eleonora follows right behind and they say the same thing. "Good, in spite of this moment of crisis."

Oscar "What about abroad? What's the percentage of sales outside of Italy?"

Elena (or Eleonora, which is actually the same thing): "30%."

Oscar "The future for us means our sales growing abroad. Every morning when you wake up remember this number: 0.83. The percentage of Italians in the world is a mere 0.83%! There's 99.17% out there waiting for us, people who want to eat and drink Italian. And if you keep thinking this way there will still be a lot to do for your children and for your children's children."

Elena "We make 200,000 bottles a year and we sell them all. We want to keep on positioning our products in the right market."

Oscar "Of course, right!"

I think Les Crêtes wines aren't cheap. But you can tell the two women are ambitious, and that they'll continue to grow.

Before saying goodbye to Elena and Eleonora and going up to "heaven," Costantino, born in 1947, shows us a picture of his parents, his grandparents, his great-grandparents. They were in the food farming business, producing walnut oil and cider. The family has only been making wine for three generations, so to speak. And while walking over to the car that's going to take us to "heaven" Costantino tells us a story about ladybugs. They were hunted for in the mountain meadows and then released in the vineyards, where they did their good deed of eating the mites that are harmful to grapes. A miracle of conservation of the biodiversity and of the natural cycle in nature, just slightly poetically prodded along by human intervention: the gathering of ladybugs. If someone like Fabrizio De André had thought of it he would have at the very least written a song about it. Ladybugs prefer to stay in places that are healthy.

Heaven can always wait. This is why Costantino, who moves about with the confidence of the perfect host, takes us to see the company's production area, recently completed with a new underground *barriquerie*, a place he calls the "emotional" tasting room that's still being built and the "wine refuge" where they will perform "proactive culture," a way of bringing wine back to the cultural dimension of being consumed on a daily basis. Costantino's company currently makes 50% white wine and 50% red wine.

Costantino "Now I'll take you to a place where you can understand what I mean by 'emotional' tasting. You don't just drink wine there—you also drink in the landscape and the apellation where the wine was born. That way the taste-smell sensation will be impressed in your mind forever. The wine takes you by the hand, it takes you inside its apellation and you go on a fantastic trip."

We're speechless. Shigeru ekes out a bashful "thank you."

Outside the cellar we're almost blinded by the incredible daylight. And then we see more mountains, on all sides. Costantino, when he leaves the house in the morning, has an amazing view. A person with the right mind and the right heart, in a place like this, simply has to make special wine.

Constantino keeps telling us stories. He never stops. His way of talking is almost musical because his words chase after each other like the notes on a music sheet. He's playing his most beautiful symphony for us, which is the story of his life, and he does so while taking us to the highest spot aesthetically speaking: the hill of Côteau La Tour, truly a masterpiece of nature. We are in the very midst of his vineyards, between the endless rows. The car can hardly get through but Costantino drives skillfully and never stops talking. While Shigeru and Simona are speechless as they see where he wants to take us, "yes, let's go up to the top," I remind him to drive carefully. "Has your car ever skidded up here?" and I look at Shigeru to see if he's doing anything to ward of bad luck. An Italian would have, but not him. That's another reason why I like the Japanese. Because they trust others.

And here we are at the top of "heaven." The grapes on this hill have a year-round view of ice, not a bad view at all. If it's true that the sea brings iodine and saltiness, then ice must be of some good, too. The place for our tasting is on the top floor of the medieval tower that overlooks the hill, symbolizing this territory. A watchtower of the ancient Via Francigena that from Augusta Praetoria, Aosta, wove its way to France. Today the watchtower is a small, self-contained guest house, Spartan but cozy, with beds, a wood stove, bathroom and on the first floor a round room surrounded by windows, in which to "savor" the landscape. We're all speechless. As we take out our four bottles, and Costantino adds his, we make ourselves at home. Shigeru sees to the bottles, glasses and, armed with corkscrew, he gets down to work. I never stop asking questions and Costantino never stops answering them. We just keep on talking in a flow of words with no interruptions.

Through Italian Wine I Represented an Alternative to the Class Struggle

Oscar "Why do you make wine?"

Costantino "I make wine because I decided to go back to the values that are a part of the Valle d'Aosta and our mountain community. I picked up on the subliminal messages that my father conveyed to me over the years, and that then emerged little by little. I went to school outside the Valle d'Aosta all the way through to the university, and I suffered terribly being so far away from this land. Paradoxically, however, although being far away made me suffer, it also made me more open to the rest of the world. I remember that when I was at boarding school the soccer matches were Valle d'Aosta against everyone else. In the boarding schools I went to only a few of us were Valdostani, but we were so attached to our land that we wanted to represent it at all costs, even when it meant there would be fewer of us on the team."

Oscar "Did you make friends?"

Costantino "Yes, tons!"

Oscar "You're an outgoing person, you're not what they call a *muntagnin*, reserved."

Costantino "I think I'm a *muntagnin* and an introvert, too, but I'm also very inquisitive, and this has allowed me to open up to the world and to people. In the 1980s I'd try to make some sales with our Vin de La Sabla. In Verona I met Romano Dal Forno; he had calloused, rough hands like mine. He with his Amarone and me with my wines that were unheard of at the time. We were enterprising and eager to try new paths."

Costantino continues to speak without ever stopping, like a sequence of endless musical notes. My job is to interrupt him abruptly every now and then, forcing him to change the rhythm and the melody.

Oscar "Did you get along with your father?"

Costantino "No way!"

Oscar "Why not?"

Costantino "Because we had very different personalities and besides that, from the ages of twenty to thirty-five I was a skiing instructor, I became a national coordinator for ski instructor courses, so my projection toward the outside world grew even stronger."

Oscar "You've always been good at representing other people. I'll bet you were class rep when you were in elementary school."

Costantino "I can't remember, but I've always been inclined to protecting people who are weaker or different. I've never taken the easy road. On the other hand, here in Valle d'Aosta there aren't many easy roads. That's why I've always felt I should represent the difficulties experienced by the people who live in my territory. I feel like a man of the borderlands, I live somewhere between Savoia and Vallese, and was elected president of the independent winemakers' association (FIVI) precisely because I stood for an alternative to the class struggle of Italian wine: Piedmont against Veneto, or Piedmont and Veneto against Tuscany, or Tuscany against everybody else. There are lots of winemakers who act like ostriches, sticking their heads in the sand, when instead, the right thing would be to see what others are doing in order to improve yourself. This is my criticism of my own category, first of all, and then of Italians in general. We don't know how to form a network. FIVI, which was started up in 2008 in Montepellier from a wonderful idea that Carlin Petrini had, could have become one big family. Instead, there are 700 of us, but there could be many many more members, and we're finding it hard to grow any further. This is my second tenure as president and I'm going to work really hard until 2014, but at that point I'll hand over the baton. In France, a similar organization has more than 4,000 members. In any case, we're making a qualified critical and constructive contribution to the world of Italian and European wine."

Oscar "My father taught me to dedicate lots of time to the hard things, because others always give up before, but also not to waste time on things that are impossible. Sometimes I think that for Italians forming networks is just something that's impossible. We're not cut out for it."

Costantino "Maybe I'm fooling myself."

Oscar "No, in the meantime you keep growing. The problem is convincing the other people in the business that we're not competitors. There's a big world out there, facing it together makes it easier, plus it's more beautiful."

Costantino "Our real goal is to create a virtuous lobby in Brussels and little by little we're succeeding."

Shigeru, in the meantime, with his usual concentration, has tasted the first wine and poured it into our glasses, too. Opale 2011 produced by Mesa, a Sardinian Vermentino. While Shigeru gets ready to tell us about it, I feel like talking about the person who makes it.

Oscar "A good friend of mine makes this white wine, Gavino Sanna, the biggest ad man of all time."

Those who don't know me will be amazed, while those who do know me are probably smiling. The expression "of all time" is part of my usual emphatic, exaggerated exclamations that charge me up, make me enjoy and above all help me to attract people's attention. I love finding the superlative sides to life and the people I know. And in Gavino's case, I'm not exaggerating. Gavino Sanna, who emigrated from Sardinia, made it all the way up to becoming president of Young & Rubicam, one of the biggest advertising companies in the world, with a huge office in New York. One day, when he was at the height of his success as a manager, right in the middle of a galactic meeting in the New York skyscraper where he worked, Gavino went into the bathroom, a galactic bathroom, looked himself in the mirror, and asked: "What am I doing here?" So he went back to his desk (needless to say, a galactic one) and wrote a letter of resignation. Then he took a plane and went back to Sardinia. Fabulous! Near Carbonia, in the Sulcis-Iglesiente region, he set up a beautiful cellar and called it Mesa, which means table, the place where people eat and drink together. He bought the best land, found an enologist and an agronomist, both great experts, and now he makes wine. And he did all this even though he doesn't have any kids. Just him and his wife. Good for you, Gavino!

"This Opale is a Vermentino and if you look at the bottle and the label, both designed by him, you understand just who Gavino Sanna is." It's all quiet for the first time since we got here. Costantino is very focused on the wine he's tasting, and Shigeru, who is ready now, is waiting for his turn to speak so that he can describe the wine to us. But Costantino catches us unprepared. We came here with a thoroughbred, our Japanese friend, but Shigeru hasn't even finished inhaling so that he can begin when Costantino jumps in.

Costantino "This is a wine with a nice straw color and green hues. This tells us that these grapes can maintain both acidity and fruitiness. It has a full floral smell with mineral notes. Sardinia is a land of sea and cliffs so the roots of these plants draw from a substratum that's capable of expressing its entire personality."

Oscar "From those vineyards you can see the water, in the same way we can see the mountains up here."

Costantino "There's a total stylistic perfection in the aroma, a frankness without any lapses."

Oscar "I agree. Tell me about the taste."

Costantino "It starts out strong, but there's softness and sweetness as well. I think 2011 was a hot year there, too. This wine is 14 degrees proof, but you can't tell because there's substance in terms of its aroma and taste. It's well balanced, mineral and sapid. You don't realize it until you get to its expressive phase in terms of its pulpiness in the mouth. So I find it's well balanced. No doubt it's a wine with a low yield per hectare, and let me add—I'm getting this a little at a time—that it's a very long wine."

Oscar "Shigeru, do you agree?"

Shigeru "He's said it all! Usually the wine producer doesn't have the ability to explain wine this well. He's very good! In this wine, first we have the minerality, the Vermentino vine is very fragrant: there's dried fruit, vanilla, chamomile and honey. The taste is round, sapid, smooth, balanced and it isn't strong despite the fact that it's 14 degrees proof, it's fresh and persistent. I'd pair it with tuna stew, spaghetti with fish roe, or else with provolone or fresh pecorino. And I would also match it with lumpfish sashimi, dogfish, with bonito tuna, the small smoked tuna the Japanese keep in the house. It's a large blue fish, actually, not tuna. To finish, some soy sauce and ginger."

Oscar turns to Costantino: "Do you agree?"

Costantino "Definitely!"   .

(He's realized that this Japanese person isn't just prattling, quite the opposite. He looks at him admiringly.) I think watching the two of them describe wines is going to be an exciting match. We're going to enjoy ourselves.

I'm the Son of a Poor Culture

We go back to Costantino's "concert." All you have to do is prod him and he starts "singing again."

Oscar "Tell me more about your father. When did he pass away?"

Costantino "In 1979, at the age of seventy-six. He was the son of a poor culture, the culture of bartering, trading things, he was a hard worker. He believed that I, his son, should never have to experience the hardship he himself had gone through. He'd already lost two children before me, so my sister and I came along after those two losses. I never met those siblings of mine, but I did grow up with the stories my parents told us about their great pain. And I felt that pain physically. So helping me study, and paving the way for a steady job was my father's goal. He made me study mechanics, a subject I didn't like, in Ivrea, again a long way from home. As soon as I finished studying he found me a job at Cogne (the special steel industry in Aosta), but I didn't last long there, just a month. I quit and registered at ISEF, where I met Imelda, the woman I have always loved with all my heart, and married forty years ago. As soon as I got my degree I found a job and I taught phys ed for twenty years. But when I had the chance to leave I did so right away. Now I'm a youthful pensioner."

Oscar "So, when your father died you were thirty-two. Did you ever have really big fights with him?"

Costantino "Yes, wild ones!"

Oscar "And do you get along with your wife?"

Costantino "Wonderfully so. That's why I say I love her with all my heart. I think you should only get married once. I have this moral rectitude, which makes me kind of square, and it's something I had to come to terms with in 2003 when I had cancer."

Now Costantino tells us the story of his disease, which he's been free from for a few years, thanks also to the marvelous support he got from his wife and daughters, thanks to his combative nature, and thanks—my words—to his luck. But special people are often lucky, too. He came out a winner, but he also changed. He has a "mellower" approach to life now. Costantino is almost like someone who's been brought back to life, he's much more tolerant than before. In next to no time we're talking about family and children again.

Oscar "You're sure you love your family and children more than your wines?"

He doesn't answer right away, he thinks it over, but when he does answer his "yes" is so full and so self-aware that it leaves no doubts: yes! Costantino loves his daughters and wife more than his wines. And I'm happy to hear this, because it's not always like this. Lots of people say so, but not all of them do it.

Oscar "Are you happy that your daughters have decided to go into the same business? How did that come about?"

Costantino "For Eleonora, my younger daughter, it was physiological, because she's very sensitive and feels the call of the earth, she feels the seasons. That's why she studied Agricultural Sciences and then came to work with me. Elena studied Law instead, and for a few years she worked at the Chamber of Commerce."

Oscar "So for a while Elena thought she wouldn't be working with you, and how did you feel about that?"

Costantino "It made me feel bad, because I could really envision this winery being run by two women, also because they have different skills and can share the work by compensating for each other."

Oscar "Do you remember when Elena was born?"

Costantino "Yes, I remember, but I wasn't there. I was in the country working. In those years I was very involved in my work and Imelda had a friend of mine take her to the hospital."

Oscar "Did she forgive you?"

Costantino "Yes, Imelda has a generous heart. You know, Oscar,

I'm enjoying my daughter's pregnancy more than I did my own wife's back then."

Oscar "That's unbelievable! And did you find out it was a girl when she was born, or did you already know?"

Costantino "When she was born."

Oscar "How did you react?"

Costantino "It was a great feeling!"

Oscar "Sure about that?"

Costantino "I said to myself… You have plenty of time. I wanted a boy when my second daughter, Eleonora, was born. I think I made her feel this, I must have sent her some subliminal messages. You know, children soak up everything, they're like sponges, and you don't have to use too many words. If you bring them up with the right sensibility they'll understand. Eleonora understood that I was counting on her to carry on with the winery. That's why she majored in Agricultural Sciences."

You're so right, children understand, that's so true!

We move on to the second wine: Mille e Una Notte 2007 from Donnafugata. Since Costantino is an expert sommelier he talks about wine in scientific terms. Whenever I hear someone talk about wine as well as he does I think about the fact that all the exercise I've done in my lifetime as a wine enthusiast has given me lots of fantastic emotions but never the pleasure of being able to talk about wine like this. And I don't spit the way they do, I just can't do it. I drink wine, I love it, so I drink it. Luckily, all this exercise has helped me to learn to hold my liquor, otherwise it would be a disaster!

Speaking of this Sicilian wine Costantino mentions the "warm sun" as opposed to the "cold sun" of the Valle d'Aosta.

Oscar "Is global warming any good for your wines?"

Costantino "Over the past years we've felt the impact of the change that's underway. These are phenomena you can't prevent, so even our grapes have had to adapt. Black grapes have been ripening better these past few years, but white grapes risk losing their freshness and acidity. Fortunately, our production area rises up to 50 meters in altitude, and this helps us a little. Consider the fact that our temperature swings between day and night, especially during the last stages of ripening, give Valdostani wines aromas and fruitiness that are very intense and immediate. At this time in history, I'm content to have vineyards in

Valle d'Aosta instead of in Veneto or Piedmont or Tuscany. Today, our marginality within the world of wine is actually winning out."

Oscar "Of course it is. If you consider the fact that humans have always reacted to the climate by finding the best ways to adapt."

As I say this I glance at Shigeru whose turn it is now to describe the second wine, and I think he's thinking: "Polca miselia, Costantino is stealing my job!" I still haven't mentioned how Shigeru uses the Italian expression "polca miselia," which is actually "porca miseria," and means "damn it." Mispronouncing certain words in Italian is something I think makes him even more likeable. He often uses this particular expression to comment on positive or negative situations, with emphasis, and as though he were fully aware of a situation that unfortunately is all around us these days: "miseria," that is, real poverty. Simona always smiles when Shigeru uses those words.

Shigeru "Costantino is right. In this wine I can taste blueberry, tar, licorice. It has a pleasant and intense balsamic component which is why the fact that it's 14 degrees proof doesn't make it aggressive. It has good body and soft tannins. It's a complete wine that has a beautiful personality and can be drunk alone, without food."

Oscar "Because it's a wine that fills you up?"

Shigeru "Right! It's an important, almost meaty Nero d'Avola. But if we were to drink it while eating I'd pair it with pan-fried rib eye steak seasoned with pink peppercorn, or grilled lamb dressed with Dijon mustard and soy sauce."

Shigeru is amazing! All those years spent in charge of Suntory, the finest Japanese restaurant in Milan, have left him with a very personal taste in matching Japanese dishes and Italian dishes with our very best wines.

I Became a Wine Expert While Looking At Myself in the Mirror

Oscar "Costantino, let's get back to you. So you're not much like your father?"

Costantino "No, not much. I found it hard to love him because my relationship with him wasn't easy. But I did appreciate him a lot when, during times of economic hardship, he made some sacrifices so he wouldn't have to lose the old family house. He made some bad investments because he was involved in too many things. However, he did manage to get out of that situation without having to sell, and he left me everything. He was a very generous man. Today I think of this inheritance as a treasure, an incredible wealth. That house is a piece of the history and the poor culture of the Valle d'Aosta, a heritage site, and as soon as I've finished with the work on enlarging the cellar I'm going to work on developing a project that I'd like to talk to you about."

Oscar "So who do you take after? Yourself?"

Costantino "Yes, looking at myself in the mirror!" (They laugh.)

Oscar "Do you remember the exact moment you decided you wanted to be a vintner when you grew up?"

Costantino "No, because it was something I gradually became aware of. I thought back to my roots, to my grandfather whom I never met, to the handing over of the baton from the old house of the 'turn-taking' mill. In the late 1970s, I was twenty-nine or thirty and teaching phys ed in a scientific lyceum in Aosta and working as a ski instructor. One day I decided to take a wheelbarrow and empty the old cellar in the family house of the soil that had accumulated there over the years, because for a certain period of time we kept the livestock there. When I finished with that chore I discovered that there was a microclimate inside that was just perfect for aging our wines."

Oscar "When did you set up the Les Crêtes winery?"

Costantino "In 1983–1984. I was still teaching, but I had already started making wine. That was when I bought these Côteau La Tour vineyards in Aymavilles."

Oscar "That mill you keep mentioning, do you remember it working?"

Costantino "Of course, my mother ran it until I was nine. We would receive walnuts from all the valleys around here. It was a 'turn-taking' mill, in the sense that people would bring their walnuts and use it as if it were their own, paying to use it. My mother kept the rental records for the mill, and I still have them today."

Time really does go by slowly in this corner of heaven, and I'm trying to set the rhythm of our meeting because I don't want to waste a second of this fabulous day.

Now it's time for Brunello di Montalcino 2007 Mastrojanni. This historic cellar in Montalcino was bought by the Illy family from Trieste in 2008. They're the ones who produce coffee. That's why I chose it, besides the fact that this is one great Brunello. I'm a friend of Riccardo and Andrea Illy, and I respect them very much. They're very professional and they put love and poetry into everything they do. We know that's true for their coffee. But it's also true for their wine, chocolate, chestnuts and tea. They've invested in lots of quality food businesses.

Costantino tastes the wine and it's poetry again. He's amazing! We're on our third tasting. He says this Brunello is ready, it has to be drunk now if we want to enjoy it to the max and I agree with him wholeheartedly. I'm not a fanatic about aging wine at all costs. So many people have cellars that are full of excellent wines they allow to age and never drink. Wine has to be drunk. And then there are some that have to be kept so they can age properly, but when the right time comes they have to be drunk, and then maybe the empty bottle should be left out for others to see, which is even better, that way we can look at it and enjoy it again as we think about when we drank it.

Oscar "Shigeru, do you like this wine?"

Shigeru "Yes, in this wine I taste excellent balsamic, licorice, leather, coffee notes… It has a very pleasant, velvety persistence. The mouth-feel is sapid and full. You can taste the dry red fruit, and the tannins are full and elegant. This wine is ready to be drunk, possibly paired with Tuscan-style meat stew or pan-fried beef seasoned with Japanese mustard and miso, but also with good Parmigiano Reggiano aged sixty months."

Oscar "*Bravo*, Shigeru! You managed to add something about your native land and its specialities this time, too. But let's go back to the vineyard and the 1980s."

Costantino "I told myself that it was time to make some choices. I chose to invest in wine, my dream was to create the biggest cellar in the Valle d'Aosta. That was 1983. At the time, in our region there were only cooperative cellars, and a market leader was lacking. I decided to buy land in the Les Crêtes zone because it's famous for being ideal for winemaking. But it wasn't easy. You probably don't know that the average surface area for a vineyard in Valle d'Aosta is 1,200 square meters. Around here everything has always been divided based on inheritance. So I'm lucky because all at once I put together 14,000 square meters and managed to buy land without falling into debt. I borrowed money years later when the cellar was enlarged."

Oscar "Did you spend your money well?"

Costantino "Yes, I did. Plus, money invested in agriculture is always a good investment. I never gave in to the illusion of making easy money with financial products."

Oscar "How much of your wealth did you invest?"

Costantino "All of it! 100%"

Oscar "And did you talk to your wife about it before you did so?"

Costantino "No, only afterwards. It was another one of those choices I made while looking at myself in the mirror!"

Oscar "Was she understanding?"

Costantino "Yes, because she's a remarkable woman and because she knows I'm loyal to people, and to the things I do. And I succeeded in transmitting this value to my daughters, to my great joy."

Oscar "The same way your father passed on his generosity to you."

Costantino "Yes, that's true. And little by little I continued to buy land. Today we own 20 hectares of land, plus 5 of conferrers distributed over five towns in the Valle d'Aosta."

Oscar "And how many bottles do you make with 25 hectares?"

Costantino "200,000 bottles."

Oscar "How many people do you employ?"

Costantino "Eighteen, this is another asset for my company."

Oscar "When did you start building the cellar?"

Costantino "In 1990, when I stopped teaching phys ed."

Oscar "So, let me guess, you became a wine expert while looking at yourself in the mirror again."

Costantino "In a certain sense yes I did, I was actually already a wine expert, I just needed to improve. When I start something I always finish it off. Sometimes I can't meet the deadlines I'm given, but I always finish everything, at whatever cost."

This man who looks at himself in the mirror and makes important decisions about his life all by himself is very brave. He has the courage to choose, to change and even to make mistakes, but he always does so honestly, forthrightly and, I think, with the idea of there being a limit. These are the qualities that have made his company great in so little time.

We taste the fourth wine, Rubesco Vigna Monticchio Riserva 2005, made by Teresa and Chiara Lungarotti, the "daughters" of a truly great man, Giorgio Lungarotti. Their story is very beautiful, and I'll get them tell it to me when I go see them in Torgiano, in the province of Perugia. Rubesco is made from 70% Sangiovese and 30% Canaiolo grapes. Costantino keeps analyzing it with great curiosity and he agrees with Shigeru that this is a very fresh wine even though it's eight years old. Shigeru reminds us of the effects of the climate: 2005 was a cold year, so the grapes ripened less. He says that this elegant wine can ideally be paired with pigeon with black truffle or a beef roast served with Japanese mustard, or else seasoned toma cheese.

I've Always Thought I Was Cool

Oscar "How many bottles were you making in 1990?"
Costantino "12,000."
Oscar "And now you're making 200,000. Did you, at a certain point in your life, realize you'd become cool? Today there's a demand for your wines in America and in Japan, places where they have no idea what the Valle d'Aosta is."
As a fanatic about the marketing of substance, to my mind becoming cool is the best thing that can happen to you. Because managing to join the quality of the contents with the image is something really great that very few people know how to do.
Costantino "Maybe this isn't the answer you'd like to hear, but I've always thought I was cool," and he says so, with marvelous dichotomy, almost whispering, very, very humbly.
Oscar "You aren't disappointing me, actually, I like the fact that you say that! I'll shake your hand on that!"
Costantino "I've always had a certain amount of self-esteem. For instance, I've always believed I'm sexy."
And those of us listening to him don't find it hard to imagine him young, tanned, wearing a ski instructor's outfit, with lots of young admirers all around him, forcing him to come to terms with his idea of faithfulness that we were talking about before. But Costantino continues to play his song, note after note, and he continues to talk.
Costantino "The best thing is that I always believed my job could be cool and that my land could arouse the consumer's imagination."

I really do have to play the orchestra conductor with him, but it's easy to get the best out of him.

Oscar "Let's go back to being cool. You may always have been aware of it, but in Rome, New York, for example, no one knew who you were. Today they do. What happened?"

Costantino "It's hard to say. I've always tried to communicate my style and the style of my wines. In all the official moments, for example, I've always worn a bolo tie."

This is something everybody knows. Costantino has always fastened his shirt with a piece of leather secured with a wooden and stone clasp, in mountain cowboy style. He's always had the habit of wearing one, so that you can pick him out, and especially to make himself known.

In the meantime Shigeru has poured Costantino's wine into our glasses. He's decided to have us taste his Fumin 2008. Shigeru tastes it and studies it in silence, highly focused, as always. Instead, as soon as I drink it I blurt out a *"Fantastico!* Be honest with me, what do you do to make it like this? Do you do what D'Osvaldo does to his prosciutto? You know he smokes them in the fireplace. What do you do to make wine like this? Do you smoke your bottles too?" Everyone laughs, including Shigeru.

Costantino "My father produced Fumin and he'd already understood that it has to be left in the barrel for two years. Continuing to believe in our autochthonous varieties, we saved two from extinction: Prëmetta and Fumin. Today we have just slightly more than 2 hectares of Fumin and we make 15,000 bottles. I place it in large white wine barrels, which give it very soft tannins because Fumin has a note of leather and animal, it's sort of wild, which is part of its make-up. If this note isn't excessive, the wine tastes better. The hard part of our job was finding the type of wood most suitable for the process of fining."

Oscar "Was the wine you made in the 1980s bad?"

Costantino "My wines have never been bad. They've always represented my way of thinking. It's also true that a person's way of thinking changes over time. But I've never changed my way of making wine. As I was saying before, there's a basic rectitude that has always been my hallmark, and that's the distinctive style in my way of working."

Oscar "Are you searching for the perfect wine?"

Costantino "No, I'm not. I'm searching for wine that will create the utmost pleasure for the drinker. Wine has to be a pleasure to drink."

Oscar "How many harvests have you done?"

I'm going to ask everyone this question because it's something that really interests me. I'd like to figure out the total at the end. Calculate how many harvests I talked to in these twelve encounters.

Costantino "Personally, I've done thirty of them, since 1983. But I've taken part in lots more, since I first learned to walk on my own."

Oscar "Is there one harvest you're particularly fond of?"

Costantino "I remember the harvest of 1980, one of the last years I helped my father and mother with the harvest; it was an extremely cold year, and it was already snowing at the end of September. I can still see my elderly parents picking those frozen grapes and taking them home. I have bottles from that vintage that I'm holding onto."

We're still not friends enough for me to ask him to open one of those bottles with us, besides that, it's not the right time. But I do hope that one day he'll invite me to drink one of those bottles from 1980 with him. I swear when that happens I'll drop everything and rush to Aymavilles.

It's Shigeru's turn to talk about the last wine, Fumin 2008 Les Crêtes. I tell Simona that she has to drink this one with us because it's good. She, like me, doesn't spit. She doesn't drink a lot, but she finishes off the glass. Shigeru describes his feelings; he says the color is ruby with purplish hues and that the aroma is of leather and spices. He can taste blackberries, blueberries, undergrowth, graphite, cooked prunes and vanilla. The taste is elegant, softly tannic and very fresh. He says its an original wine in which you can even taste the flint. He says he'd pair it with cold cuts, but also with a bean soup drizzled with olive oil and seasoned with black pepper.

Shigeru "In Japan I'd pair it with our black pork, which is a very fat meat, adding a few drops of Japanese mustard. Here in the Valle d'Aosta, I think it's excellent with your fontina cheese, too."

It's almost lunchtime, and Shigeru's description has made us all feel hungry. Before Costantino takes us home to meet his wife, and then to a trattoria to have a bite to eat together, I want to ask him a few last questions.

Oscar "Why do they call it Fumin?"

Costantino "Because these grapes are rich in pruinosity, and when they're fully ripe, if you rub the grape with your finger you remove the bloom of the pruinescence, which is of a smoky gray color."

When I Grow Up I Want to Go Back to the Wine Cellar

Oscar "You're sixty-six now. Do you feel it?"

Costantino "No, I don't. And I'm lucky not to! I still enjoy skiing."

Oscar "Now that you're sixty-six, do you think you'll enjoy making wine when you grow up, or will you prefer to go into politics, meaning polis, of course, as in FIVI, as in Europe…"

Costantino "I want to go back to the wine cellar!"

Oscar "Really? If I'd bet on it I would have lost! How much time do you devote to 'politics'?"

Costantino "These days, lots of time, and my daughters miss me at the winery. Plus, making wine is something I really like to do."

Oscar "Wouldn't you be afraid to be in the way if you were to go back to the winery?"

Costantino "I have to do so without taking away any of the spaces my daughters have managed to earn for themselves."

Oscar "Listen, let's go back to politics, but this time let's talk about real politics. Are you happy about how you voted at the last elections?"

Costantino "Yes, I'm happy, also because I have an alibi, regionalism, and I voted Union Valdôtaine as I always have. Oscar, I believe in the polis."

Oscar "I know you do. And this is why, in my view, you have to continue to be involved in it! Politics should be run by honest people. Only honest people can improve things by making choices for the common good."

Costantino "My father would often repeat the Savoy motto, *bien faire et laisser dire* (do well and let them say what they want), and I've always kept this in mind. Always."

I'm not so sure he's only going to go back to the wine cellar. It's obvious he also very much likes real politics. He could be an excellent resource for his land. Who knows, maybe I made him feel the urge.

Our chat is almost over and as we get up to join Costantino's wife and daughters in their mill-house, I think that the figure of the father he talks about, whom he says he doesn't resemble, did leave a strong mark on him after all. I can feel it, I can make it out from the way he speaks. Back in the car, we now face the steep dirt roads but backwards this time, and while I remind him, the way I did coming here, to keep an eye on the road, he does everything he's not supposed to: he's not wearing a seat belt and he makes a phone call without using a headset. He wants to tell the restaurant that we'll be arriving late. "Here in Valle d'Aosta—he says—we're always careful about these things." Right, careful. So this time I don't buckle up either and I let his car wheeze and sputter until we get there. As we descend from "heaven" I can't help but look around and think that landscapes as beautiful as these are a pretty tough competition for even the most picturesque views in the Langhe. I love making top ten lists, but this time I don't want to think about it.

Oscar "What do you think about the words organic and biodynamic?"

Costantino "These are choices made by the producer that head off in the direction that I share, such as attention to sustainability, but they aren't certifications that I'm personally looking for. I certify myself with the ethics of my work, and I don't like it when someone comes to my house to tell me how to work."

Oscar "*Bravo!* I agree! I consider it to be a vital form of virtuous anarchy."

Costantino "Today, with the question of natural wine or free wine, as you call it, the fragrance of wine is changing. We're going to have to make choices. DOC certifications will have to be changed because otherwise certain deserving wines might not fit in. The decision not to use 'sulfur,' for instance, changes the expressiveness of wines in terms of sight, smell and taste."

Oscar "Has the era of the banana finish come to an end?"

Costantino "Yes, that too. These are wines that struggle to stay within the context of a strict certification determined by norms that have become too tight. I'm thinking, for the next FIVI meeting, about getting a debate underway between people who use one style and those who use another. I would like a discussion to come out, because new steps always lead to an evolution. And maybe in thirty years, when you and I are very old, sweet, fruity wine that immediately gives pleasure won't exist anymore."

In the meantime we've reached his home and Costantino introduces us to his wife, Imelda: a beautiful, spontaneous, smiling woman. "As you can see, she's Piedmontese," I mention this to Shigeru. Right away she tells us that at first she refused to leave her land, the Astigiano, filled with vineyards, to come and live in another land with a man who was bent on making wine. But then, as they say, you can't rule the heart, so she found herself adopted by the Valle d'Aosta. "It's fate," she remarks.

And then she had her daughters. Costantino gloats among his women. This really is a beautiful family. We have an apéritif with them and toast to "Kanpai!" in honor of Shigeru, who can at last enjoy a drink without having to think about what to say. But he can't control himself. We toast to Neblù, the Les Crêtes Classical Method. Shigeru starts in with "very good, persistent bubbles...," we stop him, we're famished.

I Say What I Do and I Do What I Say

In no time at all we're sitting around a table in a family-run country trattoria that we like right away! They bring us a nice big plate filled with typical appetizers, cold and hot ones, and as we begin to eat we go back to our chat.

Oscar "We were talking about something very serious: the question of cleanliness. They used to make clean wines because nothing was added to them, but they were often bad-tasting too. Then came the methanol scandal and the quest for very good wines began, but without disdaining chemistry. Things are clearly changing now: less sulfur, insecticides, chemical fertilizers, weed killers, so we need to find a new balance, we need to make wine that's clean, but good too."

Costantino "I think this balance should be made in the country, in the vineyard. We haven't used insecticides for twenty years now because all we need is to use the sexual confusion method for insects that would otherwise attack the grapes. We don't add chemical nitrates to the soil, but horse manure instead, and we've come to the understanding that we get a good effect if we apply microbiological sowing, which recreates humus in the soil, making it rich in nutrients, with immediate and direct benefit for the grapes. In the 1990s no one was willing to make choices like this, and pesticides and chemical fertilizers seemed to be the panacea for all diseases. Fortunately, it's not like this anymore. But before we decided to go against the grain, chemistry wreaked a great deal of damage on the plants and on the land."

Oscar "Just think, I'm lucky enough to be able to use the manure of sixty-five stables in La Granda, cows that are properly fed and produce fantastic fertilizer for my vineyards in Fontanafredda and Borgogno. Now, I swear, this is my last question, let's talk about vines. Autochthonous? International? What's your opinion?"

Costantino "I cultivate autochthonous (Petit Rouge, Fumin, Petite Arvine, Gros Rouge, Cornalin, Mayolet, Prëmetta) and international (Pinot Noir, two Chardonnays, Classical and Cuvée Bois, Syrah) varieties. I don't find the topic you're suggesting to be entirely relevant. I love the vine, which is a plant that has no state, no nationality, it's a migrant. I cultivate it in a difficult zone, i.e. the Valdostana mountains. I tend to it and respect it, letting it give itself in producing characterizing grapes, which will give me wines that are absolutely in harmony with my land of origin. Without forgetting, however, that if I manage to save an autochthonous variety from extinction, then I will have made a small contribution to the safeguarding of the biodiversity and to the culture of the territory. This is what I say and do in Valle d'Aosta. Saying what you do isn't hard, what's often very hard is doing what you say with great sincerity."

Shigeru can't wait to back Costantino's line of thought. We're drinking Chardonnay and Petite Arvine. In both of them he tastes Valle d'Aosta. He's enthusiastic about the acidity and the freshness of these white wines and attributes those features to the particular orographic, climatic and morphological conditions of Costantino's lands. These wines are comparable with the best French white wines. After all, we are very close to France. But we're still in Italy and what a beautiful piece of Italy this is! This is how we say goodbye, proud and happy.

The last thing I say to him is that his wines are his children, so he has two daughters and eleven sons. But Costantino wants to be sure we understand that he loves his daughters more than his wines. This story about the skill of a businessman, divided between his children and his work, has touched him. He's in earnest, and I believe him.

Notes for Wines Tasted with Costantino Charrère
Shigeru Hayashi

Vermentino di Sardegna Opale 2011 Mesa
Type white wine
Grapes 100% Vermentino
Vinification and fining fermentation at 16 °C, macération *sur lie*,
fining in steel and later in bottles
Production area Sardinia

The color is yellow with golden hues. The aroma features vegetal
notes (tomato leaf) and Mediterranean maquis, then hints
of chamomile, honey and vanilla. The taste is round and fat,
but at the same time fresh and smooth.

To be enjoyed with tuna stew, spaghetti with fish roe, smoked
swordfish, medium-aged Tuscan pecorino, or else with dogfish
sashimi seasoned with soy sauce and ginger.

What a great Vermentino this is! It's a wine that tastes of the sea
and the Mediterranean, that makes you feel like taking a vacation
in Sardinia and discovering that beautiful island. And yet it's
also a wine that opens up to the world, with its linear, direct flavor
that everyone can understand and love.

Contessa Entellina Mille e Una Notte 2007 Donnafugata
Type red wine
Grapes prevalently Nero d'Avola
Vinification and fining fermentation in steel with maceration with
skin contact for about 12 days at a temperature of 26–30° C. Fining
in French oak barriques for 15–16 months, and after that in bottles
for about 30 months.
Production area Sicily

The color is intense, impenetrable ruby red. The aroma is ripe fruit,
violet, tobacco, coffee and mineral elements. The taste is very
strong but also very elegant, with soft and embracing tannin.

Pair it with pan-fried rib eye steak seasoned with salt and pink
peppercorn. Deliciously combines with grilled lamb served
with Dijon mustard.

Everything about this wine—from its name to its label and to the
magnificent land where it is produced—reminds you of a fairy tale,
something exotic, sensuous and warm. Red wine that's first
and foremost an ode to Sicily and the Mediterranean, crossroads
of histories and peoples. For us Japanese, a wine like this one
"has got everything."

Brunello di Montalcino 2007 Mastrojanni
Type red wine
Grapes 100% Brunello (Sangiovese)
Vinification and fining Allier oak barrels of different sizes 15,
33 and 54 hl) for 3 years, further fining in bottles for 6–8 months.
Production area Tuscany

The color is intense ruby red with garnet hues. The aroma is violet,
tobacco, coffee, cocoa, leather and licorice. As for taste, it starts out
severe, almost nervous, then it melts into a joyride of embracing
softness and elegance.

I'd always drink it with grilled red meat, but I'd also like to try it with pan-fried Kobe-beef served with Japanese mustard. And how about a Grana Padano cheese aged more than 48 months?

As I taste this wine what comes to mind is a middle-aged man with penetrating eyes, a man who is kind but also demanding, with a strong, elegant, self-assured character. This, to me, is what the image of Brunello di Mastrojanni conjures up! The 2007 vintage is already delicious now, so I can't imagine what it will be like in ten–twenty years' time.

Torgiano Rosso Rubesco Vigna Monticchio Riserva 2005 Lungarotti
Type red wine
Grapes 70% Sangiovese, 30% Canaiolo
Vinification and fining fermentation in steel with maceration with skin contact for 15–20 days, matured 1 year in barriques and fined several years in bottles
Production area Umbria

The color is intense ruby red with purplish hues. The aroma is unmistakably violet, mixed berries, spices, coffee, cocoa and some minerals. The taste is very complex and elegant, with a very pleasant balsamic aftertaste. Silky and persistent.

Pair with fillet seasoned with pepper and served with Japanese mustard. Pigeon with black truffle would be another great match, as would beef roast with wasabi. I'd like to try it with some *formaggio di fossa*, i.e. cheese covered in leaves and left to ripen in humid caves.

The passion of a man—Giorgio Lungarotti, whom I met in the late 1980s—created this wine. I still remember how, when I went to see him, the first thing he did was take me to Vigna Monticchio, the finest winery cru. Torgiano owes him everything: the Wine Museum, the Oil Museum, a five-star hotel, cultural events of all kinds. And nowadays his daughters are doing an excellent job at keeping his dream alive!

Valle d'Aosta Fumin 2008 Les Crêtes

Type red wine
Grapes 100% Fumin
Vinification and fining fermentation in steel, long maceration and fining for 1 year in small French wooden barrels, followed by rest in bottles for another year.
Production area Valle d'Aosta

The color is ruby red with purplish hues. As for aroma, fruity and wild berry (blackberry and blueberry) notes emerge. Pleasant hints of spices, cooked prune and vanilla. The taste is tannic, soft and juicy.

This wine should be paired with Felino salami and Piacentina coppa (cured meat). Excellent with porcini mushroom soup drizzled with olive oil and sprinkled with black pepper. Also savor it with roast made with celery and blueberry sauce, or else with cheeses such as toma and fontina.

A great red mountain wine, rich in character and strength, just like the people who live in the Val d'Aosta. Its structure and elegance remind me of certain Montepulciano wines from the Marches, such as the one produced by our friend Ampelio Bucci.

Gaja: Angelo Gaja
Quality Personified

*Whoever Has Been Successful and Fortunate in Life
Must Be Forgiven for It*

The landscape around us influences the formation of an interior landscape, which corresponds to the one created by Nature. I've always believed that a person who is born and grows up surrounded by hills imagines tables that are round and houses with undulating roofs. By the same rule, a citizen of the Dolomites should prefer sharp corners. I'm happy to have grown up surrounded by the roundness of the Langa hillsides. And where I come from, in the background, you can even see the mountains that separate us from the sea. Those are the Maritime Alps, among which Monviso towers over all the rest. The perfect mountain, shaped the way a child might draw it, chosen among all of them by Paramount Pictures in Los Angeles. How many times have we been asked to look at that mountain, Monviso that is, at the movies or on TV, as we settle down to watch some great movie.

I like to carry around with me, etched in my personality, the contradictions of the people from the Langhe, the so-called "Langhetti," the strongest features of my territory, but also its roundness. Fields of hazelnut groves that alternate with the ubiquitous vineyards reminiscent of a woman's breasts. The Tanaro Valley and the crown of Alpine mountains, the destination of so many of our excursions when we were young. In the Langhe where Barolo and Barbaresco are produced the landscape is one continuous, picture-perfect row of hills dotted with fortresses and steeples. I think I was lucky to be born so close to these marvels.

These were my thoughts as I drove from Barolo down to Alba. I was imagining Angelo Gaja probably driving down from Barbaresco at the same time. The sun was shining brightly and the colors were intense, with a sky that was bluer than blue, and not a cloud in sight. Sunlight all around and a breathtaking view. Angelo arriving from the East, I from the West, with the Tanaro Valley in between, seeing that our appointment was in Pollenzo, at the University of Gastronomic Sciences. I'd start the interview with a question about the landscape, I'd ask him what the difference is between the hills of Barbaresco and those of Barolo? That was going to be my first question.

First I have to stop off in Serralunga to pick up Shigeru and Simona. I can't help kidding with Shigeru, telling him he'll never see a sky as blue as this one in Japan. But then he reminds me that he was born in the country, too, near Mount Fuji, and that the sky can be as blue as it is here. "All right, so you've got blue skies in Japan, too, but this morning I'm feeling proud and I want to show you how fabulous our hills are. Whenever I go to Japan you never take me to see places as fabulous as these!" Shigeru laughs, at last. My aim is to get him to laugh at least once a day. So I'm all set for today.

When we finally get to Pollenzo we barely have time for a cup of coffee. Angelo doesn't want one: "Aren't we supposed to be tasting wine?" He's as punctilious as ever. I wonder whether he succumbs to a contradiction now and then like the rest of us, and I promise myself that I'm going to try to find out during the interview. This is what's going through my mind as I somewhat shamefully gulp down my espresso.

Oscar "Is there a difference between the landscapes of Barbaresco and Barolo?"

Angelo "No, we're all enthralled by the same mountain view, and this year especially, because the mountains are exceptionally covered in snow. I remember the year 2003 when there was no snow to be seen, a sign of climate change. This was to the advantage of the Nebbiolo that grows around here, because it can ripen more fully. But there's a negative side to it, too. Anyway, the snow makes me happy!"

We don't need to be introduced to each other. We say hello, banter a little, the way everyone does around here. I'm always ready for his "Don't you ever quit making money?" And then we're off.

Angelo Gaja is "Le Roi," the absolute king of high-quality Italian wine, one of the most famous and much-acclaimed wine producers outside of Italy, probably the *coolest* of them all, as the Americans might say. He still runs the wine tastings himself, speaking English fluently, although you can hear the wide vowels of our Langa dialect when he does. A dialect he's proud of, even on the most glamorous occasions. "Good for you, Angelo!"

Today, at the age of seventy-three (although he looks ten years younger), he's a very successful man, whose charisma and devotion to his work are so universally acknowledged that he was nominated to run as President of Italy by the Associazione delle Enoteche Italiane. This really did happen during the hectic presidential elections in April 2013. It was the association's way of sending a message, but not just that. I can't help but wondering whether, had he accepted, he would have done what Luigi Einaudi had before him: no sooner was he elected president than he took his wines off the Quirinal's list. A gesture of moral and intellectual honesty from a distant past. My answer is "yes," he would definitely have done the same thing. Gaja and I have discussed politics so much I know how his mind works.

Oscar "The first thing that impressed me about you was when I heard you say that 'whoever has been lucky and successful in life has to devote a part of their time to ask for forgiveness,' to quote Enzo Biagi."

Angelo "That's right, and we have to teach our children the same thing: I pay the price for this directly. Agriculturers are proud of what they do, and sometimes pride arouses envy in others, who become unwilling to see you for what you are. So success shouldn't be flaunted; actually, we have to be forgiven for it. My greatest fortune was having had a father whom I'm convinced was the most complete artisan of all in the world of wine in Piedmont. He wanted me to learn to plow the land and graft the vine. 'Seira' he'd say, meaning yesterday. But 'seira' also means evening. And 'seira seira' means yesterday evening. Maybe it's a subliminal way to express the widespread feeling in these parts of always being late. The past catching up with you. Saying 'yesterday' as it's already coming to an end, 'seira.' Another thing he'd always say was 'if bread had legs you'd be dying of hunger.' My father wasn't someone who wasted time."

Angelo's Legendary Compliment

There's never any time to waste with Angelo, like father like son, so we dive right in with the tasting.

The first wine we try is Les Crêtes Chardonnay 2009. Angelo has known Costantino Charrère for years and he has a lot to say about him: "I like Costantino very much and whenever I drink one of his wines I always try to understand what he's trying to tell me. In Valle d'Aosta he's made some important choices, insisting on autochthonous grape varieties, as well as international ones. Just think: in Italy we have 350 varieties, including autochthonous and international ones, that are cultivated regularly. Why should we limit ourselves to autochthonous vines? What we really need to do is dispel some of the confusion. Which variety to grow should only be of concern to those who want to sell it. Costantino's wines express his feelings and the character of the territory he comes from: a difficult, harsh, pungent one. He's also interested in the impact of climate change on his region. In Piedmont, for instance, I'm not sure what the consequences of global warming will be on the longevity of our wines. To be able to figure that out and, if need be, change direction, lots of research will have to be done, and human beings will have to learn to adapt to climate change. The positive side of all this is that nowadays we have science to help us out."

Oscar "About climate change, did you know that in 2015 Giovanni Soldini and I will attempt to navigate a 'Northwest Passage' by boat? The glacier retreat is so great right now that it's opened up the fastest route between New York and Tokyo, crossing just under the North Pole. The world as we know it is changing, and fast, too!"

Angelo "You're crazy!"

Oscar "What do you think of this wine, Shigeru?"

Shigeru "Yes, it's a very mineral wine with a scent of aromatic herbs, banana, pineapple, vanilla. This wine is soft, persistent and mineral. I'd pair it with Piacenza-style salt cod. But also with a Milanese cutlet sprinkled with lemon juice."

Oscar "Angelo, do you agree?"

Angelo "Absolutely! However, Shigeru is much better than me at descriptions. He always manages to find the words I just can't think of."

Here's something else about Angelo that stands out, his compliments. He's not one to withhold compliments, quite the opposite, he uses them in abundance. He has one for everybody and he dispenses them wisely, with words that always make their recipients proud. Of course, it would be easy, at this point, to butt in with the saying: "Voi piemontesi, falsi ma cortesi," meaning that the Piedmontese may be courteous, but they're also insincere. That's not at all the case with Angelo and I rush to defend him because to some degree I tend to do the same thing. Sincerity means knowing how to find something good about everyone, because, believe me, it's always there. Goodness, maybe with a little shrewdness thrown in, pointing it out and doing so right away, maybe even exaggerating a little. Why waste your time trying to figure out what's negative about the person in front of you? If you can see something positive, something nice, something you don't have, then that's what you should focus on. Explore it, comment on it, get the other person to tell you more, there's always room to learn more. And in any case, is there anything nicer, sweeter, more joyful than feeling good in another person's company? Other people are the only animals in the world we can spend time with as equals. It's worth it to seek harmony because it will mean a better life. And compliments help and are even more appreciated when the other person respects you.

Oscar "Let's go back to Costantino."

Angelo "He represents FIVI (Federazione Italiana Vignaioli Indipendenti) and I really admire him. Italian artisans never have a say in anything, and Costantino works hard to earn respect for them."

Oscar "I have a hard time understanding associations, all of them, including the ones that have to do with wine. In my opinion, all these associations, societies, clubs and whatnot, with all their presidents, vice presidents and board members, who work hard solely for the good of their own kind, are one of this country's biggest problems."

Angelo "Although I agree with you that there are too many politicized lobbies, I still like FIVI. If it were to manage to send a representative up to Brussels it might be a good thing, but they'd have to send the right person for the job."

Oscar "What can Brussels offer us?"

Angelo "A stricter wine code with the interests of artisanal winemakers in mind. Today there's no code of conduct acknowledging artisanal wine, and the aim of such a code would be to distinguish it from industrial wine."

*Doing, Knowing How to Do, Knowing How to Get Someone
Else to Do Something, Making Something Known*

Oscar "When did you decide to start making wine?"
Angelo "I'd always assumed it was the only line of work for me.
When I was a child I spent a lot of time with my grandmother on my
father's side; her name was Clotilde Rey, although they called her
'Tildin.' She was an elementary school teacher in Chambéry and
she'd married my grandfather in 1905. He was a viticulturist at the
time. My grandmother was a dominator, a person with an amazing
personality, who died when I was just twenty-one, unfortunately. I
would often do my homework and have meals at her house. My
grandmother was the one who drew out my skills as an artisan. She'd
always say that there are four steps to being successful: doing, knowing how to do, knowing how to get someone else to do something,
and making something known. Just think how modern, how powerful her vision was. She was an extremely lucid, intelligent woman.
One day she asked me: 'What do you want to be when you grow up?'
That day I was smart enough to keep quiet and let her speak. What
she said to me was: 'You have to carry on your grandfather's and
your father's job, because you'll earn threefold from it: in terms of
money, hope, and glory.' I was just ten."
Oscar "So how did you start out?"
Angelo "I started working with my father in 1961. For the first seven
years he wouldn't let me set foot in the cellar, only in the vineyard. I
majored in Business and Economics in Turin. In those years Gino
Cavallo was in charge of our vineyards and I learned so much from
him. In 1964, under the Center-Left government led by Aldo Moro,
the sharecropping law was abolished. It was an old stranglehold con-
tract that in the world of wine no longer had a reason to exist. Well,
in 1948, that is, sixteen years earlier, my father had already transformed all the sharecroppers into salaried workers. He'd understood
long before that it was the right thing to do because the sharecropper
focused on quantity, whereas my father aimed at another way of producing wine. As salaried workers their earnings were guaranteed,
and my father could decide what he wanted them to do, how he
wanted them to work. He sought quality. My father was a liberal, a
very tolerant man who knew exactly what he wanted. He kept his

nose to the grindstone but was never discouraged. In those days, the person in Langa that everyone looked up to when it came to wine was Bartolo Mascarello, a talented man, but a moaner. Maybe back then he was the only one to be successful. My father was very different from him. Those were years when we spoke with irony and well-founded malice about the entrepreneurs who made money with Southern wine that traveled from the South to the North in tankers. Instead my father never criticized anyone! Never! He was the one who taught me how to communicate."

At last I catch sight of a contradiction in Gaja, a weakness. Although he did pay Bartolo Mascarello a compliment, saying that he was a "talented man," he also took a little dig at him when he added that he was a "moaner." It's the first time I've ever heard him say anything but good things about a fellow winemaker. And what a winemaker! We're talking about Bartolo Mascarello here, a Partisan in the war, an intellectual, a legendary figure when it comes to Langa wine. The standard-bearer of true Barolo wine, cultivated and vinified according to the most genuine and strictest canons of tradition, the inventor of the slogan "No barrique, No Berlusconi!" But it can't just be politics that divides them to this extent. Angelo may not be a Socialist like Bartolo, but he's no great fan of Berlusconi, either. I think he simply feels like pointing out the difference in their style of communication and at the same time emphasizing an inclination to complain about things that in Langa, but probably wherever there are farmers, finds fertile terrain. Although I agree, I have to say that in Bartolo Mascarello's case his great analytical skills, the richness of what he had to say about the land and traditions, the poetic element of his interpretation of his roots were so strong that any tendency on his part to moan the way farmers are inclined to do was almost imperceptible. When Gaja produced a Barolo and called it "Sperss" (inspired by his father's reaction), Bartolo remarked that you couldn't give a Barolo the name of a laundry detergent! I wonder what he would have said, if he'd still been alive, about my Barolo Borgogno 2008, which in 2012 I called "No Name," in protest against the excessive red tape in the world of wine. Maybe he would have said "you're right about the red tape, but Barolo is Barolo and you can't change its name. And what does English have to do with it anyway? At least Gaja used a name in Piedmontese."

Oscar "Is communication a value?"

Angelo "Naturally! In 1965 AIS was founded in Milan. My father was one of its first members. That's how I got to know the owner of the Savini restaurant. In 1966 we came out with our 1961 vintage, which we were selling at four times the normal price for Barolo. Savini bought fifteen crates of it! I happened to be with my father at the restaurant that day, and they served me some yellow stuff that kept spreading out on my plate. I'd never seen anything like it! Risotto alla milanese, with a wave to it. Quite different from my grandmother's sticky version of it."

Oscar "Let's go back to talking about communication."

Angelo "Let me tell you a story about something that happened one evening at the Circolo Sociale in Alba, nicknamed the 'high society club,' because it's where the well-heeled citizens of Alba would go. One evening Gianni Brera, the sports journalist, had been invited to give a talk, and when someone from the audience asked him 'What can our area do to make its wine more famous?' he answered: 'Do what Gaja does!' My father, who was there among the audience, sank through the floor!"

I Had to Steal My Father's Trade

Oscar "When did you start having a say at the winery?"

Angelo "Toward the late 1960s. Between 1958 and 1983 my father was the mayor of Barbaresco, and for a quarter of a century he divided all his time between wine and politics. He never actually taught me anything, he simply handed his experience down to me; I had to steal his trade, so to speak."

Oscar "Did you learn to love your father *after* he died?"

Angelo "I loved him before, of course, although we were often on opposite sides. Sons tend to want to do things their own way and they're unwilling to come to terms with their fathers. My father used to make phone calls from the public phone booth in the Galleria San Federico in Milan, and I had to be quick enough to drop the tokens into the slot, or else! In those days he only sold bottled wine to his private customers because the restaurant business totally ignored us. He'd sell bottles of wine to Mario Morra, son of the legendary Giacomo, who managed the Hotel Savona in Alba. I remember them having huge arguments over prices. Whenever Morra ordered the wine he never wanted to talk about prices. My father would remind him that the price had gone up. Morra would reply that he'd already sold the wine, so he couldn't pay him anything more."

Oscar "When did you take your first trip abroad."

Angelo "I was already traveling in 1961, when I went to Switzerland. In 1972 we decided on Germany and the United States, which in time proved to be an excellent route. I've often chosen things at random, and that time I was very lucky. Even today the United States and Germany are two important countries for our exports. At the time the United States had an influence on communication, its goal being to get the Californian wine business to grow. Their strategy was to identify leaders in other countries who would be willing to be part of a group of producers that could then offset France's stronghold. I traveled a lot in the United States in those years, and I learned English. Young people were taking over for their fathers because they could speak English. My father had understood this before everyone else, and he'd said to me: 'Go abroad,' which is what I did."

Oscar "While Shigeru gets ready to tell us about the second wine, Tignanello 2009, can you tell me about Sperss, your Barolo? You have a very personal taste for words in the traditional dialect. Doesn't 'sperss' mean nostalgia in Piedmontese?"

Angelo "Yes, it does. It expresses the idea of a distance from the present that encourages us to remember. Let me tell you about it. My father wanted those vineyards at all costs, the ones in Serralunga d'Alba, with complete southern exposure. Those were the ones he wanted. If I think about all the other great pieces of land I could have had…! In those days you could still buy land on which to make Barolo in Langa. I still remember times when Dolcetto cost more than Nebbiolo for Barolo. When the opportunity came up, in 1988, to buy those pieces of land, in Marenca di Serralunga, my father scooped them up, without giving it a second thought. They do have a unique position and today the wine that's made from that small patch of vines has a flavor that's typical of that land. When my father first tasted that Barolo his words were 'Iera propri sperss.' Not easy to translate, literally it means, 'this was really lost,' meaning, I really missed this. So I simply had to call it Sperss. Thanks to the incredible and painstaking work carried out by Guido Rivella we managed to valorize my father's desire."

Oscar "What happened in the 1980s? I'm asking you this question because I remember that in those years there was sugar, which in itself was an innocent form of adulteration, in lots of cellars."

Angelo "Of course! I remember that in 1983 Renato Ratti, one of my teachers whose articles I would read in *Civiltà del bere*, organized a symbolic protest in Alba in the form of a rally in favor of adding sugar. Veronelli was there, too. To be honest, sugar was a bland and harmless form of adulteration. What happened a few years later with the methanol wine scandal was something very different."

Oscar "Let's taste the wine now, and tell me what you think of it. Actually, first, I want to hear what Shigeru has to say."

Shigeru "Just a moment, please, I'm not ready yet."

From 60,000 to a Million Bottles

Oscar "Angelo, do you know Piero Antinori?"

Angelo "Of course I do! I have great respect for him and for the great things he's done. When Senator Paolo Desana put some order in the Italian DOCs, managing to get law no. 930 passed, in 1963, Tuscany found itself in a quandary because Chianti Classico was being required to also contain, along with the higher percentage of Sangiovese, a part consisting of poor-quality grapes, white ones no less, such as Tuscan Trebbiano. But Piero Antinori and Giacomo Tachis refused to have anything to do with it, and in 1970 they oversaw the release of a Chianti Classico Riserva made from grapes from a single vine, aged in barriques. And the following year they came out with another twist in the plot. Their wine, called Tignanello after the name of the vineyard, came out as simple table wine. Their departure from the Chianti Classico denomination was a logical step forward. Piero showed great courage. He didn't agree with the industry regulations, and he was the first to insist on using international vines, such as Cabernet, in addition to Sangiovese. Giacomo Tachis, a great expert on blends, gave him a hand in this bold move. He was number one back then because he had a huge amount of experience in the cellar. But it was Piero who had the greatest insight when he decided to call Tignanello a 'table wine.' Tachis's creativity and inventiveness, together with Antinori's courage, breathed life into the miracle of Tuscan wine."

As we discuss all these things Shigeru tastes the wine, completely focused and apparently in another world. I'm curious about Angelo's opinion on Tignanello 2009 because later I'm going to have him taste Rosso dell'Abazia produced by Serafini & Vidotto.

Oscar "Are you ready, Shigeru?"

Shigeru "I am now. The aroma in this wine is cocoa, coffee, violet, licorice, vanilla and pepper. It's a full-bodied wine with delicate tannins, I'd say they're velvety, sapid. This is the right wine for beef fillet seasoned with salt and black pepper and Japanese mustard. It would also be good with aged Bitto cheese."

Angelo "Yes, I agree with you about the delicate, velvety tannins, but I have to confess that I'm not good at pairing wine with specific dishes. I don't know how to talk about wine the way Shigeru does, but I find his descriptions to be lots of fun. I can taste some *umami*, the fifth flavor, in this Tignanello, but it might just be a feeling."

Angelo is magnificent. He detected the *umami*, the flavor identified by someone from Japan in the early twentieth century. This makes Shigeru feel proud. He's already crazy about Gaja's wines, and after this interview he won't be able to stop singing their praises. Angelo knows perfectly well that our Japanese friend has a say in the Italian wine that's sold in Japan; he knows exactly which strings to pull. You can tell Shigeru's in raptures. The bottle Angelo brought for the tasting is a Barbaresco 2008. As I watched Shigeru uncork all the bottles I had the impression he was being especially careful with this one. His eyes looked like they were sparkling.

Oscar "Tell me right out, Angelo. When did you start making the decisions, without having to ask your father for permission first?"

Angelo "In 1972–1973, when I was thirty-two. It's a good thing Guido Rivella had a very important job in the cellar. So important, in fact, that it worried my mother, who would ask me 'What are *you* going to do?' She didn't think there would be room for both of us at the winery."

Oscar "Give me some numbers."

Angelo "In 1973 we had 21 hectares of vineyards and we made from 60 to 65,000 bottles because we didn't bottle everything; some of what we produced was sold in casks. Today we have 100 hectares in Piedmont, and we make 350,000 bottles. As of 1994, instead of expanding our estate to include Barbaresco, we invested in Tuscany, Montalcino and Bolgheri. Exciting areas. Today in Cà Marcanda di Bolgheri we make about 500,000 bottles in 100 hectares of vineyards, while the 27 hectares in Pieve Santa Restituita di Montalcino yield about 100,000 bottles."

Oscar "So, from 20 to 220 hectares, and from 60,000 to a million bottles."

Angelo "Yes, but not the way you do everything—in a hurry. It took us four generations!"

Oscar "The third wine I'm going to have you taste is Rosso dell'Abazia 2006 produced by Serafini & Vidotto. Shigeru, can you describe it for us. And please, give it a glowing report!"

Shigeru "You can clearly smell the raspberry, vanilla, cocoa, coffee, pepper and black currant. It's a full-bodied, clean and elegant wine. It can easily be paired with dishes that have a strong flavor. It would be ideal with chicken cacciatore, spicy gorgonzola cheese or aged taleggio."

When Shigeru gets to the word "taleggio," he says "tareggio" instead. We all look at him in disbelief. How can this be? He's always changing the letter "r" to an "l," and now that the word finally has a friendly "l" in it he's managed to change it to an "r"! There are some things about the Japanese I'll never understand!

Oscar "Do you like it. Angelo?"

Angelo "Wonderful, it's a superb wine. You can send my compliments to your partner in Veneto. This is an example of how we Italians are also capable of making these great red wines that I'd describe as being 'worldly.' You can tell there are lots of grape harvests behind it."

I'm going to tell Francesco Serafini. On second thought, I'll write it down so he'll believe me.

He Who Knows How to Drink, Knows How to Live

Oscar "Angelo, what are the basic stages in your company's success?"

Angelo "In 1977 with Gaja Distribuzione I started selling Romanée-Conti. That was a very important moment for me because, while visiting the producers as a merchant for that immense wine, they would open up to me and tell me all about their values, their philosophy. Ten years later we became the Italian distributors of RIEDEL glasses, a brand that allows you to enjoy the wine to the utmost. In 1985 we started importing Robert Mondavi's wines to Italy. Thanks to him I really grew a lot. I remember when Robert came to the Langhe for a few days, I took him to admire the view from the Belvedere at La Morra. He was astonished at what he saw and kept saying: 'There's a certain sound in the air, there's a certain sound in the air.' Then I accompanied him to Serralunga, where there was another great view. And again he kept repeating the words: 'There's a certain sound in the air.' Finally, he looked me straight in the eyes and said, 'I can hear the sound of people snoring, I can hear you Langaroli sleeping. With land like this you ought to be the masters of the world of wine.' He thought he could produce great wines in bulk. A few years later everyone was copying him, and it's thanks to him that wine tourism got off the ground. He was so farsighted that in the 1980s he was doing ads that said: 'Drink in moderation.' Before then I'd never heard any of the major European wine distributors invite consumers to drink in moderation!

My father believed that the family was responsible for teaching their children how to drink wine properly. I was just fourteen years old when, during a meal, my father poured a tablespoon of Barberesco into my glass for the first time, telling me to drink it with what I was eating. My grandmother, Clotilde Rey, who was also there, berated him, saying he was wrong to make me drink wine because I was still too young. They argued for a while, but in the end my father got the better of her, saying: 'He who knows how to drink, knows how to live. Since then I only drink during meals, and never in between meals.'"

Oscar "Your father went into politics, why didn't you?"

Angelo "Because I was involved in politics through him, even too much so. Later on lots of people asked me to, but at a certain point you have to back out. I refused to accept all the acknowledgments, even a knighthood, Cavaliere del Lavoro (Order of Merit for Labor). Sometimes it's hard to say no, it makes you look arrogant."

This is one thing about Gaja I really like. His low profile, his not wanting to appear. He'll sometimes turn up at meetings just to listen, when the organizers would gladly pay him in gold to have him speak. He sits in the back rows with the public at large, listening and taking notes. He even refused a knighthood! The guy's a legend! I swear that if they ever offer me one I'm going to do the same thing. There are far too many people, who are full of themselves and only interested in their own personal affairs and not in those of the community, who carry the symbol of this award on their lapel. Besides, I think to myself, I never wear a jacket anyway!

The Family Is a Gatherer of Talents

Oscar "Tell me about your family today..."

Angelo "In 1976 I married Lucia, who was working as a secretary for Gaja. She was a native of Barbaresco, a genuine DOCG [*laughter*]. We started going out when she moved to Genoa to take a cooking course with Osvaldino. One day I happened to see her in the kitchen and I thought this is the woman for me. Our relationship changed. I was thirty-six. Until then I hadn't really done much with my life (even when he's talking about women he wants to sound modest, but he lets a smile show through and we don't believe him). At a certain point I felt the need (but we read duty) to start a family. Once again I was lucky. My wife works with me now. She never gets tired of what she does."

Oscar "Tell me about your children..."

Angelo "The eldest is Gaia. When I went to register her birth, the clerk told me I couldn't use that name for her because there was no saint with that name on the calendar. But I didn't give in. Gaia is radiant, simple, kind. She's better than I am at relationships, but I am the way I am because I need competition. Then Rossana was born, more mischievous than Gaia but in a good way. We named our last child Giovanni. He's twenty years old now and has taken after his mother, which makes me happy. He's reflective, careful and mild-mannered. He needs room to do what he wants. My daughters work for the company, they sell, and they both have a fine palate."

Oscar "When do you plan to leave the winery to your children?"

Angelo "Everything that has to do with exports is already in Gaia's hands, the only place she lets me go to now is Mozambique (we don't believe him!). Rossana deals with PR and the Italian market. We're patiently waiting for Giovanni to join us. I'm lucky to have had two daughters. Being a son myself I think that sons always seek more independence, while daughters are still eager to get advice, especially from their father. Gaia and Rosanna have given me some great ideas. The family is a gatherer and it has to valorize talents, characters, styles and personalities, all things that have to be a part of the wine."

I think about his website. What a gem. It starts out with the Gaja logo, then you get a few pieces of information, no video, no special effects. A real beauty, in my opinion, in the digital world where three days after you've uploaded your new website they tell you it's obsolete. I think Gaja has made a superb choice. It's not expensive and it's always modern. I tried to convince my kids to do something similar. One page with the Eataly logo, and the words "We're more on land than online! Come visit us," followed by all the addresses. But I didn't manage to convince them, nothing doing. In my neck of the woods a lot is spent on the web. We've even set up a dedicated company. I wonder whether Angelo shared this analog idea with his daughters, or whether he forced them to accept it. I can't hold back so I come right out and ask him.

Angelo "First I forced it on them, and it wasn't easy. Then, with time, I'm not sure whether out of laziness or as a matter of conscience, they agreed. But I don't know how long it's going to last."

It's time to taste the fourth wine, Barolo Riserva 1982 Borgogno. This time Angelo's description precedes Shigeru's. He says there's something "sexy" about it.

Angelo "It almost feels like the prelude to a strong emotion that slowly gets better and better. The pleasure I get out of waiting is very strong, because this wine changes when it's in the glass, and then changes again to the palate. It's a mature, elegant woman to be discovered slowly. Elegance has no need for perfection."

As Shigeru describes the wine he continues to use the female metaphor, but with great embarrassment, which is typical of the Japanese. So after mumbling something I can't quite make out, filled with shame, he goes back to the velvety tannins, the elegance, the sapidity. The scent is thistle, wet wool, smoke, and licorice, and he'd pair it with braised beef stewed in Barolo and Castelmagno.

I Expect a Proposition from You

Oscar "Whom did you vote for?"

Angelo "You know quite well, we talked about it for ages."

I think about the fact that lots of smart people whom I know very well and respect voted for Grillo. The biggest mistake Bersani's Democratic Party made was to have openly underestimated the theme of the costs, efficiency, honesty and representativeness of politics. Sometimes I wonder whether these issues were underestimated in good faith or deliberately overlooked.

Oscar "Do you regret it now?"

Angelo "No, but I'm not proud of it either. This is a very delicate phase, we need a deep-seated moral revolution, the country needs good examples. Speaking of wine, the COAM (Common Organization of Agricultural Markets) allocates 350 million euros per year to wine. Is that indispensable? Not really. I wish there were some way we could really and publicly trace that money. I'd like to know who gets it, who uses it and for what reasons. We have to restore value to public funding."

Oscar "Of your forty-harvests as head of the winery which one do you remember best?"

Angelo "Nineteen eighty-two because it was a lucky vintage, it started out well, with successful projects also owing to randomness. And your Barolo reflects the outstandingness of that year!"

The last wine. We've almost reached the end of the course. It's time for Barbaresco 2008 produced by Gaja. Shigeru savors it quietly, as always he's highly focused, but this time he seems to be even more so. Our Japanese friend is completely bowled over by Angelo, who loves playing the virtuous ham. The aroma fills the air each time the wine swirls in the glass. It's almost time for lunch, the fragrance of the Barbaresco makes me dream of having a plate of thin, crispy egg *tajarin*, maybe eaten in the company of my family. But I want to hear what Shigeru has to say about the pairing: I'm always telling him off for not pairing typical Langa dishes with our wines.

Oscar "Shigeru, go on, tell us about the last wine." I'm curious about those pairings.

Shigeru "Yes, the aroma of this wine is violet, rose, ink and some leather. It's soft and delicate. Very elegant wine! I suggest drinking it with grilled fillet of beef sprinkled with white pepper, but it can also be enjoyed with a Parmigiano Reggiano aged forty-eight months."

Oscar "Let's at least hope the ox is from Carrù. But how about some ravioli *al plin*, don't you ever imagine them served with the wine?"

Shigeru "Of course, if you want... But this Barbaresco is also a meditation wine, to be sipped slowly, while discussing important issues."

Oscar "That's a good idea! Pairing the wine with thinking about certain issues. A specific conversation for each wine. A subject, a situation. Listen, Angelo, let's use your wine to talk about something important. In your lifetime as an entrepreneur you've dealt with at least four generations. The generation that went to war and took part in the Liberation of Italy. That of the economic miracle, your generation, in other words. The generation that buried Italy in debts, mine, unfortunately. And now the generation of the young people of the third millennium, those who can't find jobs. Which generation of Italians do you respect the most?"

Angelo "I always see the glass as being half full, I still have faith in this country. We need to believe in our young people, show them we have confidence in them, but the older generation, before being sent off to the scrap yard, should pass down their experience."

Oscar "Well, let's end on this note of optimism about young people. Speaking of young people, what do you want to be when you grow up?" I see Angelo stand up and look me straight in the eyes, grinning. Ten long, drawn out seconds go by, time is suspended in silence. He knows what he wants to say, but his mind is trying to figure out how to say it. You can tell he isn't unprepared for this question, and that he's also pleased to have been asked. He's visibly content about the fact that we're aware he's in excellent physical shape, and that mentally he's still oriented toward the future. Who knows how many plans he has in mind. I'm ready for whatever he has to say, seeing that today he feels like speaking in confidence. Like, I'm going to make a Gaja "bubbly" wine, and I'm going to call it just that, "BollicinaGaja." And guess where I'm going to produce it? In Britain. But instead, he catches me completely off guard.

Angelo "I expect a proposition from you. Setting up a company together. I'm willing to accept whatever proposition you make." I can't help smiling back. Maybe we could find a way to work together... and it would be great to be able to pool our courage at the same time.

Notes for Wines Tasted with Angelo Gaja
Shigeru Hayashi

Valle d'Aosta Chardonnay Cuvée Bois 2009 Les Crêtes
Type white wine
Grapes 100% Chardonnay
Vinification and fining fermentation in 300 l French wood barrels,
fining *sur lie*, continuous *bâtonnages* for 10 months, 8 months
of rest in bottles
Production area Valle d'Aosta

Bright golden color. The aroma is very complex, with hints of fruit
such as pear, papaya, mango and pineapple. Delightful aromatic
herbs and mineral touches. Sapid, soft, long and elegant taste.

I'd pair it with Piacenza-style salt cod (whipped with parsley, garlic
and olive oil). Or else mackerel cooked for a whole day on embers
with a touch of salt and ginger. In Japan I'd like to try it with
kaiseki ryori, Kyoto's traditional meal, which includes some thirteen
different courses! Instead of sake...

If you easily get dizzy, then be careful when you drink this white
wine: it comes from the highest vineyards in the world! And
the wine seems to be born right in the mountains: it's mineral,
as sharp as the rocks, upright and deep. Delicious!

Tignanello 2009 Marchesi Antinori
Type red wine
Grapes Sangiovese, Cabernet Sauvignon and Franc
Vinification and fining soft pressing, fermentation in contact
with the skins, fining between 12 and 14 months in wood
Production area Tuscany

Intense ruby red color with purplish hues. Very vast and
multi-edged aromas, with cherry, violet, vanilla, cocoa, coffee,
licorice and pepper. Full, sapid and embracing taste thanks
to the very velvety tanning. Persistent aftertaste.

To be paired with beef fillet sprinkled with salt and pepper.
Excellent with an assortment of grilled meat, soy sauce and onion.
And I think it's perfect with all aged Italian cheeses.

The "international Italian wine" par excellence, it was the first
Super Tuscan. It was originally a Chianti, then Piero Antinori and
his enologist Giacomo Tachis took up the challenge: no more white
grapes in red wine, the way it used to be done! Made that way this
wine could not (and didn't want to) be Chianti, and it ended up
changing Tuscan enology once and for all.

Montello e Colli Asolani Il Rosso dell'Abazia 2006 Serafini & Vidotto
Type red wine
Grapes Cabernet Sauvignon, Cabernet Franc, Merlot
Vinification and fining maturation from 15 to 24 months in oak
aged at least 30 months; followed by fining in bottles for 1–2 years.
Production area Veneto

Ruby red with a garnet edge. As for aroma, initial burst
of fragrances of red fruit such as raspberry and black currant,
followed by the surfacing of vanilla, pepper, coffee and cocoa.
Broad palate, full and sapid. Very delicate tannin.

Pair with chicken cacciatore, steak with Japanese mustard, aged cheese such as taleggio or gorgonzola. Ideal with pan-fried Japanese meat, soy sauce and white turnip (daikon).

I think it's the greatest Italian Bordeaux-style wine! In Veneto these French vines have existed for more than two centuries, so by now they have become Veneto wines (they might even speak the dialect). In 2006 it was as fresh as a newborn child: Rosso dell'Abazia is made to last!

Barolo Riserva 1982 Borgogno
Type red wine
Grapes 100% Nebbiolo
Vinification and fining 12 days of fermentation followed by submerged cap maceration for 15 days; at least 4 years of maturation in large 60 hl Slavonian oak barrels
Production area Piedmont

Dark garnet red color. Rich, clear aromas of undergrowth, moss, sweet spices, leather, tobacco, coffee and graphite. Warm, embracing, elegant and very long taste. A symphonic wine.

Pair it with braised meat cooked in Barolo, of course! But it's also perfect with aged Castelmagno cheese or else—why not?—with pan-fried Kobe-beef dressed with soy sauce, rice vinegar and Japanese mustard.

A 1982 vintage Barolo Borgogno, need I say more? Italy even won the FIFA World Cup that year! Borgogno is the Ivy League of wine, it has practically always existed. I celebrated my thirty years in Italy with this wine, and I'm going to celebrate my fifty years in Italy, in 2032, with the same wine!

Barbaresco 2008 Gaja
Type red wine
Grapes 100% Nebbiolo
Vinification and fining 12 months of barriques, 12 months of large barrels, final fining process in bottles
Production area Piedmont

Concentrated garnet red color, almost impenetrable. The aroma is intense, with notes of red fruit, undergrowth, spices and leather. Licorice adds a nice final touch. Warm, sapid, dry taste, the tannings are velvety and embracing. Very long finish.

Let's pair it with grilled beef fillet sprinkled with white pepper, or with a beef and wasabi stew. Perfect with Parmigiano Reggiano (exclusively from a Reggiano Red Cow) aged more than 48 months. Superb meditation wine.

I almost cried when I saw Angelo coming my way holding a bottle of Barbaresco 2008: a very beautiful scene, quite romantic! Wine always reflects the producer, and this red wine is a reflection of its creator's entire history and charisma.

Rinaldi: Beppe Rinaldi
Blessed Among Women

At the Heart of Quality Lies Scarcity

Here in Langa, Beppe Rinaldi is "Citrico" to everyone. He was given that nickname when he was in Wine Academy. He used to draw funny cartoons on the blackboard, and one day his teacher, upon seeing the umpteenth cartoon, blurted out: "Rinaldi… you're caustic." At which point one of his classmates added: "As caustic as citric acid." After that everyone starting calling him Citrico. And for all of us he's still Citrico, even though forty-five years have gone by since then. Beppe is a rambunctious guy, it's great to spend time with him. His outbursts are some of the happiest, but also meaningful moments ever for me. Ever since, more than forty years ago, we used to walk up the "Rosa" together. I remember that once, at an altitude of 4,100 meters, after hiking for eighteen hours, 300 meters from the peak of the Castore, there was a huge crevasse that kept us from climbing all the way to the top. That's when Beppe, wearily stooping over his pick axe, shouted out: "Let's go back. Sometimes the things that are left unfinished are the most beautiful of all." He was twenty.

We enter the courtyard of Beppe's house in Barolo. The first "picture" in both a literal and metaphorical sense is dedicated to these hills from which we take in the view from the back of the Rinaldi house. We Langaroli, better still Langhetti, which is how we refer to ourselves in dialect, are accustomed to this spectacle that has inspired melancholy or joy in all the writers who have passed through here. My generation has Cesare Pavese and Beppe Fenoglio in mind, but anyone would be moved before this spectacle. Of course, you have to identify a few specific observation sites because the 1960s and 1970s wreaked devastation and façades of houses that have no respect for traditions, history and a balance with nature. But fortunately, from Beppe's courtyard we only see carefully designed hills with trees, vineyards and the by now rare meadow in the distance.

We sit down around a garden table and can't get Beppe to budge, which condemns us to the noise of the cars that pass by his house. This is to the detriment of our voice recorder, which will be of little help in reconstructing this afternoon of conversation. No problem! The sun's out, we're relaxed, and surrounded by old friends. Beppe, Shigeru, Simona and I, with Annalisa, his wife, whom he calls "the Tigress." Others will join us as well. Citrico's home is always a cross-roads of friends, fellow townspeople and clients.

We're off to a flying start. The economist Zingales, who would be my guest at the Fontanafredda Foundation that same evening, gives us an excuse to talk about the damage that the free market has produced in society, and the need to renew capitalism. Boom! Now I'm going to say something explosive that's sure to warm up the atmosphere.

Oscar "How about you, Beppe. Do really think it's possible to bring back capitalism? What are you hoping for? When we were young we dreamed of Socialism."

Beppe "Yes, but seeing the obvious failure of the Socialist model, it's hard to imagine our generation witnessing the birth of a society based on Marxist and Leninist ideology…"

He speaks slowly, the way intellectuals do when they're trying to find the right words from who knows where and choose them as though they were distilling wisdom with every verb. If we add to this the fat Tuscan cigar that keeps coming and going from his lips with the typi-cally calibrated movement of the cigar smoker, the longish gray hair that falls down on his neck and is slightly unkempt, and the scarf hang-ing down in front (so that it doesn't fulfill the task it's worn for), may-be we can get an idea of the kind of person whose company we're in. A man who knows how to think, who tells his story, who gathers ideas, who has things to say and who watches how we react with curiosity.

Beppe "We're more likely to see the reform of capitalism than a re-birth of Socialist ideals. I come from a family with a Socialist tradi-tion, but the failure, even recently, has been so great… Our generation was dominated by ideals that, it's sad to say, I no longer see in my daughters' generation. Ideals that also come from the Catholic world. Remember the 'Catho-Communists'? The death of ideals is a very sad thing, because dreams are the source of great enrichment."

Oscar "Trust, hope, dreams, all these things we once had, are missing now. We dreamed of a world of equality, justice, freedom for all, and we were sure we'd get there someday. Today it's harder for youngsters to dream."

The "Tigress" comes in, Beppe's charming wife, who tugs the strings and pulls us back down to Earth. "Where should I put the glasses? How many do you need?" The spell is broken.

Beppe, who says he'd rather fly low, instead goes back to what we were saying before: "For our generation, lofty ideals were a source of individual and collective enthusiasm. The last few generations instead had to undergo a 'consumerism dictatorship,' as Pasolini called it in his *Scritti corsari*, attracted by the comfort and ease promised by consumerism (which we, instead, still didn't know about). That's how it ended: the ideal pulsations are dead."

At this point a long digression begins on Sandro Luporini, a multifarious artist, Beppe's great friend and a lyricist for Giorgio Gaber, the protagonist of a celebration at the Teatro Regio in Turin, for the tenth anniversary of the singer-songwriter's death. Beppe was at the Regio, and he was pleased to see so many young and even very young people in the audience, finding a pretext to rekindle a sense of hope. Some people never lose the bad habit of capturing and interpreting the weak signs. Right!

In the meantime, Annalisa has kindly taken out the glasses and placed the white wines on ice to cool. You can tell she's the real master of the house!

Oscar "Simona, write down his wife's name, because he calls her 'Tigress,' but her name's Annalisa. He lives surrounded by all these women: his wife, two daughters, Marta and Carlotta, and his dog and cat are females, too. You're blessed among women! Beppe, now I'm going to tell you why I'm here..." and I go on with my explanations and my reasons.

Oscar "...and this morning I met up with Angelo Gaja."

Beppe "Ooohhh!"

Oscar "Simona, make sure you get that howl down in your notes! I've read that he wants to put wi-fi in the vineyards... But he does make good wine."

Beppe is Bartolo Mascarello's cousin and the natural heir to his ideals, along with Maria Teresa, of course, Bartolo's daughter.

Oscar "Everyone in Langa remembers the differences of opinion between Angelo and Bartolo. During the interview Angelo returned to the scene, telling us that we in Langa grumble a lot. Like when at funerals, at the start of the procession, everyone sings the praises of the deceased, then someone starts in with that fateful 'you know, now that he's dead...,' and that's the signal. From that moment on all the bad things that had been carefully censored behind everyone's good manners come pouring out. But the truth is that Gaja spoke well of Bartolo today."

Beppe "It couldn't be any other way. Bartolo was one of the greatest, a visionary of immense quality. And Gaja has also done a lot for our land, especially abroad. But, like Bartolo, I'm against both international vineyards and barriques. They're just not a part of the Langhe."

I Ferment My Grapes in Josko's Vats

This afternoon, I'm sure, the Pindaric flights will take us far. I talk to him about the fact that we're also going to go see Josko Gravner, in Gorizia, but he won't even let me finish the sentence.

Beppe "He's a great friend of mine! I have some vats in my cellar, which I use for the process of fermentation; they were given to me by Josko, when he shifted to amphorae. I'm still fermenting my grapes in those vats."

Oscar "How did that happen?"

Beppe "I just came out and asked Josko if he'd give me his vats when he shifted to amphorae, because he wasn't going to need them anymore, so he did."

I smile to myself, to hear this story, because the idea of this long-distance collaboration, this cultural but also tangible thread that joins winemakers who come from such different backgrounds is exactly what I would like to see become more generalized in the future of this country, which until now hasn't known how to build networks of common interests around essential values. And wine is one of them.

Beppe, in the meantime, keeps talking to us about his cellar: "I ferment everything in wood, not because wood's better, but owing to a sort of obsession."

No, it's because he thinks it's better, I'm sure of that.

Beppe has decided not to go on explaining: "It's a mystery, it's like trying to explain sex, too much effort." We have to be content with this answer, at least for the time being, because what Beppe wants to do is finish the story of Josko's vats that have now become his. "And so, after the first time I fermented my grapes in those vats, I called Josko who wanted to be reassured. I'd found them to be very efficient, and I told him so, but adding a drop of venom along with it, 'it's the first time ever those vats have fermented noble wine.'"

Oscar "Of course! From Ribolla Gialla to Nebbiolo!"

We're all laughing, showing complicity, competition, provincialism and pride. But great respect for our friend Josko, too.

I go back to the plan for these interviews because he's acquainted with everyone I'm going to go visit. I want him to understand that I have the highest admiration for him and that I consider him among the greatest of vintners. We comment on the fact that there are cellars managed by women alone, like his own will be when (the reader can probably imagine the typically Italian gesture to ward off bad luck he's making right now) they are finally handed down to his daughters. And that gets him going against minimum guaranteed quotas for women and a priori statements such as "a woman at the Quirinal, a woman as President of this or that." Annalisa agrees with me, merit, skill, honesty come before everything else. Whether it's a woman or a man doesn't matter. She's shrewd and sensible just like her husband. After all, there must have been a reason for them to have gotten married. Their constant bickering, "she's a Tigress," "he's always off in his own world," is clearly a habit that conceals their complicity and their love for each other.

Randomness Rules Our Lives

I start over again with my plan. The question I'm going to ask everybody: "Why do you make wine?"

A long pause for effect, my friend is an artful storyteller. There's no

way he really needs to think about it for such a long time before answering the question!

Beppe "It all happened quite by chance, for me as well as for my father. He had an obsession with bricks, he liked to build things, but
his father, his grandfather and his great-grandfather were already
making wine. And family traditions are important. In the olden days
the idea that the children would carry on with the family business was
something that was taken for granted. And, of course, it's easy to become passionate about winemaking and wine. And if you're born into
that world it's even easier. And besides that, randomness rules our
lives. First of all, the randomness of a person's birth. I actually worked
as a vet for sixteen years. I was born in that room on the other side of
that glass wall. In this house, which my grandfather built in 1916."

We all go on a tour of his house. Nice and solid, made with old-
fashioned bricks, with amusing chimney-tops, each one of them different, and like many of our country houses it's built in an L-shape.
Solar panels that are of great use but seem ashamed to be there,
slightly hidden on the roof. With this beautiful, natural terrace that
overlooks the hills where wine is made. And meanwhile, it's a stroll
down memory lane: the story of his family, grandfathers, great-grandfathers, uncles and aunts, great-uncles and great-aunts, who bought
and sold farmsteads in the most strategic locations of the Barolo vineyards, when it wasn't yet called Barolo. And Beppe's story, how he
feels he was lucky to find this house already made. Stories about
brothers who argue because of their wives. (Ouch! I can just feel the
negative vibes from the women sitting around the table.)

Beppe "Women are jealous, they make sure they don't have less than
other women, a ring, a fur, a special gift. Women, in Piedmontese
dialect, *a l'an goj d'ruse* (like to squabble)."

The clinking of goblets is beginning because Annalisa, my accom-
plice, and I are organizing the wine tasting.

Oscar "By the way, how come Eataly is so often out of your wine?
Wait, I know the answer: it's because it's always sold out. You sell it
right away and then you don't do anything about it. You're lazy!"

Beppe "The truth is that I don't deal with sales, and besides that I
love laziness, and not just laziness, but tedium, boredom, the chance
to think, to sink into slothfulness, which can also mean melancholy. I
find it all very enriching."

We Have To Stay Artisanal!

I go back to the topic of the wine that's always out. "Why do you produce so little? You're wine's so good…"

Beppe "It's because of an analysis I made: we don't know how to be entrepreneurs, so we make wine the way artisans do, which means that we are and will always be an artisanal winery. And this also explains why we decided never to increase the number of bottles we produce."

Oscar "You're using the plural, so do you mean you and your father together?"

Beppe "Of course! There's never any doubt about that here! We wanted to stay artisanal. I think my father was very important to this zone, he was always involved in public and social themes, the ones pertaining to this territory, naturally. He was also Mayor of Barolo, as well as assessor and councilor, he founded the Enoteca Regionale del Barolo and was its first president. The idea of not just tending to your own garden but thinking about the territory as a whole instead is certainly beautiful and worthwhile, and it makes you livelier intellectually, but it also makes you waste a whole lot of time that you could devote to your own private affairs instead."

Oscar "You were assessor and councilor for fifteen years, too, but you're much less public than your father, isn't that right?"

Beppe "I've never been a great communicator like my father, something he was really good at."

Oscar "But what are the deep roots of this decision to continue to be artisans, which must have run against the grain at a time of economic growth, during the boom when vineyards were even being planted in land with a northern exposure?"

Beppe "In 1995–2000 there was a boom in Barolo. This meant that the population that had practically alway lived on the edge of poverty suddenly found it had a huge fortune in its hands. And it lost its sense of measure. Let me explain: the Consorzio di Tutela del Barolo e del Barbaresco (Consortium for the Safeguarding of Barolo and Barbaresco) was founded in 1932, and these great old men managed to push the lawmaker, drawing the attention of Senator Desana, who lay the foundations for the law on DOCG (1966). So the Consortium played a key role in the regulation and management of the apellation. The term 'safeguard,' which is very broad, means tending to the hills, the cellars, the territory and not just the economic well-being of the producers. It also affects the genuineness, quality and goodness of the wines..."

Oscar "It also meant safeguarding the quantity of the supply. Is that what you're getting at?"

Beppe "That's it! The bottles had to be limited. At the heart of the quality of a product lies its scarcity! When you end up having too much and start replacing hazelnut and peach tree groves, meadows followed by woods with vineyards, you're doomed! Those who planted vineyards in the north, where our elders would never have dreamed of doing so, just got lucky. It's all about climate change!"

Oscar "They didn't do it out of farsightedness, they were greedy! What made Barolo boom between 1995 and 2000?"

Beppe "We went from just slightly more than 5 million bottles to 12–13, and soon there'll be even more, when the most recently planted vineyards start to produce."

It's not really an answer, but I've come to realize that Beppe likes to talk like this, he likes to leave the topics of discussion unfinished and somewhat up in the air.

When the Female Continues the Species, the Male Can Be Scrapped

As we chat my wife and I quickly text each other: it's about our children. I feel like changing the subject for a moment. I turn to Beppe's wife: "Why do women love their children more than their husbands?" The Tigress, of course, answers unhesitatingly: "It's normal! Men love their children more than their wives, too."

Oscar "Is that true Beppe? Do you love your daughters more than your wife?"

This time Citrico doesn't hesitate: "Absolutely!"

Oscar "Write it down Simona, write down the word: 'absolutely!'"

Beppe passes judgment: "Once females have babies, in many species, the male can be scrapped and left in the undifferentiated waste pile."

Andrea, my son, arrives. It's a chance to tease him with my dream: "To see one of my sons married to one of your daughters, and raise Rinaldi production to 300,000 bottles. Think of the two of us together, old, with you beating me over the head because I destroyed the legend of artisanship. And then seeing your wines in chain distribution along with Grignolino, Asti Spumante with the Rinaldi label."

Annalisa laughs. But Beppe doesn't. "If that were the case, I'd make sure the Farinettis got scrapped!"

Everyone laughs. Beppe knows perfectly well that I'm just teasing him. I've always had the utmost respect for artisanal winemakers. We go back to talking about more serious things.

Beppe "My family's history has always lived alongside the great nobility of our wines: Nebbiolo and Barolo."

Oscar "Even though it wasn't so easy to understand it back then, so that in some years Dolcetto grapes cost more than Nebbiolo grapes."

Beppe "But already in the days of the Fallettis, late eighteenth, early nineteenth centuries, the nobility of the wine that wasn't called Barolo was known of, and in the days of the marchioness, it was listed in the cellar records for Palazzo Barolo in Turin as 'Nebbiolo di prima qualità vecchio o stravecchio amaro.' After the marchioness passed away, after 1864, that is, the first bottles labeled Barolo were produced. Barolo was born in Turin in the Falletti cellars. The term 'dry' wasn't used at the time, wines were either sweet or bitter. Strangely enough, in Piedmont and Valle d'Aosta the majority of the grapes produced were Nebbiolo and not Barbera. But the wines came out sweet, because the food people ate back then was often fat, so to cleanse their taste buds they'd order *moussant* wine."

Oscar "Let's talk about the wines I brought you. In my opinion, wine has to have four qualities: good, clean and fair, as Carlin Petrini says, but it also has to be produced by someone to my liking. There are some producers whose wine I would never drink. I'm looking for likeability. The first wine I brought you was produced by Sergio Mottura and it comes from the Lazio region. He's a real nice guy. The wine is organic. It's called Civitella Rosso. Shigeru, what's the vine species?"

Shigeru "Merlot and Montepulciano!"

Fads Get on My Nerves

Oscar "This wine is organic. Do you or don't you like the word organic?"

Beppe "I like it."

Oscar "So why don't you use it, seeing that you've always been organic?"

Beppe "Fads get on my nerves. And right now it's a fad: things are organic, biodynamic, natural. If it's a fad it's a fad, Giorgio Gaber used to sing, but it still gets on my nerves. Fads make everything the same, flat, stereotypical."

Oscar "I couldn't agree more! Fads do away with all the imagination and creativity."

Beppe "But, what I say is, long live the organic, the biodynamic, the naturalistic ethic. I hope it brings change, that it encourages us to respect the land and its products. This area could be the first to launch, by way of the Consortium, a set of rules concerning the abandonment of insecticides and weed killers, and then move on to chemical fertilizers. At the same time, you also have to keep an eye on the price of grapes, so that a family of farmers can lead a dignified life through viticulture. Let's bear in mind that if we abolish weed killers and chemical fertilizers, we significantly increase the cost of running a vineyard."

Oscar "Here are some figures. Fontanafredda, after abolishing weed killers and chemical fertilizers saw a 10% increase in labor costs."

Beppe "Furthermore, the problem of insecticides stems from the multinationals, which force us to treat the vines, but we wouldn't need to. It's the regulations that force us to do two–three treatments."

Oscar "Now Shigeru, one of the finest connoisseurs of Italian wine, will describe the wine as he tasted it… Then you can comment."

Shigeru doesn't need to be asked twice: "It's incredible how, in an area where white wines are produced, Sergio Mottura knows how to make such an important red wine. There's 80% Merlot here, and the rest is Montepulciano. I can smell prune, pepper, coffee, tobacco and licorice. The mouthfeel is sapid, warm, robust and has good persistence. Even the tannins are soft and ripe. I'd pair it with a roast leg of pork seasoned with juniper berries, or else roast shoulder of lamb with black pepper. This wine should be drunk on special occasions. For instance, the two of you at the top of that mountain."

Oscar "I like the fact that Shigeru tells us what he'd like to eat with this wine. Because wines make you hungry for specific dishes. Beppe, do you agree with Shigeru's pairings?"

Beppe "Not really. I'd drink it while eating a Langa 'tuma' cheese, I wouldn't pair it with strong-flavored meats. It's very good, but I find it to be somewhat low in acidity. I like wines that have a high acidity level."

Oscar "So you like Barbera."

Beppe "Yes, I love Barbera, after Nebbiolo. Barbera is a great wine, unfortunately it's been depreciated because people said it was the kind of wine a drunk might guzzle from a huge bottle (we actually call it *pintone* here). It has a huge capacity to adapt to climates, soils, it isn't complicated like Nebbiolo and Dolcetto. On top of that, it ages a lot and well. I make 5,000 bottles of Barbera."

Oscar "And how many of your other wines?"

Beppe "3,000 bottles of Dolcetto, 15–16,000 of Barolo and 5–6,000 of Nebbiolo."

Women Can Even Read What Isn't Written

Oscar "In the end it's always about 30,000. And what do you expect for the future?"

Beppe "40,000."

Oscar "So you expect an increase of about 30%." I'm amused. "For your information it's the growth of a multinational. Why do you predict the increase?"

Beppe "Because it's right. I'd like this winery to be leaner, I have too much machinery, I'm in the habit of having everything, of being self-sufficient, but that's a mistake, and I know it. I'm only like this because I need reassuring!"

Oscar "Have you talked to your daughters about this?"

Beppe "There's no need to, they can see it. Women can even read what isn't written! They have very sensitive feelers."

Oscar "They look at you, and then do they do what you do, or do they do something different?"

Beppe "For the time being they more or less do what I tell them to."

Oscar "I noticed that today we were only on our first glass and you were already talking about your father. You usually talk about him when you're high, I mean at about the eighty-second glass." I feel free to talk like this because I know Beppe very well. "Today you conveyed the idea of a great idyll, of being madly in love with your father... and I really appreciate that."

Beppe "Not true."

He's lying and he knows he is.

Oscar "I asked around, I asked Carlin and a whole bunch of other people. Everyone told me that your father was a great man. Why did you fight with him?"

Beppe "My father had a difficult personality, he'd been in the army, he was a firm believer in order and hierarchy, but he was democratic. He was the captain of the alpine artillery, and was especially authoritative. A character trait he'd inherited from his mother and that was for sure a dominant one in the family."

Oscar "When did you have your first differences of opinion? Was it during puberty and adolescence?"

Beppe "Right away. My father came back from the war a physical and moral wreck. We would have terrible fights, I would insult him fiercely. Once, during an especially heated discussion, he threw his war pictures down on the table, and said: 'Look at what they made me do when I was your age!'"

The war, that war, is still at the root of our present. Around here, in Langa, you still hear the stories of the torment experienced by the soldiers while they were coming to terms with the reality of the Fascist regime and its militia. There are personal traumas that have affected the lives of their children and that continue to affect behaviors, which is what Beppe is telling us.

Beppe "My father was in Albania. In those days there were many deserters, the victims of the indolence and ineptitude of our army that sent them to certain defeat. If these deserters were caught during searches, they were shot by the firing squad! My father's job was to take pictures before and after they were shot. The pictures were then sent to the Ministry, while the families were told their loved ones had died in combat. After this experience, my father became cynical, he rejected everything he'd been through. He'd look at the pictures and say: 'We must have been crazy, this was one of my soldiers.'"

Oscar "So it was because of all these arguments with your father that you decided to become a vet."

Beppe "Not really, I had in any case been to Wine Academy and was happy about it, but then..."

At this point Beppe tells us about his admiration for a vet who lived in the house opposite his, and who, in 1905, had invented pliers to neuter calves, a tool that was sold across the world. He became immensely rich thanks to this patent. Much of the money he gave to charities, especially to the hospital of La Morra. A small forgotten pearl of the Langa area that he likes to remember. The vet's name was Burdizzo. Beppe is like that. When he thinks of something he has to talk about it, even if it means changing the subject completely, but still managing to keep everyone's attention drawn to himself like no one else I know.

So, thanks to a beautiful story, and with some dialect thrown in, we understand the origin of the passion for animals that convinced him to major in Veterinary Science. And while we enjoy these chats, we see a toing and froing of clients that leave empty-handed because there's no Barolo, and he has no wine left to sell. Around here they run out of Barolo fast. A couple of Germans walk by. Beppe says hello to them smiling. Then he looks at me and says: "In the past, if you heard German being spoken in Langa, you'd flee to the hills."

My Father Never Bottled Because He Had No Patience

Beppe "But even when I was working as a vet I lived here and I worked in the wine cellar. My father never labeled a bottle in his life, he didn't have the patience to. It was up to me. Certain jobs, bottling, labeling, my father just didn't want to do. He thought such jobs were only suited to people with a high and uselessly broad forehead..."

I burst out laughing and say: "He only liked to make wine, he wasn't even interested in selling it!"

Beppe "We didn't just make wine, we had livestock in the stables, we grew some wheat, we had two pigs, I raised rabbits... You know, the way things used to be done, we were almost self-sufficient."

Oscar "Sounds great!"

Beppe "I'd like to go back to that way of life! I'd like to go back to beekeeping now."

Oscar "I really like this father who loves to make wine but can't be bothered to deal with all the rest of it. So how did you come to quit your job as a vet and go back to winemaking full-time?"

Beppe "I was forced to, because my father got seriously ill. He had always entertained the clients under that palm tree over there with hours of conversation. But ever since my grandfather's time we had always sold our wine in demijohns, except for Barolo, which we sold in bottles. He would send the demijohns from the station in Monchiero, which has closed down since, to Liguria. I still have the letters my grandfather wrote to my grandmother while he was traveling around making sales. One of his clients was the Hotel de Paris in Montecarlo."

As he jumps from one subject to another Beppe's like some dancing monkey.

Oscar "While your father was sick, did he actually witness the handing down of the family business?"

Beppe "The truth is I never stopped making wine, not even when I was a vet for the local health authority."

The clinking of goblets: a Chardonnay from Planeta. "Are you familiar with this, Beppe?"

Beppe "Yes, I am, he used to 'barrique' it more, he does so less now. It hasn't got such a woody taste. Does it taste woody to you?"

Oscar "I'll let Shigeru answer, since he's the biggest expert of all of us."

Forget the woodiness! Shigeru really likes this wine.

Shigeru "This is a wine that changed the image of Sicily to being one of pleasure. Chardonnay 100%, since 1985. The color is intense yellow with green hues. The aroma is fruity, peaches, apricot, golden apple, and pineapple. And there's also a strong scent of orange blossom honey. The taste is soft, fresh, smooth and well balanced. I'd pair it with fried chicken and ricotta with papaya, or onion soup with Parmigiano cheese, but it's also ideal with veal medallions in exotic fruit sauce, or baked fish with aromatic herbs. And cheese too. Fresh Bra cheese. In other words, it's a remarkable wine that you can pair with almost any kind of food. Try to imagine drinking it on Tokyo's Sky Tree, the tallest tower in Japan, 643 meters tall."

Oscar "Do you agree?"

Beppe "This Japanese guy sounds kind of nutty to me. But he's right about the aroma and the taste. He got the smell and taste right."

Shigeru "How weird!" Shigeru's being ironic—he's learning!

We return to Beppe's story and find ourselves steeped in tales of land that's bought or swapped between neighbors. Nothing important, because the company's size doesn't grow under Beppe's management, as had been agreed on with his father: 30,000 bottles for the rest of his life!

The story gets sad here when he remembers something terrible that happened: Beppe's brother, his only brother, Paolo, drowned in a sailing accident when he had barely turned twenty. It happened in 1974, on Easter Monday, in Liguria. Paolo, Beppe and two other friends were on the boat together. Suddenly the sea became choppy and the boat capsized. Everyone was saved except Paolo. Beppe was there, trying desperately to save him, but failed. He hung on to the boat until help arrived. Beppe's eyes are shiny with tears, he stops talking.

Oscar "Would he be here now making wine with you?"

Beppe "No doubt about that. And maybe with him here we would have grown even more. Maybe we would have made 50,000 bottles." He changes the subject.

Oscar "I know you've been married twice: the first marriage was childless, and then you broke up. After that you met Annalisa and remarried."

Beppe "No, she married me!"

Simona whispers in my ear: "He sounds just like my father, what do these 'Langhetti' think, that they're so special that women can dream of nothing other than marrying them?!"

Beppe "There comes a time when women want to have children. I've never had a particular urge to have any."

Oscar "Really? Not even to have someone to hand the winery down to?"

Beppe "I was young…"

Oscar "You were thirty-seven when Marta was born!"

Beppe "No, I wasn't thirty-seven…"

A good five minutes go by while he does all the basic math to figure it out. But, as everyone knows, I love numbers. I keep subtracting Marta's age from Beppe's. In the end he's forced to admit, although reluctantly, that I'm right, when his first child was born he was thirty-seven! Seeing that he's not very reliable, Annalisa-the-Tigress arrives to re-establish the truth about the family. So two daughters were born to their father's joy, but to the poorly concealed disappointment of the grandfather, who thought, true to the spirit of those days, that the future of his wine would have been looked after best by male heirs.

Oscar "And did you think that too?"

Beppe "Not at all!"

Oscar "Are you happy that your two daughters have instead decided to carry on with the family tradition?"

Beppe "Very much so!"

Blurted out like that the words are unbelievably beautiful! I'm always especially interested in family dynamics. The changes in perspective brought about by the birth of one's children, the reactions of the rural, traditionalist society to the evolution of thinking, especially the ways by which revolutions reverberate in everyday life and influence what happens. Sons versus daughters, that is to say equal opportunities transferred, with great effort, to the most elementary aspects of progress.

Oscar "And I'm sure you're very happy that your daughters agree with you about how this winery should be run. It's an asset for the territory."

Beppe "And I'm convinced they'll be better at it than I am."

Oscar "I also believe my children will be more successful than me. A father who doesn't think this way isn't a good father!"

Beppe "Also because your children know when you're not being sincere and when you don't have faith in them, especially if they're girls!"

I try to delve deeper into these ideas of an art that's handed down. I want to understand how such a clean, flawless idea that leads to a winemaking process that's absolutely genuine, can be preserved, and at the same time evolve so that it will continue to exist.

Beppe "I think that to be able to do things right you need to have studied the right things, enology, agricultural sciences, but without allowing science to do away with knowledge, I mean, without losing the richness of past experience."

"And," I add, "without letting science and knowledge do away with conscience!"

Beppe "It would be highly presumptuous of us to ignore the experience that, over the centuries, had established certain practices, certain habits in cultivating the vine, in making wine, in preserving the barrels. What's at stake is the work and commitment of the generations that came before us."

Weighing upon the history of wine are at least five millennia on the path to perfection, and these people who are building the image of our wine in such a grandiose way feel all the weight of those years on their shoulders. It's as if they considered innovation for its own sake to be a personal affront, too far-removed from history and from the thinking that was disseminated and handed down. We'll see how. In our visits we'll find that two substantially different paths have been taken toward what's best, and how these two different paths influence and characterize the methods, manipulations, the approach to wine tasting and, lastly, even the relationships between the great winemakers from one school to another.

Beppe "Observation and the contemplation of what had already taken place was the only method in the past to try to seek improvement. Our elders didn't have a microscope. Our great-grandfathers knew that wine fermented, but, until Pasteur discovered yeast, no one knew why it did."

Oscar "The task of science is to solve mysteries—I like the way this came out, so I decide to downplay—and now let's see if we can solve the mystery of Shigeru's thinking about the sparkling wine that I brought here for the Tigress, who's sick and tired of your red wines, it's always Nebbiolo, Dolcetto and Barbera!"

Here's a sparkling wine made in the Classical Method. It's a type of wine they've been producing in Langa for about a 140 years. The first to produce it was Gancia, who imported the method from Reims, followed by Fontanafredda a few decades later. So we have a certain know-how in the way we treat Chardonnay and Pinot Nero, to get fermented bubbles in the bottle.

Oscar "What do you think, Beppe?" We're tasting my Alta Langa Contessa Rosa Brut Riserva 2008.

Beppe "Very good!"

Oscar "This is an absolute novelty, research that I carried out personally to give Alta Langa a personality. The secret of the Champagne producers lies in the *liqueur d'expédition*: some add Armagnac, Cognac, or something else. We add Barolo 1967, can you taste it and smell it? Can you see it in the color?"

Beppe "I'm a Champagne lover. After all, if you want to get a woman into your bed you'd never use Moscato or Barolo to do so. Only Champagne! Like in that song by Peppino di Capri. There's no one who doesn't like Champagne and bubbles!"

That's it! In the language of the Langa we have described a specific marketing operation of world value. The French were able to link one type of wine to a strong metaphysical value: love, anniversaries, courtship. But us... Cesare Pavese, who was one of us, used to say: "Barolo is the wine you drink when you want to make love in the winter days, but only women understand such things." Even Gaja, while drinking some Barolo said, "It's a sexy wine!" But, there's no way around it. For now the French can't be beat when it comes to knowing exactly how to bestow their products with intangible values.

Beppe "But going back to the bubbles... the *liqueur d'expédition* is an addition that served to preserve the wine's quality level even during difficult years; then it became a specific characteristic of the winery, so that the product would always be clearly identified."

Oscar "This is why I think adding Barolo as a *liqueur d'expédition* could become a formidable identifying element over the years."

And at this point Beppe goes off on yet another tangent to tell us about the attempts made in the nineteenth century to use Nebbiolo grapes to make Champagne, the point being to make up for the scarcity of the original raw material. High-sounding names: Marchioness Falletti, General Staglieno, French consultants that make Champagne in Genoa. Maybe we've gone overboard with the tastings and I want to test my friend's well-known objectiveness.

Oscar "What do the French have that we don't?"

Beppe "They were born with Joan of Arc, and the first laws protecting Champage date back to the eighteenth century. We were born as recently as 1861, and maybe we still haven't developed completely. They have a dignity and pride that we Italians are still trying to grasp. Consciousness and the strong belief in the true value of their terroirs and their wines."

Oscar "This pride takes them to thresholds that for us are still unattainable. We have 47 million tourists, they have 80; the Louvre on its own earns more than all our museums put together; they export 11 billion euros' worth of wine, as compared to our 5."

But now Shigeru is ready to tell us about these bubbles and I'm curious to hear how he describes them. When Shigeru drinks sparkling wine he shuts his eyes and his expression changes. Like all good drinkers he adores Champagne.

Shigeru "The color is a strong yellow with pink edges. You can see how it's contaminated by the Barolo. As for aroma, the Pinot Nero prevails over the Chardonnay, you think you're smelling a red wine: dried fruit and lots of minerals. The sweet scent of breadcrust is very important. To the palate it's fragrant; the bubbles fill my mouth. It's sapid and fresh, but above all it's long. It's one of the few wines you can pair with artichokes, but I would suggest stuffed artichokes. It's perfect with seafood antipasto and cold cuts, but also with smoked buffalo mozzarella. But the dish this wine really makes me feel like eating is sushi with salmon roe and sea urchins, without overdoing it with the soy sauce."

Our mouths are watering now, but the face that shows the most enthusiasm is Annalisa's. I'd brought this wine just for her. I know it's one of her favorites.

Sex? Too Much Effort!

The Tigress, who's carefully following our ranting and raving, goes looking for the Cannubi for the next tasting. This gives me a chance to introduce a thorny subject, playing on the effect of the close multiple tastings.

Oscar "Once, during an important interview, the journalist, after forty questions on wine, asked you what you thought of sex, and you replied: 'Sex? Too much effort!' Can you tell me now what you meant by that?"

Beppe "It's a thought that has to stay unfinished. Everyone has to find their own conclusion."

And he smiles, looking like the cat who ate the canary, which is the way people look here when they mix wine with talk about sex.

Beppe "The continuity of the species, which is linked to sex, can be very heavy, but also very light. Sex is the same, either it's very enjoyable, or very hard."

Now I turn to Simona. "Did you get that Simona?" She's sort of embarrassed, but won't help me out, she's blushing.

Beppe "Giving continuity to the species can be very hard..."

Oscar "It depends on the species that comes from it, doesn't it?"

Beppe "So even sex can be a great effort. I'd rather say no more than that."

The Unfinished Is Beautiful

I try to interpret this. There are three great ideas in the minds and the hearts of men and women at every latitude: the quest for Utopia, that is, the planning of one's own future; the fear of death, with the effort to overcome it; the great question of procreation, trivialized with the word "sex." Of these three riddles the last is like an idea trapped in an elevator and you never know which floor it's going to stop at. If it stops at the lower floors, scenes in the alcove, material and technical efforts come to mind (sometimes professional ones too), to be able to give and receive pleasure. Sometimes for some people it's an effort. If the elevator stops at the floors in between, the pantomimes of court-ship come to mind, preys that think they're hunters, women whose "yeses" are responsible for the quality of future generations and, see-ing the topic, you think of the rivers of Champagne that are going to be needed. If it stops at the top floors, the statement "sex is an effort" seems to be a balance of one's life, an evaluation after the results, the offspring, the future that takes shape before us. It sounds like the words of someone who is disillusioned, who sees tears and blood ma-ture, so sex, which is at the origin of everything, can be a wasted ef-fort. I wonder if this is what he meant.

Beppe's thoughts remain romantically incomplete and suspended. Let's heed the lessons of the great Tonino Guerra!

Beppe "Seeking completeness is a form of conceit. Only God is fin-ished and perfect. Faith itself, in any form, can be none other than doubt."

So true! But I think the elevator has gone up too far. Let's come back down to the clinking of our goblets. I suggest drinking Teo Musso's beer, Terre 2010, the one that's aged in red wine barrels.

Oscar "What do you think?"

Beppe "It's not really a beer, is it: this is something else, I really like it. I consider beer to be a beverage, among other things the fruit of lots of processes, which start out from the raw material, barley." It's hard to describe the tone he uses to pronounce the word "barley," as if he were talking about some vile material, suited at best for making ersatz coffee.

Oscar "Let's go back to the future of our wines. Let's talk about the Consortium. You were responsible for getting me involved in one of the most boring and pointless evenings of my life, when you took me to the meeting of the Consortium to elect the president. There were two candidates. I was expecting to hear their speeches with a list of the things they would do so that I could choose which one to vote for. Instead nothing doing, we went straight to the vote. How was I supposed to decide who of the two was better for the future of our wines? There were lots of people sitting there passively, casting their vote with no debate whatsoever. It will soon be time to re-elect the president. What do you think?"

Beppe "I'm hopeful for a change. This wine zone could really do with a farsighted plan."

Oscar "Do we have examples of consortiums that actually work in Italy?"

Beppe "None at all!"

Again, the French are more serious than we are. We Italians don't know how to be part of a team. We have immense assets that are just waiting to be told to the world. We even have the individual champions who would know how to do this. But the institutions are soporific, even when they elect their own representatives.

Beppe "The best men hold themselves back. But this may also be because the companies are overburdened with bureaucracy that forces the entrepreneur to work hard, to waste time with dull and tedious tasks that don't leave him or her free to think about common interests, those of the territory. On top of that, in consortiums you always find two souls: the retailers' lobby and the producers' individualism. Retailers aim for big numbers and globalization. Artisanal producers, besides the fact that they thrive on envy and trivia, also have the huge defect of isolating themselves socially, despite the fact that they're the zone's healthy backbone. It's the small companies that have valorized this territory. Unfortunately, though, the small ones have acted individually, and this isn't a good thing."

Oscar "Is our inability to do things together a throwback to the past?"

Beppe "It's the legacy of feudalism. In fact, what's lacking in the consortiums is information being shared, a network, democracy. This is why some of them opt out. It's easier to rule if you keep people ignorant. History teaches us this."

The Consortium as a metaphor for the whole country! I wonder if an outside president of great stature, someone like Carlin Petrini, for example, would be accepted. He probably has much more important things to do. But it would be fabulous…

Time for politics.

Oscar "Now that we know how things went, would you change your vote at the next General Elections?"

Beppe "Yes, I'd vote for Renzi."

They almost answer in unison, Beppe and Annalisa. I was talking about the General Elections, they answered about the Democratic Party primaries. But the concept is clear. I'm happy, I think to myself, it's never too late.

Oscar "What do you think will happen now?"

Beppe "It's a mess now, and I don't know why you're asking *me*."

Oscar "Because you've gone through so many harvests I think you know a lot more about it that anyone else. People who harvest know more."

Beppe "My father could never imagine that there would be someone in the family who wasn't giving a hand. As soon as I learned how to use my hands he put me to work in the vineyard. You can't imagine the number of harvests he put me through…"

Oscar "So let's consider fifty-one harvests for you, starting when you were fourteen, of which twenty-five as head of the winery. Did I get that right?"

Beppe "Yes, fine. You deal with the numbers."

Shigeru wants to talk to us about Baladin Terre 2010 beers and he sets in: "I remember that Teo Musso gave me a CD with Spanish music on it. It was September 9, 2008—it's incredible how the Japanese are always so accurate—. Warm, sexy music, like this beer that tastes like wine."

But we interrupt him. The beer is already finished, so good and fresh that we gulped it down. Now we feel like having Barolo.

Oscar "Shigeru, why don't you write down a nice description of this beer, right now it's time to talk about Beppe's Barolo."

Annalisa comes back up from the cellar with a bottle of Cannubi 2009, unlabeled, just bottled. Naturally, no sign of any of the previous vintages. All sold out. Except for a few magnums that Citrico jealously preserves for important evenings, with real friends. I'm honored to have participated in a few of them. Outstanding wines. But now I'm curious to be the first to try his Barolo 2009. I've never drunk such a young Rinaldi before.

Beppe "Come on, forget about it, I just bottled it. It's not ready yet."
Like hell I'm going to forget about it.
Oscar "Annalisa, uncork it. Don't listen to him… the way you always do, as usual."
And, as usual, Beppe's Barolo is magnificent. Makes me lick my moustache, which I'm lucky to have. So good! I really like Citrico's wines. What a shame he makes so few of them! This time we let Shigeru describe the Cannubi. There's no holding him back.
Shigeru "This hill that only gets southern exposure is legendary. The wine it produces is of unparalleled elegance. The aroma is of roses and violets. Also cherry, herbs, lots of herbs, pepper and licorice. But I can also smell stone, Langa stone. It tastes sapid, warm, it has good body, but you can tell it still has to age in the bottle some more. These velvety tannins are typical of Cannubi. I'd pair it with Barolo stewed meat, but made with the same Barolo. Also hare cacciatore with green peppercorns, and aged cheeses. Here in Piedmont you have a re-markable variety to choose from."
We end with Cannubi 2009, and talk about the future.
Oscar "What are your daughters like? Are they like each other?"
Beppe "Yes!"
Annalisa adds: "They're both more intelligent than me, but more than him, too!"
Oscar "You love your daughters so much. What a beautiful family!"
We take off. There's one question I would have liked to ask but didn't. Maybe in the future. Maybe when he reads this he'll call me… from the land-line… since he's thrown his cell phone away. Why is sex such an effort if the result of it is two daughters you can be so proud of? But, most importantly, why is it that trying to achieve per-fection in the winemaking processes, getting through bad seasons, worrying about the results, sweating from harvest to harvest, spend-ing your life pondering over the meaning of wine in this particular zone and in the world in general, talking for hours about the history of your family, doesn't for a single instant make Citrico say: "Wine? It takes a great effort!"

Notes for Wines Tasted with Beppe Rinaldi
Shigeru Hayashi

Civitella Rosso 2010 Sergio Mottura
Type red wine
Grapes 80% Merlot, 20% Montepulciano
Vinification and fining fermentation in steel, fining for another
6 months also in steel
Production area Lazio

Impenetrable ruby red color. Fruit (prune) seeps through its
aroma, followed by black pepper, undergrowth and licorice.
The taste is sapid, dry, round, with a definite acidic backbone.
Mature tannins, long and harmonious aftertaste.

Pair with fried meat mix, pork stew seasoned with juniper, roast
shoulder of lamb with black pepper. Savor it with aged Parmigiano
Reggiano or Grana Padano.

The challenge wasn't just to make a good wine, but to make a great
red one in the land of white wine. Sergio Mottura succeeded in
doing so, and every time I taste this blend (international and
autochthonous grapes) I feel just as moved as I was the first time!

Chardonnay 2009 Planeta
Type white wine
Grapes 100% Chardonnay
Vinification and fining fermentation and fining in barriques that
are half new, half second passage
Production area Sicily

Golden yellow with green hues. As for aroma, fruity hints of peach,
apricot, golden apple and pineapple emerge. Honey flavor on the
back palate. The taste is soft, fresh, smooth and balanced.

I would pair it with fried chicken, ricotta with papaya, Parmigiana-
style onion soup or veal medallions with exotic fruit sauce. Perfect
with oven-baked fish and aromatic herbs.

An incredible white wine, capable of changing the image of Sicilian
wine in the 1980s. I never get tired of drinking it, and I'd like
to taste it at the top of the Tokyo Sky Tree, a 643-meter-tall tower,
the tallest building in Japan. Just like this wine, the "tallest" wine
in Sicily.

Alta Langa Contessa Rosa Brut Riserva 2008 Fontanafredda
Type sparkling wine
Grapes Pinot Nero and Chardonnay
Vinification and fining after the first fermentation (half in steel,
half in barriques), the cuvée is made and the secondary fermenation
is carried out in bottles, where the sparkling wine goes though
a long process of fining on its own yeasts.
Production area Piedmont

Intense straw color and intriguing, compact perlage. Complex
and rich aroma, with notes of dried fruit, breadcrust and yeasts.
Fragrant, sapid, fresh and persistent taste.

Pairs well with seafood antipasto and cold cuts. Excellent with smoked buffalo mozzarella, stuffed artichokes, salmon roe and sea urchin sushi dressed with soy sauce and sake. I will never tire of saying that the bubbles are great both with a meal or on an empty stomach.

Fontanafredda and Gancia were the first cellars in Piedmont to produce sparkling wine in the Classical Method, that is, with the same one used to make Champagne. In my opinion, Contessa Rosa is a super sexy wine. The secret might just lie in the *liqueur d'expédition*: Barolo Borgogno 1967!

Baladin Terre 2010
Type Barley Wine beer
Made from Nerone black rice from Cascina Belvedere and barley grown directly on the estate
Vinification and fining for a long time in barrels and barriques inside the Cantina Baladin
Production area Piedmont

Deep amber color. The aroma features an initial burst of notes of barley, cherry, prune, vanilla, coffee, tobacco and walnuts. The taste is warm, soft, sweet and structured. The aftertaste is long and harmonious, you can taste the toasted barley and the caramel.

I suggest pairing it with Piedmontese fondue, fried eel with marasca (cherry) sauce and toasted barley, pork shank with shallots and balsamic vinegar. But it's also perfect as meditation beer.

Another magic trick by Teo Musso, his gift to his "land," the Piedmont. I wish I could always have a bottle of it with me, it makes me feel safe and I know it makes me feel good, too. On September 9, 2008, Teo gave me a CD: every time I listen to it I think of his beers and feel happy!

Barolo Cannubi San Lorenzo-Ravera 2009 Giuseppe Rinaldi
Type red wine
Grapes 100% Nebbiolo
Vinification and fining long maceration, fining for 3 years in a large
barrel, then left to rest for 1 year in a bottle
Production area Piedmont

The color is ruby garnet with an orange edge. As for aroma,
you discover notes of rose and violet, cherry, aromatic herbs, black
pepper, flint and licorice. The taste is sapid, warm, it has robust
body but without any roughness. Subtle tannins.

Pair it with braised meat cooked in Barolo, hare stew seasoned
with green peppercorns, pan-fried beef fillet with pink peppercorn
and wasabi. Excellent with game and aged cheeses like toma
or spicy gorgonzola.

One Barolo, one style, one land. One man: Beppe Rinaldi,
the prophet who can see the future. His wines are the slowest
in the world: you can open a bottle today, head out for a vacation
to the Hawaiian islands, come back in a month and the wine will
just about be ready to be drunk: but it's so enjoyable!

Vigneti Massa: Walter Massa
Smiling Eyes, Embracing Arms

The following story is not just about a person named Walter Massa. It's the story of a wine, Timorasso, a wine he totally reinvented. It's the story of a border territory, between the Italian provinces and northwestern regions, in search of an identity. It's the story of a lunch in Fellini style on the square of a small town, with a group of very special people, organized in our honor by a phenomenal person: Walter Massa.

Wine is the Balancing Point above the Madness

Monleale is not a place you just pass through. It has nothing to do with the Via Francigena, the road that heads in the direction of the Gallie, the one that Costantino mentioned to us. You have to come to Monleale on purpose. You arrive from Tortona, heading toward the hills that emerge from the plateau between Alessandria and Pavia. Looking southward you can see mountains and small valleys across which the breeze from the nearby Genoa sea blows in. It must be this unusual encounter between the border winds that gives Timorasso the sublime fragrances and flavors of long lost places. Close by is Volpedo, famous for being the birthplace of Giuseppe Pellizza, and for its fabulous peaches. Monleale Alto is the place where Walter Massa lives. Walter is famous for his wines, especially his white wine, which ages as well as Barolo does.

It's another marvelous spring day, we're all in a good mood, and we like the place right away.

"Zoccolo" is the first of Walter's friends we meet. Mid-morning, he's kneeling, bent over a large casserole atop a makeshift gas burner that he's set down on the ground, right on the paved square. Zoccolo, which means "clog," and who was no doubt given this nickname because eight months a year he doesn't wear shoes (and he isn't wearing any today either), is a chef who's cooking chicken for lunch. There must be at least five chickens in the pot. They spent a joyous life in the barnyard of some nearby farm—he tells us reassuringly—and they only ever ate natural food, never animal feed. Fabulous! It's already plain to see that there are going to be a few big surprises today... we're so lucky!

Walter has smiling eyes, and when he says hello he gives you a hug. So we embrace and then go into the house to put down the four bottles we brought with us. It's nice and cool, the windows overlooking the valley are wide open so the fresh air can come in. This is where he, his mother, the great and beloved mother of this family, Walter's sister and her husband, a niece (the princess) and two young nephews all live together. Walter's son instead lives with his mother in Tortona. That's a special story, and we'll go back to it later. We only stay in the house for a few minutes because Walter wants to take us to see the vineyards, which he says "are a hundred steps from the house." A hundred steps aren't that many, but they're enough to meet one of Walter's nephews, Edoardo, driving a tractor with a sense of purpose. "Do you have a license?" I ask him. Of course he doesn't, he can't be more than thirteen...

At this point I realize that to be able to talk to Walter the *vigneron*, the winemaker, I have to talk about his tractors first. You can't really tell the story about someone like him if you don't understand just how important Caterpillars are to a winery like his. There are tractors everywhere: in the air, because you can hear them working, in the landscape, because they emerge like dots of color, in the open garages where they peek out showing all their beauty, in the imagination of the children who, when driving a tractor, feel like they're adults already. Tractors are the farmer's arms and legs multiplied by a thousand, and knowing how to use them represents the art that strikes a balance between the farmer and his land. The real farmer knows how to drive a tractor skillfully and lightly so that he doesn't damage his land, twisting and turning on the hills the way Soldini does on the ocean waves. A hundred steps later and we're overlooking the vineyard-filled landscape, which reminds us that, besides the fruit, and the tons of grapes that are produced here, these terroirs have a vocation for winemaking. A natural amphitheater filled with vineyards that reminds us of the Langhe, and that we weren't expecting to see around here. Looking down from above you can barely see the different eras of the planting. Walter tells us that the winemaking tradition here is as old as it is in the Langhe. "If not older," he says. Walter's pride for his land is boundless.

Oscar "Did you learn your trade from your father or on your own?"

Walter "I learned it while looking in the mirror, and driven with the proud desire to give meaning to this land."

Incredible! It's the same answer we got from Costantino Charrère. I'm starting to wonder just how often these men look at themselves in the mirror?! Then I think about the fact that we're dealing with the generation that had to invent a new relationship for itself with the vineyards, so that they could achieve the quality we're familiar with.

Walter "I was born surrounded by vineyards: in this territory there were 8,000 hectares of vineyards. Today, that number's down to 2,000. Until the 1930s, the Tortona market was one of the most important ones for Italian wine, because it had both white and black grapes. When the phylloxera struck, which happened when there wasn't enough labor to tend to the vineyards anyway, people started growing fruit and the vineyards disappeared. When I was a child all the business in this area was aimed at Asti, Milano and Stradella. On the street where my house is situated, during the harvest, there were four active presses and almost all the wine was sold in demijohns. The wine at the time was mostly Barbera, of which there were two kinds—as he tells me this Walter's already laughing—there was type A (acidic) and type B (*brusc*)." We laugh along with him. (In Piedmontese dialect "brusc" means "acidic.") "In the 1970s, some people, and us too, started adding 'Cortese': we're 30 kilometers from Gavi."

Oscar "So your family was already into winemaking?"

Walter "Yes, my great-grandfather came to live here in 1879 and he bought a lot of land. I personally own 6 hectares in this valley. In 2006 I bought the last parcels of land, the ones down there—he points to them—they face the southeast, a fantastic exposure! I uprooted the Cortese down there and planted Timorasso because I thought to myself... there's no point keeping Claudia Schiffer in the kitchen washing the dishes, I'll switch her over to reception and get more out of it!"

Oscar "Was your father, like his father before him, a farmer?"

Walter "One step back. My father and my uncle have always worked together, sharing a TV, washing machine and the great friendship between their wives. Thanks to this I was able to put aside some resources. They believed in fruit harvesting and in the 1960s they planted 400 American Red Haven yellow peach trees that sold at a price that was four times that of the traditional Guid Buns. Thanks to those peaches my father and uncle were able to build a six-story condominium, and then the house I was born in. I'm proud of my ancestors because there were some pretty amazing people among them. Just think, my great-grandfather on my mother's side, Bartolomeo, who in the 1930s was the first person in town to have a bathroom in the house, got married for the second time when he was eighty-one. He used to say, 'If we don't have any children it's not my fault...,' because he'd had four boys and a girl from his first marriage." So that's who Walter takes after, we all laugh.

Walter "I couldn't waste all the work that had been done by my family so I decided to go into winemaking, but the way *I* wanted to! My parents were stubborn, and they refused to accept changes. During the early years I would prune the vineyards secretly! It was thanks to this that we finally started making good wine. The first harvest of grapes I myself grew was in 1978, the year I was doing my military service. Back then I had 10 hectares of Barbera and 2 hectares of white grapes with some Timorasso, but not too much."

White Wines Are the Jewel in the Crown of Tortonese Viticulture, and They Will Have a Wonderful Future

On our way back home, Walter tells us that in 1300 the magistrate from Bologna Pier de Crescenzi, who was an agriculture enthusiast, after living for a period of time in the Asti area wrote a *Practical Treatise on Agriculture* in which he stated: "White wines are the jewel in the crown of Tortonese viticulture. They will have a wonderful future." Evidently, the treatise never ended up in the right hands because Tortonese viticulturists didn't believe in their white wines. When Walter began making wine, a small amount of Timorasso was sold in demijohns on the Swiss market under the name of Torbolino, because it started out murky in November and was then processed and filtered in Switzerland. Or else it was blended with Cortese, which was the only white wine that was known of.

Oscar "Is this Timorasso a hard grape to process?"

Walter "It doesn't produce well, it's not regular, it tends to rot, in other words, you have to keep a sharp eye on it. Just like you would for Nebbiolo. Problematic grapes, when you know how to process them, produce unique wines."

As we stroll along we run into Walter's other nephew, Filippo, who's busy with a tractor as well. In this family everyone works, even on a Sunday, the way people used to.

Walter adores his nephews and they adore him. That's for sure.

I ask Walter, "You went to Wine Academy, didn't you?"

Walter "Yes, I did."

Oscar "Was it your own choice?"

Walter "No, my father made me go, and it was my grandmother who convinced me."

Oscar "Did she see you as a future vintner?"

Walter "My father, Augusto, was a staunch Christian Democratic, a diehard anti-Fascist, and a dogmatic anti-Communist. He envisioned me in Alessandria in a position of power so that I would be able to take care of all our friends and relatives. He didn't see me going much farther than that."

As we talk we go inside the house and Beppe, Walter's brother-in-law, comes to greet us. Walter introduces him as his biggest intellectual sponsor. Beppe apologizes to us, saying: "I don't drink, so I'm leaving." "But his children, my nephews, have a drink every now and then, it's a good thing they didn't take after him!" Walter adds. We all laugh, his brother-in-law too.

Oscar "Let's go back to the Wine School..." As we talk we make ourselves comfortable around the table. In the house you can still feel the fresh air from before, and Walter starts putting the tasting glasses on the table, while Shigeru, as always, very carefully takes care of arranging and opening the wine bottles.

Walter "In 1973 they convinced me to go to Alba to study. When I came back home an enologist, I got right down to work on the Barbera. Finally, in 1979, I made my first 10 hectoliters of Croatina, arguing with my Uncle Renato, my mother's brother, who even today, at the age of ninety-one, thinks he's an expert on everything. My father, instead, was always interested in the vineyard and politics. When he passed away in 2000 he was the mayor. I cut my teeth in the wine cellar in the company of my Uncle Giuseppe. I felt like making another white wine to be added to the Cortese. I had just under 10 tons of grapes from which, in 1987, I made the first 560 bottles and went to sell them at the Fiera di San Giorgio. I called it Timauss."

Oscar "So you hadn't called it Derthona yet?"

Walter "No, because ideas usually come to you when you're in the middle of the job!"

It's almost time to taste the first wine, Roycello 2010 Tormaresca from the Salento area, wine from one of the most beautiful Pugliese wine companies, bought and run by Piero Antinori. Salento is the Langa of the Puglia region. Walter finds that the wine was "made very well": it's a modern Fiano and it has little to do with other southern wines, which are often too strong.

As always, **Shigeru**'s description is precise and delicate: "The aroma is white flowers like acacia, herbs, yellow peaches and apricots and dried hay. The flavor isn't particularly sapid, it only slightly alludes to dried fruit, it has a gentle acidity and an average body. Very soft and pleasant. It's a wine for every occasion, it's easy to drink. Ideally, I'd pair it with vegetable puré, raw fish, asparagus tempura with salt and lemon, or a nice *acqua pazza*, fish cooked in poaching liquid." I think that tasting a Fiano from Salento in the valley of Timorasso is sort of like eating typical Milanese saffron rice in Naples. But this is what makes our trips to visit the greatest winemakers so exciting. I really enjoy watching how eager they are to taste the wines made by other producers. Generally speaking, the bigger they are the more they appreciate their fellow-vintners' work.

Setting the Price

Oscar "So you made your first bottles of Timorasso. How did you set the price?"

Walter "I was at a trade fair when a man from Ovada came around. He said he had a bar in Milan, on the Naviglio, and he only wanted to serve Piedmontese and Veneto wines. He bought several bottles."

Oscar "And what about the price? Did you start out high?"

Walter "I started out right! Let me explain: since the price is usually the result of the classical economic law of demand and supply, I should have practically given it away for nothing. So I decided to use another method. I told him the truth: if I had based the price on the cost of production it would have been expensive. So I was pragmatic, as usual. Gavi, the good kind, cost from 5,000 lire to as much as 14,000 lire per bottle in the 1980s. I calculated the average and in 1987 sold my first Timorasso at 7,800 lire a bottle."

The fact that Walter still remembers exactly what the price was twenty-six years ago tells me that he has a good relationship with figures. A good sign, I think to myself.

Oscar "What did you think when you tasted your first bottle of Timorasso?"

Walter "I thought: well, maybe this is it."

Oscar "It was a very critical moment. Your whole life was at stake there."

Walter "Well, yes... I had been lucky to have some excellent teachers at Wine Academy, people like Professor Rissone, for chemistry, Professor Morando, for enology. They knew their stuff, but to make wine I used the rule that had been taught to me by my law professor, Gigi Borgogno: the judge must exercise the diligence of a good family man. And to make Timorasso I applied that diligence. In other words, I put some common sense into it. I wanted to understand who was right. Those who told me it was the best wine in the world, or those who told me the grapes were crap."

Oscar "Practically speaking, you're talking about the relationship between science, knowledge and conscience. You applied conscience, because always abiding by the rules means applying science and knowledge. But sometimes the soul can show you the right way too." Conscience is reponsible for the evolutionary leap forward that changed apes from animals into human beings.

Walter "Yes, that's what I did. In 1988 the wine was even better, but that year I tasted it in July, before bottling it, and I felt it was a tiny bit too sweet. And right there, in the cellar, I realized that Timorasso requires time: it isn't ready until at least eighteen months have gone by after the harvest."

Oscar "Back then, there was no aged white wine."

Walter "No, there wasn't!"

Oscar "But in the meantime you'd become the head of the cellar?"

Walter "Yes, I had, in 1982–1983. It's a natural promotion, the same thing happens among farmers."

When he speaks Walter expresses a rare energy and vitality. His eyes are smiling, his hands make wide, ample gestures, his cheeks turn red and he keeps on drinking. He's like me: if he likes the wine, he'll drink it. The second wine we taste is Breg Anfora made by Josko Gravner. I brought it here because I know the two of them share a mutual admiration for each other. When Walter tastes it he goes so far as to call it "orgasmotic," and he quotes Erasmus of Rotterdam and his famous words: "Wine is the reflection of the mind."

Shigeru is virtually down on his knees with this wine. He says that maybe in Japan they wouldn't understand it, but he finds it extraordinary. He'd like to explain the process of fining in amphorae, but as soon as he starts to do so Walter looks at him pityingly, as if to say: "You were still drinking green tea in the soy fields when I was already talking to Josko about amphorae." He doesn't come right out and say it, but it's obvious. And it's obvious to our Japanese friend, too, who stops talking. He just adds one sublime thing: "I'd drink it with shark's testicles." Well, I'd drink it to forget them, the testicles, I mean. But Walter doesn't manage to hear those incredible last words, because he keeps getting calls from friends, which he always ends with an imperative in just a few syllables, *Ven su co tì!* (you come on up too). He invites everyone to join us for lunch. He's practically arranged a party. I wonder how many of us will be eating…

Oscar "Let's go back to Timorasso. So you understood that it takes time. And then what happened?"

Walter "In 1992 I harvested a great grape, which I put into the first Timorasso cru and called 'Costa del Vento.' My father gave me his backing in this venture. In those days, when we weren't fighting, we worked in harmony together! He understood me, and luckily he lived long enough to find out what my utopias tasted like. I went from 5–6 hectoliters of wine to 21–25,000 bottles. This wine was good, I liked it! And since my salesman in Milan said he thought I sold it at too high a price, to prove him wrong, I decided to sell it at the same price as the Blangè: 12,000 lire a bottle! Seeing that I was increasing production I also felt entitled to raise the price. As you can see I've never applied the rules of economics."

Oscar "You do the exact opposite of what the market rules say you should do. So much for Adam Smith!"

Walter "Yes! But Smith was right when it came to normal people, not crazy ones like me."

Where I come from, in Alba, we coined a word: *gabilò*. It means a crazy person who's likable, charming, successful. And Walter Massa is one of those people, he's a *gabilò*.

Oscar "Do you sell everything?"

Walter "Absolutely everything! With the help of my sales agents."

Oscar "Is it a strategy you decided on by yourself or together with your father?"

Walter "With all the respect I owe him, I've always made these decisions while looking at myself in the mirror. My father, like his whole generation, was devastated by the war and he would never have supported a strategy of this kind."

We didn't say much about the war, but as soon as we arrived Walter told us that his uncle had been deported by the Germans (never to return) and that his father was so traumatized by it that he never again wanted to leave Monleale. Not even for his honeymoon! An incredibly close-knit family. I think about all the things these great winemakers have in common. Costantino's mirror, Beppe Rinaldi's war-traumatized father… and while I'm thinking about it all Zoccolo comes in with bread and *pancetta*, Italian bacon, which he praises with a "December 2009!" Around here they're much better at making cold cuts than in Langa, and this fragrant, crisp, fresh *pancetta* brings tears to our eyes! It can't be from 2009, no way. But who cares, it's awesome. The place has turned into a party. It's hard to steer the helm of this ship that I'm happy to set free to sail wherever it wants to upon the sea… it's a friendly sea anyway. Walter opens up a couple of bottles of his Barbera. It wasn't planned, not now, not two of them. He says he's not doing it because of the wine, that he wants to talk to us about corks: the same kind of cork was used to seal both of them but he wants to show us that the cork itself is of two different colors. The top of one of the corks is stained a lighter red, while the red on the other cork is darker. Why? Because one of the corks wasn't perfectly neutralized. Corks used to seal bottles undergo chemical phases that first basify them, then acidify them, and then basify them again, over and over again. And the cork has to be perfect, otherwise it would compromise the conservation of the wine. The matter of the corks is something he takes very much to heart . But, while we're at it, we taste the Barbera. It goes perfectly with the bread and bacon, magnificent. The whole thing about the corks is just a big excuse.

Oscar "Walter, sorry, let's go back to prices. After 1992 did you raise them again?"

Walter "Yes, because my aim was to get as high as the price of Jermann's Vintage Tunina. And I did. My revolution took place in 1995 when I went to Friuli and met Mario Schiopetto, Gianfranco Gallo, Silvio Jermann and Gaspare Buscemi, who's less famous, but what a great guy! They taught me that you can make wine without adding sulfites. I continued with the process of maceration on the lees for long periods and I learned that my Timorasso has to sit still in the bottle for a year. I had to find the balls just like everyone else to hold 5,000 bottles of Timorasso for a year, otherwise it would have meant failure! So my 1995 Timorasso was put on the market in 1997. And that's where my rule of thumb for winemaking was born."

I Hire a Wine Expert: Vasco Rossi

We're joined by Filippo, Walter's young nephew, whom he calls over, pulling him toward him on his lap. He questions him about the rule of thumb for winemaking but Filippo's self-conscious and kind of bashful. He'd rather not let his uncle get him involved, there are all these strange guests today… he stares at Shigeru.

Walter tells us that Filippo's going to go to a high school where they focus on languages, because all you really need to make wine is a formula that he can explain to him: ripe grapes, common sense and time. That's Walter Massa's rule of thumb for winemaking. Whereas if you want to learn a language you have to go to school.

Oscar "And what about your other nephew, Edoardo, what are his plans?"

Walter says that he doesn't force anyone to do anything, he just makes "suggestions," so if Edoardo takes his advice, he'll go to Wine Academy, because if these two nephews want to run the winery, they're going to have to specialize in two different yet complementary things.

"I don't say they have to do something, I just suggest that they should."
He loves them as though they were his own children!

In 1997, thanks to the success of his Timorasso, Walter decided to hire
a wine expert: born in 1952, a native of Zocca, in the province of
Modena. The wine expert is Vasco Rossi. He quotes Vasco's song
Sally, which goes: "Because life is a thrill that flies away, it's all a question of the balancing point above the madness." He changes Vasco's
words to "Wine is the balancing point above the madness." Walter is
a rocker, no doubt about that. When he was young he rode a motorbike and listened to Vasco Rossi's music, and if he hadn't had the
winery to run and expand, also out of respect for his parents, he might
have lived a life of danger, endlessly skidding sideways, just like Vasco.
This is one marvelously "crazy" guy!

We don't have to wait too long for his explanation for the rock quota-
tion: in order to make wine the way he wants to you need three things.
One of them is the raw material, that is, grapes; two of them you can't
buy: time and common sense. To be able to hold together one tangible
thing with two intangible ones, and to get them to work, you need to
find the "balancing point above the madness."

Walter "That's why when they ask me if I go to the natural wine fair I
answer that I go to the 'artisanal' wine fair. Because the artisan makes
the originals, while industry makes copies of them. But the collaboration between artisans and industry is crucial."

Oscar "Let's go on. We've reached the end of the millennium, what
happened next?"

Walter "What happened is that I took my territory to heart and I also
helped my friend Andrea Mutti to make his Timorasso. Andrea is like
me. People have always left these places to go away to Milan or Pavia.
The best have always left... Where you come from, in the Langhe, it's
different. There's always been a culture of the territory."

Oscar "That's not altogether right. In the postwar years the Langa was
a disaster. Whether or not places that have the same vocation and resources are 'lucky' depends on the people who are born there. We had
the incredible luck to have a genius like Giacomo Morra, who completely turned the fate of the Langhe around. We owe him everything.
He built the legendary Hotel Savona, and he took a huge white truffle,
which the local farmers snacked on, and gave it to President Truman,
so that he ended up being photographed right next to him and seen in

newspapers all around the world. At the Savona he had them serve Barolo and Barbaresco. In no time at all he had earned his first Michelin star. Later, he was succeded by several celebrities of the world of wine, like Renato Ratti and then Gaja, Ceretto, the Monfortinis, and others, too. People who got on their feet and started traveling around the world to talk about the Langhe. It's people who change the destiny of the territories. And you'll see that you're going to succeed in changing the destiny of your own. You're already on your way."

Walter "Let's hope so! In the meantime, in 1997, Andrea came out with his own Timorasso: a wine similar to mine except for the fact that it's made by an anarchist with a big ego, just like me. Similar doesn't mean the same. They're two different wines that mark two fixed points. And when you have two points you can draw a line between them. It was the start of Timorasso's success."

Oscar "I'm going to interrupt your story about Timorasso's success to ask you and Shigeru what you think about this third wine. In our glasses we now have a Montepulciano d'Abruzzo 2008 produced by Marina Cvetic. How do you like it?"

Walter "Aaah! Marina. Her husband, Gianni Masciarelli, was one of the many friends who carried forward the good wine revolution in Italy. Makes me remember—with a lump in my throat—all the friends and fellow winemakers who left us much too soon and just as things were getting under way: Matteo Correggia, Massimo Accornero, Marco De Bartoli, Giacomo Bologna, Angelo Rocca, Andrea Chionetti, Quinto's son, one of the first revolutionaries. It was thanks to Quinto Chionetti, in my opinion, that the 'rural wine' revolution began; with his Dolcetto grapes in Dogliani, he never produced 'good wine' but 'wine that's good.' These people are no longer with us, but their ideas, thanks to their love of their families, wineries and wine, still travel the world in the form of art, and make Italy look good. This is another perfect wine that has to be drunk across the world. It's wine that's made very well, featuring great structure and material, which is perhaps only missing that tiny defect, like the strabismus of Venus, which made her the most beautiful of all the goddesses."

Shigeru has been very quiet so far. I can imagine his Japanese rigor being put to the test by all this back and forth of Walter's friends, who keep coming and going, constantly changing the geometric shape of the group. However, at the same time, I'm sure that Shigeru is seeing all this as the best possible example of a spontaneous and welcoming attitude, the convivial spirit that's part of the Italian way of doing things. He hasn't tasted either the bread or the bacon. His palate is still uncontaminated by food, focused solely on the wines.

When it's his turn to talk about the wine he's, as usual, happy to take the floor. In the wine produced by Marina Cvetic Masciarelli he smells the aroma of violet and licorice, prune, pepper, black currant and tobacco. The taste is full and dry with fresh notes of red berries, soft, almost chewy. It has a full, well-balanced body. He'd pair it with roast made with red meat, lamb with ginger, chicken liver kebabs cooked with seven types of pepper. I complain now, jokingly: "But whenever I've been to see you in Japan you've never taken me to eat kebabs with seven peppers! You always take me to eat sushi, I'm sick and tired of eating sushi!" Of course, I'm kidding, and Shigeru is well aware of this, because I'm crazy about Japanese cuisine, and with so much variety it's almost impossible to get tired of it. Sometimes he takes me to those family-run eateries, in the more out-of-the-way parts of Tokyo, where what they prepare for you is so good it almost brings tears to your eyes. It was in one of these places that I ate shark testicles for the first time. But the bastard didn't tell me until after I'd gulped them down.

You Don't Have to Be a Communist to Be a Member of the Democratic Party

Walter goes on: "It was 2008 when F.M. Martinetti entered the field. He wanted a Timorasso, too, and I helped him. In product placement, he sells to the starred restaurants, while I continue to sell to the eateries. This way we complete the market."

Oscar "Franco is a great person." As I say these words, without thinking, I pour myself some more Barbera Monleale 1978. Maybe it's because when you mention Martinetti, Barbera is almost a must. It was there, open so that we could talk about corks, or pretend to talk about corks. I know perfectly well that it has nothing to do with the tasting, but when I find myself with a bottle of Barbera in front of me, winking at me, I can't help it! On top of that, cold cuts, lard and bread keep being brought to the table by Zoccolo, and the food keeps getting better and better. The temptation is just too great and

I have no intention of pulling back. Walter's Barbera is excellent and served with salami it's sheer bliss. This is my favorite wine! Shigeru looks at me, maybe he's slightly envious. The Barbera wasn't part of the plan, so he doesn't drink it. It's almost lunchtime and he must be hungry too. This is why I try to speed up our conversation. Shigeru won't touch a bite until he's finished working.

Walter "But before that, in 2000, other producers started coming out with their own Timorasso; believing in it, they had planted the grapes in the late 1990s: Claudio Mariotto, La Colombera, Ennio Ferretti, Luigi Boveri, the Azienda Agricola Terralba. I was no longer a heretic, but the person paving the way ahead in a sector that could finally have others with which to compare itself. We decided that the only way to defend Timorasso was to throw away the 'chastity belt' and use love instead. And you only have love when you have an identity. That's when I said: 'I'm going change Timorasso's name to Derthona.'"

Derthona Iulia is the Latin name for Tortona. As this thought goes through my mind I apologize to Walter saying "I'm distracted because I'm texting Matteo Renzi."

Walter "Tell him, tell Matteo, that next time I'm going to run along with him. And I even have a slogan ready: you don't have to be a Communist to be a member of the Democratic Party."

Oscar "Great! I agree wholeheartedly. Let's go back to the Derthona. So you practically christened the Timorasso with a name that represents the territory."

Walter "That's exactly it! Just think of it, when you talk about Pinot Nero, you're saying the names of a series of marvelous towns that represent a small, but very famous, corner of the world that's called Bourgogne. Everyone knows the identity of those villages. If I could revolutionize things I'd call all the DOCs by the names of the towns. Derthona is the name of a territory that I use as an imaginary name. I registered it with the Chamber of Commerce, with the 'h,' and without the 'h,' and spent 240 euros per version!" He's got the numbers at his fingertips.

Oscar "So you offered the name to your fellow winemakers?"

Walter "Of course! And to the cooperative winery of Tortona, which was having a rough time."

Oscar "And what did you do?"

Walter "I introduced the enologist Umberto Lucarno, who worked with Donato Lanati for seven years. Lanati is a great wine scientist

whom I very much respect and appreciate. It's important for a cooperative winery to make good, stable wine, and Umberto was the right
person. I basically believe that Timorasso can contribute to improving this territory's economy."

In the meantime I can't let go of the Barbera 1978, so I turn to Simona
and say: "This was made the year you were born, you simply have to
taste it!" It's delicious!

One of the moments I like best arrives, when I ask what the person's
"heartfelt numbers are," the ones that represent something important.
Fully aware of the fact that Walter's a whiz at numbers.

Walter "Fifty-seven harvests (I'm fifty-eight and I've done fifty-seven of
them full-time!). Twenty-three hectares of vineyards. Five is the number
of grape varieties I cultivate: Barbera, Croatina, Freisa, Timorasso and
Moscato Bianco. Four is the number of the crus where I have vineyards.
Six, my tractors: I wouldn't be able to do anything without tractors! Two
thousand is the number of hectares of vineyards on the Colli Tortonesi.
My mission will be over when this territory has understood its immense
vocation for wine, and the number of hectares have grown to 3,000.
And: 120,000 bottles sold, a number I don't want to change, I want to
stay an artisan. And four is the number of banks I owe money to."

Oscar "What's your take on debts?"

Walter "They're a primary need, along with grapes. They have an aroma,
too, they smell of the sweat you pour out to be able to pay them back."

Oscar "Fabulous, I think so too! Listen, what percentage of your total
production do you export abroad?"

Walter "33% to the United States, 33% to the rest of the world, 33%
stays in Italy. 1% for the things that are to come and for us to drink."

Oscar "And what about the revenue?"

Walter "I have no idea!"

I Married a Territory

Oscar "Walter, I want to talk about 'family' now. When you say 'family,' what do you mean?"

Walter "My mother, my sister, my brother-in-law and their children."

Oscar "Not your father?"

Walter "Him too, of course! I used to argue with him all the time, but my uncle would step in to straighten things out. We fought so hard the dishes would fly! We had some terrible arguments but I have always felt that my fate is closely bound to my family. On top of that... I think I take after the best side of both my mother and my father."

Oscar "Listen, what about these two nephews you're crazy about?"

Walter "I was just damn lucky! When you're dealing with the land there's no question about it, men are more at home. They know how to drive a tractor! Imagine this, the first time Edoardo started up the tractor, and he learned how to just by watching me without my saying a word, he was just five years old! He's the one you saw riding the tractor this morning, a complete and utter anarchist!"

Oscar "They'll take over the winery, while they wait for your own son to grow up."

Walter "I'd like that to happen."

Oscar "What about women?"

Walter "I've been trying to find one all my life, someone who's willing to move in here and live with me. Because I'm not leaving this house! This is the most beautiful town in the world, I'd be crazy to leave!"

Oscar "And when did you decide to have children?"

Walter "I didn't. My was born when I was fifty-five and I decided to keep him. It was a great gift of fate! Today Alberto is almost three."

Oscar "Did you marry Alberto's mother?"

Walter "No, I'm married to my territory. But she's a great woman. Alberto lives with her, but I hope one day he'll move to the country."

Walter talks about his son with tenderness and joy. He became a father at the age of fifty-five, and it seemed like the most natural thing in the world to him. It comes naturally to me to wonder what he's going to expect of this child when he's his nephews' age. And as he talks about his son, he uncorks the bottle of wine, this too a child of his, which we have to taste. It's the last one.

In the meantime Shigeru has started to tell us his feelings about the fourth bottle we brought here today: L'Equilibrista Vintage 2011 produced by Birra del Borgo, a brewery in the province of Rieti. Leonardo Di Vincenzo is an outstanding master brewer. In this amazing beer he sought an almost impossible balance between beer and wine. That's why he chose to call it L'Equilibrista. It's made with 39% Sangiovese grapes. You can taste the barley, hops, malt and hay with notes of vanilla, coffee and tobacco. It's a very soft beer, and Shigeru thinks it should be paired with grilled chicken or pan-fried pork dressed in Japanese mustard. I wonder what Beppe Rinaldi would have had to say since he finds beer to be an inferior beverage. Walter, on the contrary, just loves it, and gulps it down.

We've almost come to the end. There's one last wine, Costa del Vento 2006. It's a cru made from 2 hectares of Timorasso. The other cru, which we're not drinking today, is called Sterpi. The end of our conversation is up in the air. Other friends that Walter invited for the lunch prepared by Zoccolo keep arriving: among them are Riccardo Franzosi, the master brewer of Montegioco brewery, Elisa Semino, from the Azienda Agricola La Colombera, fruit harvesters, the town butcher, his nephews who are starving and can't wait to dig in... A party! And in the midst of all this coming and going we're there trying to talk about personal matters: his son, love, the future...

But Walter is unfazed. He's a traditionalist-revolutionary, someone who makes no compromises and doesn't feign modesty, someone who tells you things straight to your face, in his own way and with "his own" diplomacy. "I'm the perfection of imperfection," he says of himself, and we know it's true. I take the floor.

I interrupt the confusion to say, "Excuse me. I want to be the one to comment on this wine. Costa del Vento is fabulous! One of the best white wines in the world!" Yes, I know, it was Shigeru's turn. But he's going to say what I'm thinking anyway, except he'll go about it in a classier, more authoritative and expert way than me. In fact, he starts right in without letting me say a word.

Shigeru "The aroma is flint, gravel, dried fruit and tar. The flavor is mineral, I taste ripe apple, dried fruit. It's long, persistent and sapid. I'd pair it with a tomato soup with ricotta made from sheep's milk, Piacenza-style salt cod, fresh Tuscan pecorino. This is a wine that's made history."

Oscar "Why do you think fresh cheese goes down better with Timorasso?"

Shigeru "Because Timorasso has a great mineral quality and so do aged cheeses. So, to bring out the flavor of the wine, a fresher, more delicate cheese is preferable."

Hmm! I don't really agree with you. I turn to Walter again.

Oscar "Your future. What are you going to be when you grow up? Up to now you've done a whole bunch of new things. In line with your idea of continuity and progress, what do you want to change in the next thirty years or so?"

Walter "I want this land to become more dignified. From Timorasso to Volpedo peaches, from truffles to salami, from the landscape to food and beverage traditions."

Oscar "It seems to me that you think the only weak point are the people who live in these territory. They should believe in it more, right?"

Walter "We suffer the weaknesses of this borderland. We're on the very edge of Piedmont, a stone's throw away from Lombardy and Liguria, we've always paid for politics' lack of interest of in us. Lack of interest and lack of discussion. But I have always believed in my region and Piedmont has given me the strength to keep working in the wine business."

Oscar "And what about your future?"

Walter "I'm going to run for the Democratic Party, if someone wants me. I'd like to go into politics because I think that a person who deals with universal shafts, vine species, graft-holders, corks, bottles and many other things can also deal with anthropology and thus improve this country. But without ever giving up winemaking."

I think I'll definitely vote for him. I think that if he put the same courage into politics that he's put into wine he'd be a real asset to help change this country.

Oscar "And now what? Should we go have some chicken?"

Walter "Yes, at ease everyone!"

What happens outside, in the courtyard of Walter's home, is hard to describe. There are more than twenty of us for lunch, but there's no table. The only place we can set things down on is a dais held up by a fork lift. On the dais is a casserole with the chicken in it, paper plates, a few forks and knives and some half-filled glasses. Some of the guests have brought other dishes, in addition to the one prepared by our barefoot chef. Once again, in this country banquet we find perfection in the imperfection! And then, all of a sudden, something happens quite by chance. Walter is still talking about the role of the wine producer, whom he sees as being an artisan... but instead of saying "artisan" he says "partisan." It's a huge Freudian slip that takes everyone aback: put producer together with artisan and you get partisan! I'd never thought of that, I want to use it! I tell Walter and he answers: "Don't forget, if you use it I want 50%... for my madness."

Long live the partisans!

Notes for Wines Tasted with Walter Massa
Shigeru Hayashi

Roycello Fiano 2010 Tormaresca
Type white wine
Grapes 100% Fiano
Vinification and fining fermentation in thermo-conditioned
stainless steel, fining in steel *sur lie* (3 months), followed by bottles
(3 months)
Production area Puglia

Straw color with green hues. Nice floral aroma, but also white and
yellow fruit like pineapple, peach, citron. I can smell jasmine and
sage, too. Intense, sapid and fresh taste with mineral aftertaste.

Ideally paired with fish or vegetable dishes dressed with cream
sauce. Excellent with asparagus tempura with lemon sauce.

I can still remember the first time I went to Tormaresca: it
reminded me of Las Vegas, all you could see was this huge cellar
undergoing construction and all around the deserted, hot plains.
Today the company is in the heart of one of the most beautiful
and important wine-producing zones in Italy. But Tormaresca
was the first to believe in it.

Breg Anfora 2005 Gravner
Type white wine
Grapes Sauvignon, Chardonnay, Pinot Grigio, Riesling Italico
Vinification and fining in amphora for 7 months, with neither
added yeasts nor temperature control; maturation in oak barrels,
bottling with the moon on the wane, no clarification, no filtration
Production area Friuli Venezia Giulia

Intense amber yellow color. It releases aromas of dried fruit, yellow
flowers, aromatic herbs, chamomile, mimosa. Complex, warm,
sapid and soft taste. Very long finish, with salty aftertaste.

Pair with grilled shellfish, fish soup, seafood risotto, pickled
mackerel with Japanese mustard or medium-aged Tuscan pecorino.
And even if this makes Oscar (and maybe even Josko) angry,
I'd try it with swordfish testicles!

A legendary wine, made by a legendary man, a true samurai
of the Italian borderlands. I'm sorry I didn't know him when
he went to the Caucasus to see the amphorae for the first time:
he understood that the future of wine was in its past and
in the flavors of the ancient peoples. Magnificent!

Montepulciano d'Abruzzo Marina Cvetic 2008 Masciarelli
Type red wine
Grapes 100% Montepulciano
Vinification and fining 20–30 days of maceration, 12–18 months
of maturation in barriques
Production area Abruzzo

Intense ruby red with garnet hues. I can distinctly smell red fuit,
such as cherries, red currant and blackberries. Also emerging are
flowers (violet), then vanilla, cocoa, pepper and tobacco. Broad,
full taste with soft tannins.

Pair with important meat roasts, or with skewered chicken livers with seven spices. Perfect with Parmigiano Reggiano aged more than 24 months.

One of Central Italy's best wines, elegant and determined, like the woman who produces it and names it after herself. In Japan, when you finally get to the summit of Mount Fuji, the tradition is to make a toast for good luck: the next time I want to use this wine to make that toast.

L'Equilibrista Vintage 2011 Birra del Borgo
Type experimental beer
Made from 50% Sangiovese must, 50% beer must (barley)
Vinification and fining blending of musts, addition of *liqueur de tirage*, fining in bottles on yeasts, *dégorgement* with addition of *liqueur d'expédition*
Production area Lazio

Pale golden yellow color. The beer's aroma is very broad and winey, with notes of chamomile, violet, barley, coffee and vanilla. You can taste the toasted barley and caramel.

Pair with grilled chicken and *salsa verde*, pork shank baked with rosemary and balsamic vinegar, *sukiyaki* with onion, soy sauce, sake and sugar.

The new frontier for beer: to use wine must in order to produce a beverage that isn't wine yet, and is no longer just a beer. It's like crossing a tiger and a dragon: whatever comes out of it will be very powerful!

Costa del Vento 2006 Vigneti Massa
Type white wine
Grapes 100% Timorasso
Vinification and fining pellicular maceration, maturation
on its owns lees for at least 10 months, 12 months in bottles
Production area Piedmont

Bright golden yellow color. Bouquets of yellow flowers, dried fruit, flint, honey, tar and hints and minerality. Full and persistent taste. Bitter aftertaste.

I suggest pairing it with tomato soup and sheep's milk ricotta, Piacenza-style salt cod (whipped with parsley, garlic and olive oil), bean soup drizzled with olive oil and sprinkled with pepper.

I left this out, but I'd really like to taste this wine with tempura and different types of salt (Brittany, Mongolia, Hawaii…): salt helps you to get a better taste of things, even wine! I want to say something else to Walter Massa, but there's no room left: so let me just say "thank you."

Allegrini: Marilisa Allegrini
When I Was Eighteen I Told My Father
He Couldn't Depend on Me

Meeting Marilisa Allegrini, after having been with Beppe Rinaldi and Walter Massa, is like hopping off a cross-country motorbike and getting into a Bentley. You're still traveling, you're on your way, but in a completely different style. In both cases you experience the emotion of traveling, driven by a great engine. But the surroundings are the opposite of one another, overly so. Marvelously so. Moving from the country homes of Beppe and Walter, with their barnyards and tractors, to the Renaissance stuccowork of Villa della Torre is definitely one way to cross the biodiversity Italy is famous for. Which doesn't just consist of wine, food and landscape, but of lifestyle as well. During our long journey we'll have the chance to see that this is true. We look forward to such beauty.

We Have to Fight Like Lions

Marilisa Allegrini has a name as delicate as that of a flower, but she has the character of a lioness. I know this is true because we've met before. I wonder if it's true that a person's facial features hide their soul. I don't know enough about physiognomics, but I can safely say that Marilisa has the sort of broad forehead that's typical of people who have faith in others as well as in life. Big eyes, a steady gaze, high, nicely shaped eyebrows: these are things that make us imagine her as having strong, insightful intelligence. She has the high cheekbones of someone who's strong and brave, the gaze of someone who's always ready to face challenges. Marilisa is a beautiful woman, with a very elegant manner about her, but she never makes you feel ill at ease. She's wearing a jacket made of shimmering fabric with wide stripes that seem to be gray and black; it reminds you of the Renaissance, as do the prominent padded shoulders. Completely different from the corduroy jackets, sweatshirts and sweaters the other winemakers got us accustomed to seeing.

The first woman of wine on our tour immediately marks out the difference, also in terms of clothing. Consciously? Unconsciously? I tend to think that women leave little room to the unconscious when it comes down to their appearance!

Without my asking, she says: "I was born in 1954, just like you." She catches me off guard. Women rarely tell you their age right away, or maybe she's just fishing for compliments; that would come easy, but I keep it to myself. However, I can't help thinking about all the heads she must have turned. I'll ask her about that later.

She welcomes us to Villa della Torre, a jewel in the crown of Italy's Cinquecento, now owned by the Allegrini family, and surrounded, so that it blends into the landscape, by the vineyard called Palazzo della Torre, from which their wine of the same name is produced. The villa is located in Fumane, a town of 4,000 inhabitants 20 kilometers from Verona, where it's still referred to as "el palasso" (the palace). It was Giulio della Torre, a humanist and intellectual, who had it built, commissioning artists such as Giulio Romano, Michele Sanmicheli and Bartolomeo Ridolfi.

The villa was conceived with the serenity of the body and soul in mind, according to the canons set down by the Latin philosophers so beloved by Italian humanistic tradition: Vitruvius and Pliny the Younger.

The villa's architecture revolves around the peristylium, the "heart" of the house that even now continues to welcome the guests of the many parties held here. We're surrounded by so much genuine beauty that I can't help but think: "Marilisa Allegrini is really lucky!" Marilisa leads us to one of the rooms decorated with mascarons. The first thing you notice is a fireplace surrounded by stuccowork portraying a cherub holding a sea monster by the nostrils; the monster's mouth actually serves as the central part of the fireplace. Grotesque and charming at the same time. We sit down at the table, Shigeru takes care of opening the bottles and Simona does the note-taking.

The first thing I ask Marilisa is: "How many harvests have you done in your life?"

Marilisa "I started taking part in the winery's harvests when I was fifteen, but I've been personally overseeing the harvests since 1983."

Oscar "This means a total of forty-two, of which thirty that you feel are your own. Is that correct?"

Marilisa "Right! That's a lot... you know, I'd never thought of it before!"

Oscar "I ask everyone the same question. So far we've been to see Costantino at Les Crêtes, who has done thirty of them, Gaja has done forty, Beppe Rinaldi, fifty, Walter Massa jokingly said fifty-seven, one less than his age. Just think, by the time I've finished with these interviews I will have spoken to twelve marvelous producers with hundreds of harvests behind them! Just think of all the things they can tell us about Italy, their territory, their wineries... And how did Vinitaly 2013 go? It's just come to an end, are you happy about it?"

Marilisa "I'm very happy! I think it went well and I wait all year long to open this villa for three evenings during the event."

For years now the Allegrinis have been organizing three amazing parties during Vinitaly. They open Villa della Torre to hundreds of guests and celebrate their wines, the fine wines of their winemaking friends, the territory, the food and beverage traditions... We, too, were at the party that was held here last night, and we had the pleasure of drinking Amarone Allegrini with my Barolo Casa E. di Mirafiore and with a fabulous Red produced by Chateau Musar presented by Serge Hochar in person!

Oscar "How much do you invest in these parties?"

Marilisa "300,000 euros and loads of energy."

Oscar "Why do you do it?"

Marilisa "Because the world of Italian wine is beautiful and I don't just produce wine to turn in a profit, but to convey a message of passion and love as well. I've chosen to work in this sector because I believe in it, not just to do business."

Oscar "Your strong frankness, which is plain for everyone to see, is also linked to your shrewd side. Having a network of relations must unquestionably help you to sell more wine."

Marilisa "Of course! Why should we see the two things as contradicting each other?"

Oscar "Exactly. That's what I often say. You can be honest and shrewd at the same time." The conversation gets off to a good start, there's no need to warm up the engines. I can rush ahead and ask a question that I usually save for later. "Are you familiar with your company's numbers? Do you always have them inside your head?"

Marilisa "Yes, I have a good head for numbers!"

Oscar "Do you already know how the balance will go even though you're only halfway through the year?"

Marilisa "Well, of course I do. An entrepreneur has to have limits and goals that are clearly established, but having a knack for certain things is indispensable."

Oscar "Let's stick to the topic of the relationship between honesty and shrewdness. I know you and I know you're generous, but you live in a region, the Veneto, that's selfish. There are no roads here because the land is expensive and no one ever wants to sell theirs. It's the region of the Northern League, which is the quintessence of self-ishness. The first item on the party's statute is secession, which money-wise means 'I separate from you because I think I'm better than you.'"

Marilisa "I don't think you can generalize. But I'm not like that. My life has gone off in a certain direction, and I started traveling a lot when I was young. This helped me to understand that integration and interaction between peoples are a great thing."

Oscar "Do you make wine because your own father was a wine-maker?"

Marilisa "Not really. Actually, I went into another field of work. When I was eighteen I told my father: 'Don't think you can depend on me!'"

Oscar "What did your father do?"

Marilisa "My father, Giovanni Allegrini, made wine. I'm the sixth generation to do so."

Oscar "When was he born?"

Marilisa "In 1920, and he died suddenly in 1983, when he was still quite young. But even though all these years have gone by, whenever I have to make an important decision, I think: 'What would my father have done?'"

Oscar "Is he the man you've loved the most in your life?"

Marilisa "Absolutely! He's the man of my life!"

Oscar "How did he get into wine? Did he immediately take over the helm from the previous generation?"

Marilisa "No, he rebelled when he was young too. He wanted to be an airplane pilot, but couldn't because he suffered from tachycardia. So he chose to go back to his father's business and make wine."

Oscar "Was he already well-off?"

Marilisa "Yes, our ancestors, from the very first generation, were landowners, agriculturers."

Oscar "Was your father a Fascist?"

Marilisa "Yes, he was. For him Fascism meant order, rules, work... Even after the war ended he continued to be a Right-winger, but with a strong critical sense and great skill at making judgments."

Oscar "And how was his wine? Was it good?"

Marilisa "His wine was delicious. He was a great innovator of Valpolicella. He produced our three DOCs: Valpolicella, Amarone and Recioto. He only thought he was good when he succeeded in making a good Recioto. He didn't care that much about Amarone: he thought of it as second-class Recioto."

At this point my impish humor gets going. The word Valpolicella starts buzzing in my head and I'm laughing it up inside. "In Valpolicellaaaaaa wine, the old spinsteeeeer seeks loooooove, in the osteria one glass after another..." That was what Giorgio Gaber sang in the 1960s. And quickly, uncontrollably, materializing in my mind is a thought on the changes that have taken place over the past fifty years: in Milanese osterie only Pugliese draft wine was drunk (Trani and Barletta), to such a degree that these osterie were referred to by the same name as the beverages, and women who were fortyish and still not married were called spinsters. Today we find ourselves before the Lady of Amarone and spinsters practically no longer exist.

Oscar "How many children did your father have?"

Marilisa "Three."

Oscar "Why don't you ever talk about your mother?"

Marilisa "Because she didn't have much to do with the company... and besides, the relationship between a mother and a daughter is different. I was a very energetic child and I suffered a little because so much attention was focused on my parents' first child, my elder brother, and their last one, Franco, the youngest. By contrast I started doing things on my own right away, and I really developed my independence. Well anyway, when I was a teenager, my parents realized I was like an eel slipping away from their grip. They belatedly started paying attention to me, but at that point it was hard for me to change direction."

Oscar "In all those years, did you ever think you'd be making wine when you grew up?"

Marilisa "No way! When I was eighteen I told my father he couldn't depend on me! My brothers, instead, have always dealt with the winery."

Oscar "How many bottles were you producing back then?"

Marilisa "About 50,000 with 25 hectares."

Oscar "So your story starts with 25 hectares. How many do you have now?"

Marilisa "We own 212 hectares, and lease about another 60. In Veneto and Tuscany."

Oscar "Let's go back to the 1970s, your brothers were working for the family business, what were you doing?"

Marilisa "I decided to study medicine. It was a strong calling for me and I wanted to study in Padua. My father, who knew that if I had studied medicine I would never come back to the business, told me that he wasn't going to let me go to Padua, that if I really wanted to get a degree I was going to have to stay in Verona. It was blackmail! I wanted to rebel, but I couldn't forgo a university degee, so I decided to study physiotherapy in Verona."

Oscar "Did you manage to avoid the world of wine completely?"

Marilisa "Of course not! I would spend Saturday and Sunday taking care of the invoices and some of the administration. After all, everyone in the family has always gotten along."

Oscar "What did you do after you got your degree in physiotherapy?"

Marilisa "I worked as a physiotherapist for five years at the hospital in Borgo Roma, in Verona, and even got promoted. They said I was good at it, and I liked what I did!"

Oscar "No kidding! You would have been successful at anything you did! If you'd started up a café it would have been the coolest one in town for sure!"

Marilisa "Let's say I got by. And, in fact, when I decided to go back to the company, the hospital offered me one of their top positions. But I turned it down, I was twenty-eight..."

Oscar "Were you engaged?"

Marilisa "I had started out on the wrong foot. Wanting so much to get away from my family I'd gotten married very young, to the wrong person. A doctor who was much older than me. It took us two years to decide to get a separation, and three more to make it official. Five years in all. I already knew I'd made a mistake the day after the wedding…"

Oscar "That soon?"

Marilisa "Because people ought to listen to themselves. One evening in Rome, in Piazza di Spagna (we were passing through on our honeymoon), I saw some young people playing the guitar and I felt the urge to sit down with them; then I looked at my new husband and wondered what he was doing with me, and what I was doing with him. He was fifteen years older than me. Because my marriage failed my father insisted that I come back to the winery. Despite the fact that I was one of the first to get a divorce in Fumane, and that my mother was really ashamed of it, he was happy because he really wanted me to have another chance."

Oscar "Your father wanted you at the winery at all costs."

Marilisa "Yes, at all costs!"

Oscar "He'd realized you were talented and wanted you to work alongside your brothers."

Marilisa "I think he'd realized that I could be a good addition to the team."

I Go to America to Sell Some Wine

So after Marilisa's first marriage failed, when she was twenty-six, she joined the company once and for all. Her divorce was finalized, and the prospect of doing something completely different in terms of work, from her career at the hospital to the world of wine, meant turning over a new leaf. I can't help wondering whether her father had understood that Marilisa had a lot to offer the winery, or whether he just favored his daughter, the way fathers often do. Probably a combination of both.

Marilisa "He would tease me. He said I was the intellectual in the family. Sometimes, when it comes down to work, a man and a woman get along better than a man with another man. You don't have daughters so it's probably hard for you to understand that the relationship between a father and a daughter is based on an alchemy that's hard to explain."

Oscar "I believe it. I don't have any daughters but I have lots of friends who do and they've always told me the same things you're telling me now. Daughters make your head spin! The men I know who are my age are crazy about their daughters!" But the strongest example in this sense was the relationship I saw between my father and my sister. He couldn't hide the fact that Paola was his favorite, and my sister always adored my father more than anyone else.

Marilisa "My father thought I was the most intelligent young woman in the world. The most beautiful, the most sought after." Marilisa's words must be so universally true that they encourage Shigeru to speak up: "Oscar! It's the same for me! I'm crazy about my daughter!" Shigeru would never have interrupted us if he hadn't felt strongly about what we were saying. I nod in agreement, and I think that after three boys I would have liked to have a girl too. Fortunately, my first grandchild—I'm a grandfather—was a girl, named Celeste.

I ask Shigeru if he's ready to talk to us about the first wine, Viognier 2011 produced by Calatrasi and Miccichè. The producer is a friend of mine, Maurizio Miccichè, an important figure in the fight against the Mafia. His vineyards are located near Portella della Ginestra, in the Piana degli Albanesi, where, in 1946, the outlaw Giuliano, hired by the landowners, had the peasant farmers who demanded a better life shot. The place is more than 900 meters a.s.l. in the mountains. Shigeru does an excellent job describing it and he says you can tell it's a high-altitude wine. I don't think he knew it was, or maybe he did, but I really appreciate the fact that he said "you can tell." He suggests pairing it with vegetable and mushroom tempura—but not porcini mushrooms—, hard-boiled eggs with Marsala cream, aragula omelette, or oysters, but "the fat ones." Marilisa really likes the freshness of this Viognier, but I keep asking questions: "What role did your father give you?"

Marilisa "I told my father that I wanted to lay down the terms. Just think, at the time we had a cellar, but we didn't have an office! The first thing I asked him for was an office. And this tells you a lot about a woman's contribution to a place where only men have always worked." She's right, it does tell me a lot, I think to myself, I think so too, and Marilisa hits the nail on the head when she says, "You know, Oscar, a woman is generally more ambitious than a man; she wants an image, decorum, comfort, too." As plain as day! Marilisa the woman is none other than the continuity of the young Marilisa of the past. She already knew how important image is if you want to be successful in sales.

Oscar "Who decided which role you'd play?"

Marilisa "My father, who else. At the time, my brother Franco was helping my father with the vinification, he was our enologist, while Walter saw to the countryside. There was a gap in the administration, which was the area my father assigned me to. But not just that. I showed him I'd understood that it's not enough to make good wines, you have to know how to communicate them, creating a relationship between those who make wine and those who drink it. And I had some ideas about how to make our message simple and easy to understand: by beginning to communicate our passion for winemaking."

Oscar "Of course, you wanted to lay the eggs your own way." Marilisa smiles. She knows perfectly well that I'm referring to my obsession with the idea that hens are great communicators because they cluck. Hens invented marketing. They lay an egg and then they tell the world.

Marilisa "I had some ideas and I told my father that I wanted to start traveling to sell our wine abroad and communicate its image in a certain way. Just like when I wanted to go to college, he was absolutely against it! He kept saying that if they wanted our wines, the buyers would have to come and get them from us. In those days it was normal to think that way."

Oscar "Or maybe it was a way of protecting you. So you'd already had some insight about a global market."

Marilisa "Yes. We'd been exporting wine since 1972, and in the 1980s almost 50% of our sales were abroad."

We let slip some political views. Marilisa votes for the Democratic Party today, "for the good of the country," she says, but having come this far, completely on her own with respect to her father's Fascist beliefs, must have come at some cost to her. I imagine an open dialogue with her father, and Marilisa trying to explain her reasons. Marilisa wants us to know that today she votes for the Left, but that wasn't always her political leaning. But we'll go back to politics later.

Oscar "Let's get right back to the subject of wine. Besides the way they're communicated, is there something else that's yours in Allegrini wines?"

Marilisa "In 2003, in Bolgheri, we planted the first 11 hectares. Then, in 2004, 7 hectares of Vermentino. In 2003 my brother Walter died and I found myself having to decide the fate of that wine although I knew nothing about wine agronomy. Fortunately, I was working with Stefano Bartolomei, a good agronomist. I told him I wanted a wine that was structured, not simple, with good acidity, not woody and long-lasting. And I expected all these things from the Vermentino. I'm neither an enologist nor an agronomist, but I do know what I want. When you've been hearing people talk about wine and problems related to agriculture since you were a child, it tends to stay with you."

Oscar "Yes, naturally! But was what you told him you wanted based on your own taste or on the market?"

Marilisa "It was based on my own taste. *I* want to like it. I'd worry about selling it later."

Oscar "So did they make it the way you wanted it?"

Marilisa "Yes, they did, starting from the very first harvest! Not that I'm saying that over the years we haven't ever changed our way of making wine, quite the contrary! When I started traveling I realized that our Amarone was perfect for Valpolicella's small enclave, but compared to the great wines of the world it was too rich, heavy, too sun-dried. In other words, too 'Amarone.' I talked to my brother Franco about it and he managed to remove what you might think of as its flaws. He's an expert enologist."

Oscar "Let me tell you a story about your Amarone. One day Carlin Petrini and I went to Giancarlino Ronzoni's house for lunch. He's a friend of ours who's a member of Communion and Liberation. Giancarlo Cesana was there too. Two people known to be Communists in the middle of a refuge for 'Ciellini,' who decided to challenge Carlin with a blind tasting. So he tasted one of the wines and then said: 'that's easy, Amarone Allegrini!' It was one of your 'Tre Bicchieri.' Carlin has a great palate, but your Amarone is unmistakable. The others were flabbergasted!"

Marilisa "Thank you!"

Marilisa looks at me and you can just see she's in seventh heaven. I couldn't have given her a nicer gift.

The Land Is the Only Asset That Can't Increase in Quantity

Oscar "After your marriage to the doctor, my guess is there was someone else in your life."

Marilisa "Of course. Six years later I met Giancarlo, with whom I had my two daughters."

Oscar "Did you marry?"

Marilisa "No, marriage is a mistake you make only once in your life, so we never got married."

Oscar "And when did the trips begin?"

Marilisa "In 1983, the year my father died. Not before then. My father was the head of the business for as long as he was alive. I remember that when he died many people from Verona thought that in six months' time the three of us would have squandered the whole family inheritance. They didn't think we were good enough to keep up to his standards."

Oscar "Was there something special about him? Did he always get there before the others did?"

Marilisa "He was always a great pioneer! Just think that in 1979 my father decided to plant some vineyards with Guyot, the way he had seen the French do. The La Grola vineyard, which is celebrating its thirtieth anniversary this year, is completely planted with Guyot. Until then, Valpolicella grapes were grown on a trellis, because Corvina grapes are very vigorous and require lots of space. But he decided to innovate and tried a different path. He may not have had an innovative spirit for marketing, but when it came down to agriculture we can safely say he was downright revolutionary."

Oscar "1979 was an important year."

Marilisa "Yes, it was the year my father bought the Palazzo della Torre vineyard, he built a cellar that we still use today for the vinification of Amarone and... then he ran out of money! But, still not satisfied, he finds a way to buy La Grola, a vineyard that had been abandoned for eighty years. That didn't put him off, and he decided to invest 400 million lire, borrowing money from the banks, at an interest rate of 25%. And this was while the winery was bringing in 200 million lire!"

Oscar "Had he talked to you about it?"

Marilisa "He'd mentioned it to Franco and Walter, because I hadn't come back to the winery yet. To encourage himself he'd say that land is the only asset that can't increase in quantity. If things went wrong we could have sold it."

Oscar "Of course, in plain terms, as all prices are the result of the age-old physical law of supply and demand, the only asset in the world whose supply is fixed is the land. So in time prices can only rise. You're saying, then, that when you went back to the winery in 1980 there wasn't any money."

Marilisa "That's right. There were debts."

It's time to taste the second wine, the Otello, the Lambrusco made by Cantine Ceci. Shigeru describes it as being a very pleasant wine with a bouquet of blueberry, undergrowth, brown sugar, candied fruit and dried prunes. He'd pair it with various kinds of cold cuts, including mortadella with "pistaccio" (it's not a typo, that's how he pronounces the word *pistacchio*, which is pronounced with a hard "k" sound in Italian). Then he digresses to explain to us how the tannicity of this wine is softened and mitigated by the important sugary residue. I add to this that I really like Lambrusco, that it's unjustly underestimated. I agree with Shigeru, if I had to choose I'd drink Lambrusco while eating bread with salami, maybe the one from Varzi, or culatello di Zibello Dop, and still feel like royalty!

Marilisa "I swear I had no idea Lambrusco as good as this even existed."

Oscar "Because you don't know Alessandro Ceci. He's the missionary of Lambrusco. For this particular Otello he was awarded the AIS's '5 Grappoli' prize. Lambrusco is one of the most exported Italian wines. It deserves more respect. But let's go back to the early 1980s, what were you up to then?"

Marilisa "In 1983 I took my first trip to Switzerland, to Zurich. On coming back from that tour, during which I tasted wines that I really liked a lot, I told Franco that we needed to work on structure and acidity, and make a wine that was midway between Valpolicella and Amarone, starting from that innovative viticultural idea that our father had set up. That's how La Grola was born."

Oscar "Did your brother always get exactly what you were saying?"

Marilisa "Yes! A few months later I went to the United States. That was the first time in my life. I went to New York, Boston and Chicago. Our agent back then wasn't that great."

Oscar "What did you tell your brothers when you decided to focus on America?"

Marilisa "It was still 1983, and we had debts to pay... So I said: 'I'm going to sell some wine in America!' And they were very pleased to hear it!"

Oscar "Both of our stories have so much in common! Did you ever think you might not make it?"

Marilisa "No, not at the time. I did panic a little in 2009."

Oscar "You can tell me about that later, let's stick to the subject of America. What did you see there?"

Marilisa "My somewhat ingenuous agent came to pick me up and he whisked me off to New York. The first thing that struck me was the filth in the streets back then. Those of us who came from the provinces just weren't used to it."

Oscar "The first thing that came to my mind, when I went there in 1981, was that it was just like in the movies: the steam rising up from the manhole covers, the lights, the skyscrapers, the yellow cabs. The truth is that it's common for people, when they go to New York for the first time, to have the impression they've already been there. It's the TV-series effect."

Marilisa "Yes, that's probably true. In any case, what my agent asked me to do was prepare a presentation that included every single thing I knew about my winery. This phase of my work was good training, it made me realize that knowing how to communicate in an essential way, touching the chords of emotion, is an extremely useful quality to have in business."

Oscar "Did you manage to sell those days? Did you keep the promise you'd made to your brothers?"

Marilisa "After six weeks I came back with an order for 2,000 crates, which I'd sold store by store! That year, on August 15, we all took part in the bottling process, and the very next day, the 16th, the containers were already on their way. Our revenue doubled. In 1989 we were debt-free thanks to the increase in revenue in the States. By 1990 we billed as much as one billion lire."

Oscar "Good work! This means you turned the business around. From that moment on you must have felt like it was really yours."

Marilisa "Yes, that's exactly how I felt."

Oscar "Are your brothers as good as you are with numbers?"

Marilisa "They're much better than me in other things that are just as important."

Oscar "Do you remember any big changes in the way the winery was managed?"

Marilisa "There wasn't one big change, things changed gradually."

Oscar "And when did you decide to invest in Tuscany?"

Marilisa "It was the early part of 2000, but not without arguments with my brothers. Clearly, arguments between siblings who love each other deeply. The love and mutual esteem between us have never diminished."

As Marilisa continues to tell her story I can't help but think that in my situation, too, those who deal with the vineyard and production are less willing to make changes. They tend to want to repeat the gestures that stem from tradition. But, by mixing tradition with innovation, you succeed in finding the winning combination. I use up a lot of my energy convincing those who work with me to be open to what's new. This effort to convince them has two advantages: I can hone my theories thanks to their objections and trigger a phenomenon that's called "group creativity." If, instead, I force a change on my collaborators that they're not convinced of, the result is undermined. Her story continues and as I listen to her talk about the exponential rise in sales in the Scandinavian markets and the family discussions on the opportunities offered by the new markets, I find the right moment to interrupt her: "But back then, were you already the elegant woman you are today?" My attention had been drawn to the rigorous and "Renaissance" lines of her jacket.

Marilisa "Yes, I've always thought that the way we present ourselves is the first impression we give people of ourselves. And I also like the idea of conveying the Italian style. They look at you and judge you in America, and as an Italian I wanted to distinguish myself."

No Man Can Ever Ask Me to Leave My Work

Marilisa's love for Giancarlo, the father of her daughters, lasted a decade. It ended slowly, she tells us, to make way for another love story. America is a party to it. He's a big importer of Italian wines in the United States. I wonder, could the huge success of Amarone on the American market be the fruit of this love story? I laugh to myself just thinking about it. Marilisa changing the fate of a wine by throwing herself into the arms of a powerful importer. I can't keep it to myself, I tell her what I'm thinking.

Marilisa "Stop it, you're being naughty! It was the longest relationship I ever had, fifteen years, a serious one."

Marilisa intensified her business trips to the United States, making them compatible with her sentimental pilgrimage. She was in New York every two or three weeks. Mind you, although she traveled there a lot, it never even crossed her mind to move across the ocean. She would never have left Italy.

Marilisa "And he would never have left the United States. Our relationship finally ended because it couldn't survive the distance."

Marilisa's real values are in Italy. Her real family is in Italy. Even the father of her daughters stayed on to work with the Allegrinis. These are very personal topics and I don't want to insist by asking impertinent questions, but it's plain to see that as soon as she was forced to decide between dropping everything to start a new life or staying in Italy, she chose her work. In spite of the charm of New York, in spite of the interesting prospects, in spite of... love.

Marilisa is still looking at me like she wants to slap my wrist for what I'd said about Amarone being successful in the States because it was the fruit of her love. I need to change the subject and there's the perfect excuse to! It's called "25 Anni," and it's the Sagrantino di Montefalco produced by Arnaldo Caprai, vintage 1999. It's one of my favorite Italian red wines. Maybe I'm swayed by my friendship with and esteem for Marco Caprai, but the fact is there are lots of people who feel the way I do about this wine. Shigeru agrees with me, and he starts right in singing its praises.

He says it's highly concentrated with fresh aromas of undergrowth and red flowers. He finds it "long," he says it fills your mouth, but also your head and your heart. It's a wine that makes you feel like eating rare grilled meat with sea salt sprinkled all around the rim of the dish, pigeon, hare and *formaggi di fossa*, cheese covered in leaves and left to ripen in humid caves. Strong flavors that can hold up to the body of the wine. After all, he does the opposite of what's normally done; the food is actually a parenthesis that's supposed to sustain the main factor, the wine.

On the back of the Sagrantino's success we quickly move on to the fourth wine, which I am equally familiar with. Another astonishing red wine. Where Amarone is king you can't just show up with any red wine.

Oscar "Angelo Gaja always scolds me about the fact that during interviews I always talk about Barolo and never about Barbaresco. He'd be pleased today because I've brought you a fantastic Barbaresco."

I tell Marilisa about this Santo Stefano cru. Naturally, she's familiar with the one produced by the legendary Bruno Giacosa.

Oscar "This is no less so. The grapes come from the same hill. Castello di Neive is the producer, his name's Italo Stupino, the owner of the castle and of some very important vineyards in the Barbaresco zone. Including Santo Stefano. I chose the 2004, what do you think of it?"

Marilisa "You're right, Oscar, it's marvelous. I find that Nebbiolo is a great grape variety, and even if I love Amarone, Barolo and Barbaresco always give me a huge amount of satisfaction. They don't have the immediacy of Amarone, which is a good wine even when it's young. But this element of expectancy is very interesting. It makes them elegant, strong, different every year."

Oscar "I agree." Of course I agree! But I explain to Marilisa that Barbaresco in particular is also good when it's young, a mere three years after the harvest.

Oscar "Marilisa, while Shigeru gets ready to tell us what he thinks of this Barbaresco, I'd like to ask you, when you say 'family,' whom are you referring to?"

Marilisa "To my brother, my daughters and, although in a different way, to Giancarlo, who has continued to work for the company despite our separation."

Oscar "What's your relationship with your daughters?"

Marilisa "I feel so lucky to have them, and to have them the way they are. In my life, because of my work, I missed out on their most important years... I could tell you some stories."

Oscar "When were they born?"

Marilisa "Carlotta was born in 1989, Caterina in 1992. In those years I was very happy playing mommy. I breastfed both of them, even though I didn't take a lot of time off during the pregnancies. I knew the winery needed me and I jumped right back into work to sell wine."

Oscar "Hadn't you ever considered the idea of hiring a sales manager, someone who could have helped you out?"

Marilisa "I tried to, but in the end I preferred to take care of things myself. I had one for five years. With two of us traveling we could develop more business, but after that I preferred to take care of things on my own."

I think Marilisa is a solitary superstar. I'm not saying she doesn't delegate to others, she knows how to do that, of course, otherwise she wouldn't have come this far. It's just that some things she prefers to take care of personally. The company's goals, for example. I remember that when I first met her she was already one of Eataly's suppliers. She said to me: "As soon as I realized what Eataly would become, I looked for your son, I asked him for an appointment and I went to put in the first order in person."

There are certain things that Marilisa likes to take care of personally.

Oscar "I know what you mean... listen, while we drink this Barbaresco, I'd like you to give me the numbers that tell me about your winery. How many bottles?"

Marilisa "Four million and 100,000 for the whole group, more than 80% of which go abroad."

Oscar "How many of them come from Veneto, and how many from Tuscany?"

Marilisa "Two million bottles of Allegrini, 1 million and 500,000 with the Corte Giara label, about 200,000 of San Polo in Montalcino and 400,000 bottles of Poggio al Tesoro in Bolgheri."

Oscar "Revenue?"

Marilisa "Twenty-seven million euros."

Oscar "How many countries do you sell to?"

Marilisa "Sixty-nine."

Oscar "Well, there are 194 in the world... there's still some room for improvement! Why did you all choose Tuscany to invest in?"

Marilisa "I can't speak for the others. Tuscany is still the most famous Italian winemaking region in the world. As for us, there's the question of the continuity of Allegrinis. If necessary, our children could choose. My brother Walter had three daughters. Sadly, one died in a motorcycle accident six months after his father did. Franco has three children. I have two daughters... It's a big family. But only one of my two daughters, Caterina, will become a part of the winery, because my other daughter, Carlotta, chose to study what I would have liked to, medicine."

Oscar "And what about this fabulous Villa della Torre?"

Marilisa "I wanted it at all costs. It was the crowning of a childhood dream that I thought would never come true."

Oscar "You followed in your father's footsteps!"

Marilisa "Yes, unconsciously, I'm reliving the things my father did."

Oscar "And in 2008 the crisis hit, the great crisis, from the country that you export to the most, the United States. Did you fall back into debt?"

Marilisa "That's easy to imagine. I hate finance."

Oscar "Same here."

Marilisa "I find that investing one euro today, and after three days finding yourself with two, isn't exactly ethical. You need to work to make money. Lehman Brothers filing for bankruptcy was something that caught us all unawares. For us, 2009 started with a revenue of minus 60%! What could we possibly do with all those debts to pay? I panicked, but this is what encouraged me to travel even more! I don't think I ever traveled as much as I did in 2009... and little by little we came out of it. Even 2009 ended with a plus 8%. In the following three years we doubled our revenue."

Even in such a difficult phase Marilisa was super! Like Einstein said, a crisis can be a real blessing to those who know how to react. A crisis can generate new creativity in people who are courageous, proactive, and who roll up their sleeves instead of complaining. I tell Marilisa that Einstein drank Barolo. She's quick to answer: "That's why he always looked drunk. You can hold Amarone better." We can't help laughing, and while holding a glass of Barbaresco Santo Stefano it's a pleasure to. I swallow it joyfully almost in one breath.

Shigeru "This Barbaresco is very elegant! I taste mint, licorice and white pepper..."

Oscar "Mint too?... You're right!"

Shigeru has the ability to perceive aromas and flavors that I recognize only after his descriptions. I can't do this on my own. And each time he does, I curse myself for not having been able to. It's a good thing Shigeru exists. He is what we call an "absolute palate," an "absolute nose." Drinking with my Japanese partner is a totally different ball game.

Shigeru "Yes, you can taste it. It's fresh, dry. It's soft and has just the right well-balanced tannins. In this wine everything is typical of Nebbiolo, it's the apothesis (he means apotheosis) of Nebbiolo. I'd pair it with beef stew, seasoned cheeses and fontina or taleggio cheeses that are seasoned, but not too much."

Marilisa "I agree! Nebbiolo made and aged as God wanted it to be (and God, for those of you in Langa, wants big barrels) is one of those wines that if tasted blind cannot be mistaken for another. Like my Amarone for Carlin." She really liked my story!

Now it's time to taste Marilisa's wine. To be honest, I'm terrified, after a Barbaresco like that one, to have to get through an Amarone. Don't get me wrong, it's delicious. But not after a Barbaresco Santo Stefano 2004. But what could we drink instead? Of course, a great white wine, maybe not too young. Marilisa is familiar with my tastes and has decided to have us try her Solosole 2007, a single-variety Vermentino produced by Poggio al Tesoro in Bolgheri. It's the wine made according to her own indications that she told us about at the beginning of our meeting. Excellent idea. This way we'll finish the way we started out.

And at this point something happens that I want to try to describe. I take a sip of the Vermentino and I inelegantly blurt out: "Mother of God! What a wine!"

I've already described what Marilisa looks like: a beautiful woman, with elegant ways in both the clothes she wears and her way of speaking. A refined woman who leaves nothing up to chance, well-aware of her charm and the charm of the surroundings where she welcomes people. But this woman, as soon as she hears my comment, starts beating her breast with the palm of her hand, as a sign of enthusiasm, as if she were congratulating herself on her wine. Fantastic! Proof of my old theory of apparent contradictions. When an elegant, poised woman like her manages to give in to such a spontaneous gesture, that to me is sublime! It's something that blows my mind! I'd like to tell her she's great, and not just for her wine!

Oscar "Swear to me there's no Reisling in this wine."

Marilisa "I swear! I swear on my daughters, but not the way Berlusconi does! Maniacal viticulture, that's the key to it all! Every year, when I taste it for the first time, I get angry because I say it's not like last year's. But then, in time, the difference comes out."

Oscar "*Brava*." I can't stop telling her how great she is. "Come on, tell me about your plans for the future."

Marilisa "First of all, I have to finish consolidating my investments."

Oscar "And in your opinion, where do you think this country is headed? You observe Italy from sixty-nine different countries. You have a huge advantage compared to people who only work within the Italian market. What's your idea of Italy?"

Marilisa "When I travel around the world, in spite of everything, I feel that there's still a lot of fondness for Italy. In our field I also feel admiration. Italy is the country where humanism was born. This is a broad-ranging concept. We Italians have a depth of heart that we have to hold on to and that's our real resource. Italians are loved the world over! Of course, the current crisis will have to end sooner or later. Right now, we're in a sort of middle ages in the history of Italy, but we can get through it and we'll make it in the end."

Oscar "And in your own way, to be able to contribute to solving the crisis, in the next few years you'll continue to travel around the world to sell wine, is that right? Doesn't it bother you to travel alone all the time?"

Marilisa "I like this life. When I travel for work I don't have so many opportunities to be alone, you must know this is true as much as I do."

Oscar "Do you want to continue to grow?"

Marilisa "Not too much. I want to consolidate the wineries we have. From 27 million euros we can easily go up to 40 million, but I don't think we'll expand any more than that. I don't know whether we would be able to continue to make a genuine and identifying product beyond a certain quantity."

Oscar "Let me ask you one last question, then let's hear what Shigeru has to say about your wine. But you don't have to answer if you don't want to, whatever you say will go into the book. Do you have a partner today? Are you in love?"

Marilisa "No, I'm not."

Oscar "Would you like to be with someone?"

Marilisa "Life is always better with someone than alone."

I try to be more direct. "Do you feel like falling in love all over again?"

Marilisa "Yes!" She smiles slightly embarrassed. "How can you not want the chance to fall in love? That would be impossible!"

Oscar "Isn't the overwhelming love you have for your work something that holds back equally strong emotions?"

Marilisa "Absolutely! My work is so gratifying that it fills lots of gaps. But I'm also aware of the fact that love is something different." That's true. Love is something else... maybe bigger, definitely different. But all you men out there, careful, don't ask her to give up her work because she wouldn't think of it. It's a compromise that in the past, the present and, I think, the future Marilisa has never nor will ever be able to accept. And it is, she tells us, proof of her respect for the work she does.

Rita Levi-Montalcini comes to mind. One evening, in Bologna, I was lucky enough to have dinner with her. She had just turned ninety-nine. She told me that she'd never had a relationship with a man because of her respect for science. She could never have shared her capacity for attention. Rita was already married, but to her research. The comparison might seem irreverent but, forgive me, I think that traveling around the world to sell quality wine (and there's no way you can do that and be successful without proudly talking about history, culture, traditions and territory) is a marvelous service to our country.

Shigeru ends our meeting. He manages to stay focused on the wine from the first minute to the last. He talks about Solosole 2007, describing it as the sublimation of Vermentino: a wine with an excellent mineral nature, a soft taste in which you can savor the grapefruit, in which the aroma is long. Shigeru finds it has a very persistent, dry flavor with elegant tannins. He'd pair it with oysters, *cacciucco*, Italian fish stew, buffalo mozzarella on a thin slice of lemon, olive oil and pepper... And then he mentions one of my favorite Japanese dishes, baked eel, fabulous!

Marilisa "You know how we make this wine? We make the grapes ripen as much as possible."

Oscar "Is 2008 as good as this 2007?"

Marilisa had also put a bottle of 2008 on the table.

Marilisa "Franco says it's even better."

Oscar "Come on, we have to go now. Hey everyone, as you get into the car steal the bottle of the 2008 vintage, we'll drink it tonight with our dinner!"

Notes for Wines Tasted with Marilisa Allegrini
Shigeru Hayashi

Viognier 2011 Calatrasi e Micciché
Type white wine
Grapes 100% Viognier
Vinification and fining fermentation at controlled temperature
(12 °C), maceration *sur lie*, several months in steel before bottling
Production area Sicily

Straw color with green hues. Very floral aroma but more Sicilian
jasmine, followed by orange blossoms and fruity notes (apricot,
peach, a hint of pineapple). The taste is sapid, soft, mineral,
endowed with good acidity and pleasantness.

To be paired with all types of fish, especially shellfish and molluscs
(oysters with rice vinegar). Perfect with hard-boiled eggs and Dijon
mustard. Can also be tried with white meat, for instance, pan-fried
chicken with salt and white pepper.

The estate this wine comes from is called "Magnifico," and never
was a name more appropriate! We're at an altitude of 1,000 meters
in the conch of Corleone, where the Micciché family has been
producing wine for generations. The landscape is so harsh it
reminds you of the surface of the moon. The winery is a member
of the Vino Libero project.

Otello Nerodilambrusco Cantine Ceci

Type red sparkling wine
Grapes 100% Lambrusco
Vinification and fining maceration with the skins at a low
temperature, re-fermentation in the Charmat method
Production area Emilia Romagna

Bright purple color, bouquets of red fruit, undergrowth, wild
strawberry, chamomile, blueberry, brown sugar and grape juice.
The taste is soft, sapid, aromatic, very pleasant.

Excellent for meals, this wine is perfect with the cold cuts of
Emilian tradition, first and foremost mortadella. I'd also pair it
with a Japanese dish called *oden* (stewed gut skewers).

Lambrusco di Ceci should be enjoyed in the company of others.
Take it with you to the beach, in summer, or savor it while
watching the Champions League finals. It's easy, but not banal,
fresh, but not simple, immediate, but not passing. Your friends will
always thank you for it!

Sagrantino di Montefalco 25 Anni 1999 Arnaldo Caprai

Type red wine
Grapes 100% Sagrantino
Vinification and fining 30 days of maceration of the grapes, aging
for 24 months in French oak barriques
Production area Umbria

Impenetrable ruby red color. Intense aromas of ripe fruit and red
flowers, licorice, green peppercorn and leather. As for taste, the
fruit returns, it's persistent, velvety, soft and slightly aromatic.

To be savored with mixed grilled meat or lamb roast. It's at its very
best when it's paired with game, especially when an Umbrian black
truffle garnish is added. Try it with cheese that's spicy or aged
after being covered in leaves in a humid cave.

Caprai is the "inventor" of Sagrantino Moderno, wine that at one time was sweet and mouth-puckering, while now it's dry and elegant. It seems it got its name from the fact that it was the feast day wine, to be enjoyed only on Sunday, the day of the Lord.
In Japan it would have been perfect for the Shogun, the great samurai chief: whenever he lost a battle he would do hara-kiri.
If I were to choose the last wine to drink before I die, I'd choose this one!

Barbaresco Santo Stefano 2004 Castello di Neive

Type red wine
Grapes 100% Nebbiolo
Vinification and fining 12 days of grape maceration, 2 years of aging in large oak barrels, 1 year in bottles
Production area Piedmont

The color at first sight is sparkling ruby and garnet red. Very elegant aromas, with dried rose, violet, white pepper, licorice, leather and balsamic notes on the finish. The taste is powerful, balanced, with sweet and soft tannin. Harmonious and very long aftertaste.

To be paired with lamb seasoned with rosemary, beef stew, pan-fried veal fillet with *salsa verde* (finely chopped parsley, capers, garlic, anchovies, olive oil, pickles); fabulous with aged or hard cheeses. And it's perfect when paired with a beautiful woman, too!

We tasted this wine while watching the TV show called *Show Dinner*: a famous Japanese chef uses knives as though they were swords (and sometimes swords as though they were knives).
And indeed, this Barbaresco, which comes from the most beautiful vineyard of the apellation, is razor sharp.

Bolgheri Vermentino Solosole 2007 Poggio al Tesoro
Type white wine
Grapes 100% Vermentino
Vinification and fining after harvesting and complete maturation,
fermentation and maceration at controlled temperature and fining
in steel
Production area Tuscany

Rather accentuated yellow, almost golden color. Bouquets of
apricot, white peach and freshly mown grass. Pleasant and clean
minerality, almost salty. It has a subtle almond taste; it's very
pleasant, sapid and fresh.

It's perfect with a variety of fish-based dishes. I'd like to see it
paired with giant baked oysters dressed with cream and citron
sauce. And why not? With a fish stew, a *cacciucco*, in *salsa verde*
(see above).

What is it that drives the greatest producers of Amarone (in
Veneto) to want to make a great white wine from Vermentino
grapes (in Tuscany)? I think it's the love of their work and a liking
for a challenge. Have they succeeded? You bet they have! The
Allegrinis could make great wines anywhere (maybe in Japan, too?).

Gravner: Josko Gravner
Little Is Good: My Father Was Right

You Don't Know Which Land You Belong To

Five kilometers past Gorizia, we climb the hills overlooking Slovenia. That's where we find Josko Gravner's home and wine cellar. A single floor above ground, white, clean and basic. His wife Maria is there to welcome us because he's busy working on the land. So it's up to her, to this "wife-and-mother," to be the first to place, in Italy, in Europe and in history, this corner of a country that no longer knows or doesn't yet know exactly who it belongs to.
I say: "I came here to talk about Italy starting from your wines."
She answers right away, her intonation is clear and direct. In her voice there is no uncertainty nor are there pauses for reflection. Her thinking flows lucidly and traces the royal path we might be able to venture along to be able to understand what isn't clear about this part of Italy and the most profound experiences of this population. The father of the family, Josko, will talk to us later, as men often do, about his hobbyhorse, day after day, invention after invention, about the things that give him pleasure, about his ever-changing certainties that are always being debated. But his wife-and-mother has told me all there is to tell about the framework within which this family has lived and worked. Maria and Josko have been together for forty years; they got married when she was eighteen and he was twenty-one, but all you need to do is listen to them to understand the meaning of their being together: for her, stability and the family, for him, big projects and seasons that are ever-changing and ever-stimulating. It's the roles people play.

Women plan and cast a watchful eye, men invent.

Maria talks the way I like people to. Subject, verb, object, period. No fancy frills and no waffling expressions. She's definitely helped by the fact that Italian isn't her native language, so she manages it with care and circumspection. She never makes mistakes because she refers back to the basic structure of the language, and this too is a lesson in itself. How many people today, incapable of facing, simplifying a problem, build up complicated sentences chock-full of adverbs and parentheses, where all meaning is lost.

We have fifteen minutes before Josko arrives and in the meantime Maria tells us: " This land was Austrian until 1915, then after the First World War it became Italian. At that time, the Slovenian minority in Austria was protected, it had bilingual schools. When it came under Italian rule it no longer did; speaking Slovenian was forbidden. Now the situation is improving, but there are still some obstacles. Those who live here must know a second language, but if you learn your language and your history well so that you can express yourself correctly, and then you also learn the language of the host country— (those are the exact words she uses, 'host country')—as well as its history, you live better. As a bilingual person I can talk to you your language, but if you, as an Italian, can't talk to me my language, this becomes a great barrier."

Words on paper will never do justice to her firm, strong voice, which gives you the impression that she expresses concepts well rooted in her way of thinking, and it's hard for me to give the reader an idea of her vaguely foreign but not wholly foreign accent, which isn't German, or Slav, but I will try to describe it to help you to understand. Even these small slips, "talk to you your language," but without real errors in syntax, show that Maria well distinguishes the basics of the language (the way the phrase is built and verbs, for instance) and is careful to respect them, but that she also knows that sometimes a preposition isn't crucial to understanding, so she skips it, she leaves out the detail. It seems like a mature approach and a beautiful form of integration: it's as if she's saying, I apply the important rules of this country that hosts me, but I base things on my original culture, which likes to go straight to the point. So what Maria is telling us is that there are still some obstacles to the integration of the Slovenian community on the part of Italy.

Oscar "Do you consider yourself Italian or Slovenian?"

Maria "I'm a Slovenian, born and bred a Slovenian."

Oscar "And what about Josko?"

Maria "He's of Slovenian nationality, but he was born Italian."

Oscar "And what about you?" (I ask their daughter who has just joined us.)

Jana "I'm Jana." (Good answer!)

Oscar "What I meant was: do you feel Italian or Slovenian?"

Jana "I can't define myself exactly, I'm part Slovenian and part Italian."

Josko joins us, he gets down off a tractor. He's ploughing a new piece of land and he's using the tractor, not a pencil, to plan it directly. He and Maria look alike somehow, they're both tall and slim with light skin and hair. Their styles are similar too: what I mean is they're both wearing jeans and a flannel shirt, a heavy sweater and a smooth corduroy jacket with lots of pockets. They welcome us into a white room with off-white beams and a wooden decor. The tables are made from the same type of wood and are of the same color, the bare walls are white, there's also a cupboard for the glasses and a few chairs: no distractions, no decorations.

I tell them about the project behind this visit and about all the other visits that are part of this tour. And I play my trump card: three fantastic bottles of Barolo Borgogno (1961, 1967 and 1978) and a bottle of Riserva 2010 produced by Lune Teo Musso, because I know Josko loves Teo's beers. I chose the bottles of Barolo with Josko and his search for purity, authenticity and tradition in mind. Values that even old Cesare Borgogno knew how to put into his Barolos. I feel proud of these three bottles even if my only merit is that of having found them in a cellar when I bought the Borgogno. I open the one labeled 1978 right away. It's perfect, I'm in love with it at the very first sip and I start to sing its praises, even though it's not up to me to do so. I wish Cesare could see us seated around that white table: I express praise and joy while they all sit there listening to me quietly. Not because the wine isn't excellent, but because I made the choice: 1978 forever, no doubt about it. I'm wrong. A father (even a foster father) must never say to one of his children: "I love you more than the others," because those listening will be drawn more to the other children, to try to understand what they're really like, and they'll end up loving them more. You'll understand what I mean as you continue to read.

Jana and Filippo Polidori join us as well; Filippo is a great friend of Josko's and mine too. Filippo helps Josko to distribute his wines with the image and value they deserve. He's young, but in marvelous harmony with this man who's twenty-five years his senior. It's surprising how Josko manages to conquer the scene and take over the lead with just a few words. He keeps his head sunk down between his shoulders and bowed slightly forward, especially when he has to compose and express a thought. As if it took a special kind of energy to push these ideas out of his head. He looks at us with his eyes the color of undergrowth (I could say, if I wanted to, "the color of the leaves on the vine in the fall," but it seems too obvious), and he often smiles at us.

Forty-six is the number that characterizes Josko: forty-six harvests, which is a nice number, because it tells us about the opportunities he had to change his mind and test the viability of his inventions. And Josko has traveled a long way along the path of change.

Oscar "Tell us where we are, Josko."

Josko "We're in a small village of 250 residents who practically make their living by working the land. And it's a place where every war has been waged. So it's a land that has suffered. Each time a war ended we had to start over from scratch. The First World War was the cruelest; just think that there are 52,000 Italians buried in the Monumental Sacrarium of Oslavia alone. In addition to the many people missing and the same number of fallen on the Austro-Hungarian side. Our house was the only one left standing because it was the Red Cross's medical headquarters, there was even a red cross on the roof. That's the only reason it was spared. This was my grandfather Gravner's house, which had already been built when he got married. Then we moved on."

Oscar "This was Austria, right? So your grandfather was Austrian?"

Josko "Yes, my grandfather was an Austrian solider. My father, instead, and my uncles, his brothers, were refugees in Ivrea. During the war, the civilians were transported far away to many regions of Italy."

Oscar "So your father only spoke Slovenian."

Josko "My family is Slovenian, my father only spoke Slovenian, but we're of German stock, the name is German, originally from Lower Bavaria."

Oscar "So you were born in this house. Was it already so beautiful?"

My questions are pressing, perhaps too much so, but I'm eager to learn all about the experiences of a family that was "transplanted" several times, even without ever leaving home. It's so different from the story of someone like me who has a history that revolves around a few towns located close to each other, so that the concept of the "roots" of civilization is far more concrete. The only change my grandparents and parents experienced was that of going from the Italian monarchy to the Italian Republic. In the land of the Savoy that was a huge change.

Josko "No, it was more beautiful but then I tore it down. I remodeled it a first time with the help of a surveyor when I was twenty-five and didn't understand. I've tried to make up for it somewhat, but I still haven't finished. I still have to see about the turret. In any case, here in Italy the red tape is just terrible. It's absolutely impossible to work, I think we're living in an age of self-harm. You need to get through some red tape on the other side too, but there's less of it. But Europe is spreading there too, which means that stricter rules are on the way. On the other side you can plant a vineyard without any red tape; here, planting a vineyard is almost like building a house."

Oscar "So you were born here in 1952. You're two years older than me."

Josko "Yes, I lived and grew up in this house along with my four sisters, who have other jobs now."

Oscar "And what did your father do?"

Josko "My father was a farmer, which is what people did in the olden days. He made wine, he had livestock in the stables, fruit on the trees, cherries... My father taught me to make wine because the wine he made was really good. But most importantly he taught me the values of life."

Oscar "So your father was a good man."

Josko "Yes, he was a good man, but he didn't get past fifth grade."

Oscar "Just like mine. Did you learn more from your father or your mother?"

Josko answers without hesitation, "From my father! My grandfather, in 1926, after the war, had opened a tavern that did a lot of business. Then the tavern closed in 1932 because in Italy you couldn't work if you weren't a member of the Fascist party, and my grandfather chose to close. Fascism abolished the Slovenian schools. You couldn't talk

Slovenian here anymore. After the Second World War not much changed because there was the problem of Yugoslavia, and anyone who spoke Slovenian was automatically considered a Communist. After the war, native speakers of Slovenian had none of the benefits that Italians had, like subsidies, for instance. In a situation like that you don't know who you belong to. On this side, they would tell me to go over there, you're a Slav, on the other side they told me to go back, you're Italian. I'd tell them all to go to hell. I'm a citizen of the world. If we look at Europe, we still have a big problem because this isn't a people's Europe, it's the Europe of vested interests."

When You Work Too Much There's No Time to Think

I met him in Turin in 2008. Josko had come for a public tasting of his wines. On his second glass he said: "Let's use the familiar 'tu' form, that's what wine is for, so people will use the 'tu' form!" I find there's a lot of poetry in this sentence. I used it for one of Eataly's advertising pages. And after our meeting Josko said: "In all my life I've never spoken so much!" In fact, Josko is usually very quiet.

Oscar "Where did your father store his wine? He still wasn't using amphorae the way you do now, was he?"

Josko "No, my father stored it in barrels, in huge wooden ones."

Oscar "The way we did, in Langa. Which wines did your father make?"

Josko "Mostly Ribolla Gialla, which is a typical vine species in this area, on either side of the political boundaries. Nature knows no boundaries. Ribolla Gialla, like most of the vinestock, originates from the Caucasus."

I feel like learning more about his personal life and I barrage him with more questions. He learned Italian in elementary school, because it's not his first language. But he does speak it properly, with an accent that to us Piedmontese sounds German. Excellent grammar and basic expressions. Only when his thoughts are deeper does he draw his words from a less immediate archive, so it takes more time, but this doesn't mean he's less accurate in expressing his ideas. After middle school he attended a technical college, watched over impatiently by his father who was waiting for him to come to work and was

surprised that he still wasn't producing anything by the age of fourteen! "If you wait until you're twenty-five to choose a trade you've
already missed the train!" his father would say.
How right he was! All this youth unemployment in Italy is creating a
second disadvantage: people who don't work when they're young
don't know how to live off of their work, not because it's their fault,
but because of the lack of habit. You learn to reason with your head
and your heart between the ages of eight and twelve, but you learn
how to work between eighteen and twenty-eight: if that train passes
you by, then socially it's a disaster! Even if we do manage to come out
of the crisis we still risk finding ourselves with a generation of thirty-
to-forty-year-olds who have acquired a lifestyle that doesn't contem-
plate ongoing work activity. I get lots of applications from young
graduates who all want to work in marketing or public relations or
events management... I tell each and every one of them the same
thing: at Eataly you start out the way my own children did, unloading
trucks, waiting tables, stocking the shelves. You can't understand
anything about marketing if you don't first get calluses on your hands.
Josko "That's true... At the beginning I thought I would work far
away from my father, I wanted to drive a bulldozer because working
the land seemed to be too hard. But then I realized I liked it. I worked
all the time, even on Sundays... and I made so many mistakes... when
you work too hard, there's no time to think. My father had 10 hectares of land and now I have 35."

The French Talk about Terroir Because They Don't Have One

Good. Now we can calmly sip this 1978 Barolo. Simona, who was
born in 1978, is hesitant about drinking Barolo in the morning,
before lunch, but it's a once-in-a-lifetime chance, so she's finally
convinced and accepts the compliments all around for the excellent vintage.
Josko "Among the oldest wines I've ever drunk the best was a Borgogno from 1931, which I drank on May 1, 2001, in Gorizia. I'll never forget it. A seventy-year-old Barolo, perfect."
I crunch a few numbers about the bottles from 1961 that I still have
in the cellar. I absolutely must leave a few for 2031. Unless my luck is

rotten, I should still be alive when I'm seventy-seven. That way I too can enjoy a seventy-year-old Borgogno.

Shigeru starts in with the description of the 1978 bottle. He's in seventh heaven. He finds everything in it: animals, flowers, spices. He keeps us there ten minutes listening to the most recondite aromas and flavors he can feel. He's like a machine gun. In the end he declares he doesn't want to talk about the food it would be well paired with. He says there's no food good enough for this wine. Josko is looking at him as if he were from another planet. I interrupt Shigeru.

Oscar "And you, Josko? What do you think of this wine?"

Josko "I don't know how to make all these classifications for wine, for me, wine has to have a soul, if wine has a soul, then the soul will bring together all the rest. And if wine has a soul then it's alive, if it's not alive it's not worth the trouble even drinking it!"

Oscar "Does this Barolo have a soul?"

Josko "Of course it does!"

Oscar "How do you know?"

Josko "I don't know how to explain it! People have their own way of defining what the soul is. Even criminals think they have a soul. But you can tell whether a wine is alive or dead right away!"

Shigeru "This is interesting! We never talk about wine having a soul, this is something new and interesting!"

Filippo steps in to tell us about a famous journalist who, during an interview, heard Josko answer that when he goes into the cellar his wines understand the sort of mood he's in, whether he's happy or angry. In the same way, wines "shut themselves off" before visitors who aren't interesting. "That's all we need now: wines with a soul!" This was the reaction of the silly journalist as Josko looked at him pityingly: "There are some things a person who doesn't make wine just can't understand."

Oscar "Let me get this straight, so you're saying that one of your wines, or a wine in general, a living, beautiful wine, one that you like, if drunk by a cynical person, loses its soul?"

Josko "Listen, the value of wine in 5 or 6,000 years of history lies right there: generation after generation of vintners has sought the unattainably perfect wine, wine that's alive, wine that has a soul."

In the interviews in this book, we'll hear stories about utopias over and over again. Utopia brings these producers together. The search for beauty, which, however big it may be, will always be unfinished. Because the following year they'll try to make a better wine, certain that it can be done, hopeful that it's the perfect wine. A good as well as bountiful utopia that bestows meaning to life. Josko's comment continues, confirming my thoughts.

Josko "You can't achieve the perfect wine. Every year something escapes you, nature is always different and this constant quest to get to the top is the value of the wine, and the explanation of a history that's thousands of years long, otherwise why bother to continue?"

Oscar "How did you get these ideas, did you already have them when you were young?"

Josko "Well, no, in those days I disagreed with what my father would always say: 'little is good!' And I'd reply: 'no, Papà, you're old: a lot is good!' But he'd also say: 'vineyards fertilized by rabbits!' By which he meant vineyards that aren't forced, so very few grapes. Let me give you an example. 2012 was a year you'd rather forget, a leap year, with lots of rain in the spring, a very dry summer, and heavy rain again in the fall. Those who had used fertilizers in the spring suffered the greatest damage because the vines were too vigorous and the drought blocked them. Then the rain came along and it made the grapes rot… but this year it's the same thing all over again: two days of sun and they're already rushing to fertilize, they don't realize they're making a mistake. This is the textbook style, they do what they were taught, they don't listen to the land."

Oscar "So in the end, how did your 2012 turn out?"

Josko "Good! 165 hectoliters from 17 hectares of vineyard. I finished harvesting on November 9."

Oscar "Maybe slightly less than your average."

Josko "Yes, my average is 220 to 230 hectoliters from 18 hectares."

Oscar "Let's go back to your story. When you were eighteen you wanted to make lots of wine, lower costs, make money, right?"

Josko "I don't even know why. Maybe because that's what they teach you in school, then I'd tell my father: you're wrong, you're old, we have to get rid of the wooden barrels and move on to steel, and that's what I did. Then, in 1982, I realized that I was wrong and I made another mistake: I moved to barriques, because in those years I was traveling around France and I'd liked some of the French wines I'd tried, I wanted to do what they did. I still hadn't realized that the

French talk a lot about 'terroir' because they don't have one, so they have to use barriques to add dryness and tannins to it."

Legendary words! "The French talk a lot about terroir because they don't have one." It's a refined concept that in just a few words describes a way of seeing people across the Alps: their great pride in their land becomes marketing and makes up for potential that, as compared with our land, is inferior. We Italians should learn from them. That mythical ability the French have of describing things, their ability to add intangible values to their products, to make others perceive them as real values. This must be why they sell twice as much wine as we do abroad. We should do what Josko does, someone who has plenty of values, and really knows how to sell them. Very few bottles but with an average price that will arouse the envy of many French producers. He sure knows how to talk about his values!

Oscar "Why do they sell so much more than we do? Why do they have a much higher average price? Why do they manage to have 11 billion euros worth in exports whereas we hardly have 5?"

Josko "Because 250 years ago the British were already talking and writing about French wine, while here in Italy we drank wine, but no more than that."

Oscar "A great advantage that stems from the powers of marketing."

Josko "And also because many consumers are interested more in image than in substance, they'll pay 900 euros for a wine that tastes like horse's sweat and they'll still say it's good."

Oscar "Of course, if you're spending 900 euros you can't say it's bad."

Josko "But some people pour it down the drain, though there aren't many who do that."

We laugh out loud, at the notion of wine that tastes of horse's sweat and of some people liking it, or forcing themselves to. We're holding a glass of Barolo Borgogno 1978. After Josko said it was "alive" it seems to have improved. Could that be because it has a soul?

I Could Always Tell When It Was Time to Change

Filippo takes us back to the fundamental phases of the evolution in this wonderful winemaker.

Filippo "It's important, when you're talking about Josko's development as a winemaker, to think of several very important facts. He went from wood to steel, from steel to barriques, he got rid of the barriques and moved on to large barrels and vats for the long maceration phase, and, finally, he began using amphorae. Before going from steel to the barrique Josko was considered to be one of the biggest white wine producers in the world. At that time there were so many orders that he would fill them with whatever quantity of wine he had available. But when he had reached the peak of success, he'd become a market reference, he decided to change his method."

Josko "I could always tell when it was time to change to be able to sell... less! The opposite of you!" But as he looks at me he smiles.

Oscar "I'm starting to be a lot like you too."

Filippo "Let me tell you this story again. When Josko went to do his tour of France he started out with Romanée-Conti, but he had other visits in mind as well. When the visit ended he decided to forget the rest and go back home, because he was convinced he'd seen the best, and out of respect he went back home, he didn't want to see anything else!"

Josko "That's right. You can't go on a wine tour for the sake of just doing something; once you've seen the best you really don't need to see anything else. Sometimes I have visitors who've already seen three or four cellars and I realize they're already drunk, they're not really interested and I get teed off. I try to handle the situation as best I can because I need to sell too, but I still get pissed off!"

Oscar "Going back to your story: in 1982 you move on to barrique..."

Josko "One year in steel and one year in barrique."

Oscar "In 1982 you were already famous. You had a good market. Why?"

Josko "Because there was demand for it. Maybe there wasn't enough wine, and on top of that, as compared with other wines, there was something about mine that made them better. But it's hard to say. It's like when you talk about your children. Then, again in 1982, I pruned the grape bunches for the first time, and that's when they decided I had to be crazy. No one threw grapes on the ground!"

Oscar "Unlike everyone else, you started with pruning. Does Ribolla Gialla have a high yield per hectare?"

Josko "Extremely high."

Oscar "And how do you prune the grape bunches?"

Josko "I leave six bunches cut in half, because the sour rot starts at the mid-point of the bunch."

Goblets clink. I continue to drink Barolo 1978 and sing its praises. Damn, this is so good! I'd drink it all but I can't because too much might make me sick. We start tasting the 1967, which I find less good than the 1978, even if that year in Langa is considered to be better. For Borgogno they say the best year is 1961, also because the more you go back the more the production is natural.

Oscar "Josko, can you tell us about this wine in your own words?"

Josko "I don't know how to, but I can say that if I were asked to choose, I prefer 1967."

Oscar "Why?"

Josko "Ha! Why? Because it tastes more like wine!"

Oscar "So as we gradually go back in time you'll like it more and more because the working method at the winery was more natural. In 1961 this winery was a legend! Cesare Borgogno died in 1968, so he oversaw both the 1961 and 1967 productions, and Cesare was totally fanatical about naturalness and respect. A total fanatic! My son Andrea has decided to go back to those values. This year the first wine that's completely his will come out, 2008 vintage. I can't wait to have you taste it."

Josko "We have to start doing things like that again!"

Oscar "Let's go back to your story. You keep on using steel and barrique and grow more and more famous."

Josko "Yes, but I don't know why."

Oscar "That's normal. Great people never know why they're great. Then what happened?"

Josko "What happened is that I didn't like what I was doing anymore. I'd been wrong to bring barrique here, in this fantastic land of white wines. Here we really do have terroir, and we don't need barrique. On top of that it wasn't right to crush the Ribolla grapes right away. They have such a thick, juicy skin you have to squeeze it carefully, otherwise it squirts all over the place and the best part ends up being used by Nonino to make grappa. So in 1994, 1995 (also 1996, but there was hail that year), I made my first attempts at maceration and fermentation with the skin. I tried other things with and without yeasts, with and without sulfites. I got the worst results when I added yeasts. In that case the wine was really bad."

Filippo reminds us of Josko's California experience in 1987. "Ten days, a thousand wines tasted." When he came back, Maria asked him: "What did you learn?" Josko's answer was: "Everything you're not supposed to do!"

Josko "Yes, that's right. I'd tasted the first wines with the addition of artificial aroma. This had happened in June, and in September I tasted a few wines produced by Collio with artificial aromas added. Even right here in Italy! Because some of the people from around here worked in California and learned how to do that. It was very successful. Great scores coming in from all around."

Oscar "During your lifetime big trips shape your career: California in 1987 and you understand what you're not supposed to do, Romanée-Conti in 1993 and you understand what you *are* supposed to do…"

Josko "But I also understood that I had to abandon the barrique."

Oscar "When did you decide to start using amphorae?"

Josko "I was at Veronelli's in 1997–1998 and Attilio Scienza was there. He happened to talk to me about the Caucasus and put a flea in my ear. So I decided my next trip would be Anatolia, Mesopotamia and the Caucasus. I went there in 2000. But in 1997 I had already done my first experiments with fermentation in an amphora, and I had decided to start using amphorae to make wine."

Oscar "I'll be going there soon myself, between the Tigris and the Euphrates, where agriculture was born more than 11,000 years ago, because I want to dedicate Eataly Bari to the Levant. I'm going to go there with Attilio Scienza who'll explain everything to me."

Making Wine Is Like Searching for Clean Water:
You Have to Go Straight to the Source

Josko "Modern technologies last ten–fifteen years, after that period of time they no longer work and you have to change. This means they're already not working when you adopt them. This is why you have to go back to the beginning. It's like water, the closer you get to the mouth the more it's polluted. To find pure water you have to go back to the origins. The same thing goes for enology. Today enology is very polluted. I find there are some modern wines that are undrinkable. They hate me for saying it, but I can't help it."

Oscar "So you think it's gotten even worse since they used chemical flavoring in California."

Josko "Of course. My father would tell me that the wine in his day and age was better. I used to kid him about it, saying 'because you were all hungry back then.' But now I think he was right. Nothing was added in those days. And I'm sorry my father died before I could understand just how right he was and I went back to the beginning."

More clinking of goblets and we devote ourselves to a 1967 Barolo, but also to the one labeled 1961, which we have decided to pour right next to the 1967.

Shigeru "I have no words to describe these wines. I'm moved. And I'm embarrassed before Josko, who shoots me down with just one word. I'm going to write up the descriptions. All I can say is that there are paintings by Modigliani and Picasso that leave you speechless. You can't explain why. They mesmerize you and that's that. This is happening to me today."

Josko smiles. The fact that he's managed to tame the Japanese connoisseur pleases him. He has no doubts: 1961 is the best! It has the most soul of all!

Oscar "Let's go back to your story. Why did you move on to amphorae? What does it mean to move on to amphorae, in just a few words?"

Josko "The land has the vine that gives birth to the grapes, and the grapes are used to give birth to wine. It's a complete circle. I haven't checked the sugar or acidity of my wine in years, simply because I don't add anything, and I don't take anything away. I don't want to know, I leave it up to nature. One year one of my collaborators asked me for permission to measure the acidity. I said no, but then I thought about it again. I said: 'Go ahead and measure, but don't tell me what you find out. I'm not interested.'"

Oscar "Do you watch the weather forecast?"

Josko "Yes, I do."

Oscar "Don't you it think ruins the surprise?"

Josko "I watch the forecast... then I think: they're wrong, it won't be like that. But then they get it right. But this year I finished the harvest on November 9 anyway."

Oscar "Help me to understand in technical terms what it means to use amphorae."

Josko "I've gotten rid of all the steel from the cellar, the pneumatic press which I've replaced with the winepress, and the refrigerator which is of no use because it doesn't have any steel. I don't clarify, I don't use yeasts and I don't filter."

Filippo "For Josko, talking about natural wines and using steel is a paradox because of the galvanic currents that are created, and because steel can release heavy metals." When Filippo intervenes it's always to clarify and add something. He's a special sales agent because he's familiar with the product and the process required to make it, but also because he's emotionally involved in Josko's values.

Josko "What I don't like is that if I say what I think they give me a dirty look. Whereas if they criticize my wine I don't get upset. It's sort of like going to Mass in Italy, if you don't go to Mass they give you a dirty look, but I'm not someone who follows the crowd. I don't go to Mass because I don't need to, I try not to sin so I won't have to go to confession. There's no point in going to confession and then committing the same sin over again. And yet that's what happens, and all this has brought the world to the state it's in right now."

Oscar "Tell me what you think of the world today."

Josko "We thrive on falsehood and appearances, the only thing that's important is how you appear to others. But I've completely detached myself from that way of being. I don't have a TV, I don't buy the newspaper, I get the news when I manage to read some Slovenian newspaper, but always when the news is old. I'm not interested in politics and I think of myself as an anarchist... but not someone who's violent, not the kind who throw bombs, of course. I have to do my job well and the rest doesn't interest me. And do you know why I've reached this conclusion? Twenty–twenty-five years ago I voted for Craxi, because my family, which has never been Fascist, was Socialist. Here, after Fascism, you couldn't vote for the Right. Then we learned that he was stealing too, and that he even justified himself by saying 'everyone does it.' Around here, if you weren't a Fascist they'd make you drink castor oil if you were lucky, or burnt-out car oil if you weren't, and these are things they don't teach you in school. Italy has never formally apologized to the territories it invaded. The Germans apologized, not the Italians. Fascism crept as far as Ljubljana and there are families there that lost everything under Fascism. But no one ever talks about it. Instead they talk about the foibas. For as long as the country doesn't deal with these issues it can't move forward. It's still rotten underneath. And there's no sense of conscience."

Oscar "You're right. You know, not all apes evolved into human beings. They already possessed science and knowledge; the great transition from the ape to the human being was the acquisition of conscience, a soul, poetry, that music inside that makes you choose what's right without having to read the rules. And after Craxi who did you vote for?"

Josko "I voted a few more times for the Left. But it's been about twenty years since I last voted."

Oscar "Do you feel like talking about your family some more?"

Nature Gives Us Everything, Every Now and Again It Has the Right to Take Something Back

Oscar "At first, there was your father and mother. And then what happened?"

Josko "I had three sisters: one in Trieste, another one in Gorizia, and one died of cancer at the age of forty-seven. We've always gotten along. Of course, not all of them have an equally good opinion of me. But that's what happens when you go against the grain. I got the winery because I was the youngest. It was a question of fate."

Oscar "Then you got married. You went to get your wife 'on the other side.' How did you meet her if you were busy working all the time?"

Josko "Not quite always. I met her at a party. I married her forty-two years ago."

Oscar "In church?"

Josko "Yes, I used to go to church then. I don't anymore. I have nothing in particular against the Church, on the contrary, I know some excellent priests, but... Then I had four children: three daughters and a son."

Oscar "When did your son die?"

Josko "In 2009. Miha was twenty-seven. A motorcycle accident."

Oscar "Did his death change you?"

Josko's voice is dampened, it weakens.

Josko "Yes, very much so. My son was super. But you can't ask a father about his son. He was already working at the winery and he knew what he wanted."

Later, while talking about the damage from a hailstorm, Josko will say: "Nature gives us everything, every now and again it has the right to take something back." I think he was really talking to himself about a much bigger loss for which there's no consolation, and I can't even imagine what it's like to be in his shoes. It makes a shiver run down my spine.

Josko "He had started out at a young age working at the winery with me, and then he would have kept it going. Now Jana, one of my daughters, is working with me, but she didn't start out young like him, and it takes time to fit in."

I try to find out more: "How do you react when something terrible like this happens, what do you do in your life?"

Josko "You don't do anything, what can you do? You understand that life is a phase, that what seemed like important goals to you, aren't so anymore. Now my goal is to do vineyard architecture. These days I'm working on a piece of land down here. Sometimes I think I should move on and do it without a permit because I find it ridiculous to have to spend 15,000 euros on papers, required by people who know little about the land and who have never gotten their hands dirty. Maybe Miha would have had the courage to just do it."

Oscar "Does the red tape make you mad?"

Josko "There has to be some paperwork, but not the way it is now. In Austria, if you want to build a house, you can get a building permit in a month. The technicians go to the site along with the Mayor, they evaluate and decide. Here instead it's just piles of papers and no one ever comes out to see what you're doing."

You can tell that besides the incommensurable pain felt by a parent, his regret is also that of a father and partner, of all the great things they could have done together. Including bravely dealing with a wrongful and outrageous bureaucracy.

Oscar "Now let's talk about all the changes in your life. The future is change, but it's not necessarily progress. This is why I always try to explain to young people that a ladder can be more future-oriented than an elevator, a horse more than a car. The cell phone boomed when it was given the oldest function in the world: writing. You always have doubts. You always try to improve what you do, you seek utopia, the perfect wine, knowing full well that you'll never achieve it. Has your wife always supported you in your ideas and projects? Do you talk to her about them?"

Josko "Yes, of course I do... But, you know, right now I'm building down here, on a piece of land, a botanical garden that around here, with our species, is actually a wood. But I couldn't do that with a project because when I use a bulldozer I follow the shape of the land. For the vineyard I want to plant they asked me for a plan, but I can't draw the plan on paper. I tried to build a 'pond,' and it didn't get approval. I had to have Attilio Scienza write up a report, while in the meantime they're handing out subsidies for private swimming pools that are made to look like 'water reservoirs'! With government money!"

What he's actually saying is: I don't talk about my projects because they're not real projects, I just try to accompany nature, to follow along with it. The members of my family know this so they don't expect grandiose talk about future schemes, but they do follow me when I understand the path that nature invites me to take. The problems of bureaucracy and injustice rear their ugly heads in everything he says.

Oscar "It pisses you off, why don't you just report these things?"

Josko "Who can I talk to about it? Reporting them means wasting more time."

Filippo tells us that Josko receives lots of visits and inspections instigated by people who envy him. One of the anti-fraud inspectors even paid him his compliments for the work he's doing. Honest journalists say that at the home of certain producers they spend a few minutes talking about their own wineries and hours criticizing Josko's decisions, his only fault being that he stays home and chooses not to take part in the various trade associations and lobbies.

In the meantime, the 1961 vintage has changed its pace even more. It seems like a different wine with each glass.

Unfazed, I continue to defend 1978, and now we're joined by Jana, the daughter who works with Josko. Together we taste the 1978 vintage. She likes it, but Josko is uncompromising. He looks at the three glasses he has before him and declares: "There's no contest, 1961 comes out the winner."

Oscar "Understanding a wine is like understanding a person. The first impression is important, but then you have to delve deeper. Do you usually hit the bull's eye with your first impression?"

Josko "More or less."

Oscar "When I do job interviews I can usually tell how smart a person is, and I can also understand right away whether the person knows how to reason with their head and their heart, because reasoning with just one or the other isn't any good, you have to be able to reason with both. That much I can understand, but what I don't understand in an interview is whether they feel like working. And if they don't it's hard to find a way to fix that. But with wine it's what you say. Usually the first impression is the right one, but these three Borgognos change right inside the glass every fifteen minutes. Don't you agree?"

Jana speaks up: "Then leave some for me. I want to taste them later, too."

Oscar "If you're like your father you'll be most impressed by the 1961 vintage! Now we're going to try some beer. What came first, wine or beer?"

Jana "Beer, it dates back to the days of the Ancient Egyptians!"

Oscar "This beer is really going to surprise you, because it reminds you of wine. Teo Musso makes it, it's aged in barrels he gets from wine producers. So the beer is aged in the Baladin wine cellars in the barrels used for great white wines. This is from 2010. I think it's a fantastic idea. Do you like it?"

Josko "Yes, of the simplest Baladin beers the one I like the most is Nora."

Oscar "I like Elisir. I want you to taste some Elisir and some Super. But Teo's latest idea is this beer aged in wine barrels. Before we talk about the beer, there's something else I'd like to know: of all your grape harvests, forty-six we said, do you remember any one in particular?"

Josko "1982: a beautiful year, very dry, only a few treatments, my first pruning ever, Miha was born, everything was perfect… and now, in recent years, I've come to realize that you shouldn't classify the vintages, every vintage is great!"

Oscar "What lovely words! Every vintage is great! Was there one harvest when you didn't make wine?"

Josko "1996. And that was a great vintage too, because it made a lot of grapes ripen. I lost a vintage, I lost work, but I gained something in terms of my way of thinking. I remember it very well indeed: on

June 19 it hailed from the north and the next day from the south, and always on the same vineyards. Out of 4 hectares I picked 200 kilos of grapes. I would watch the hail and curse. My uncle said to me: 'Why are you cursing? Nature gives us everything, every now and again it has the right to take something back. It's part of our job. Our winery has no roof over it, so we have to accept things like this too.' I can still clearly remember 2008, the last year we harvested with Miha. I remember that about mid-October an enologist came by and was amazed that I hadn't harvested yet. He said to me: 'Everyone harvested in mid-September and the Ribolla was ripe,' and I replied: 'Even an eighteen-year-old boy is considered an adult, but he's not mature yet.' They're harvesting earlier and earlier now, so, according to the latest technology, you have to monitor the acidity... That's bullshit. This year the grapes weren't ripe, they were yellow but they weren't ripe, because the drought had stopped the ripening, we needed to wait for the rain to come to get the ripening going again."

Oscar "So you go into the rows and taste the grapes?"

Josko "I don't taste the grapes, I eat them, lots and lots of them!"

Filippo steps in again: "During that period of the year all he wants to eat are grapes, and during the cherry season, all he wants to eat are cherries. And the fact that he doesn't do any testing drives everyone crazy. There are some people who come here to pick his grapes and have them analyzed. But he once answered a person's questions with these words: "'Wine is in the thoughts of the person who makes it and thoughts can't be analyzed.'"

Oscar "So let's go back to talking about the future. What's in store for you?"

Josko "I want to make a great wine."

Did you get that? Gravner wants to make a great wine. It's as if Alessandro Baricco were to say: "I want to write a great novel." And in fact he does say that, and just like Josko, he's in earnest. People like them make up for the sadness of seeing so many people around who are certain they've accomplished great things, when instead they've done zilch.

Oscar "Are you pessimistic about the future of humanity?"

Josko "I'm not pessimistic, but I do see a decline in the way things are going. A farmer can't do anything without asking for the permission of people who wear a jacket and tie to work. But how can a man who wears a jacket and tie to work possibly teach me how to do my job? To plant the vineyard I was there every single day with my umbrella, in the rain, to see how the water flowed, whether there were springs, and so on. I had a picture in my mind of how I wanted the vineyard to be, and then a technician from Udine came along to tell me what to do. And on that occasion he saw the place for the first time. How can that possibly work? It's also true that not all farmers have the right vision so there has to be some form of checks. For instance, right now in Slovenia they're replanting the vineyard below a castle. This vineyard had been planted under Communist rule, but it had been done properly: small terraces and small tractors. Instead what are they doing now? Sixty-ton bulldozers as big as this house and they're lowering the hillside and underneath they find rock. They want to use mechanized viticulture, but if they were 2-meter terraces before, you can't just throw all the topsoil underneath. There you have it. That's a case where you need some sort of checks. But by people who know what a vineyard is."

Oscar "Have you noticed a decline in human relations and with the public institutions as compared with when you were young?"

Josko "Yes, I have."

Oscar "You get mad, but you don't protest. Are you a moderate anarchist?"

Josko "I've tried to get the producers and the farmers together in this room, but I ended up getting nowhere. As they got up and left they'd say 'this guy's an idiot.' And they'd go out and buy steel. It's useless. Why should I waste my time? I'm trying to change my world. Let everyone change his or hers the way they want to."

Oscar "We need to think about this, because we love the land. What can we or must we do to stop the rot? What do we have to do to convince people to give up this idea of money, of interests at the heart of everything and take in a bit more poetry? We must do something. You've already tried to."

Josko "I already live like that: I don't do the bookkeeping, Jana and my wife take care of that. I bought a small thirty-five-year-old Japanese bulldozer on the cheap. We completely took it apart, rebuilt it and varnished it in the workshop. Now it works..."

Oscar "Come on, Shigeru, tell us about the beer!"

Shigeru "It's incredible how this beer tastes like wine. *Porca miseria,* it's so good. If you're careful you can taste the barley but also the hulled wheat. It tastes like passito wine that's almost 12 degrees proof. A glass while chilling out after dinner, musing over life..."

Today Shigeru is thinking about other things. Josko's monolithic presence has obviously affected him. My impression is that he might feel he was being reductive if he only described things technically, and, incredibly, he drinks it all up, the way he did before with the Barolos. Today, for the first time, Shigeru doesn't spit it out.

In the meantime Josko has asked Jana to bring a bottle of Ribolla Gialla, our fifth wine. I say: "Josko, tell us something about this wine..."

Josko "This is the most recent vintage being sold. It's been on the market for the past ten days. It's a Ribolla from 2006: six years of fining of which one year in the amphora and five in the barrel. The next one will be 2007, after it has spent six years in the barrel and one in the amphora. These grapes are left with their skins on until March, then they're pressed and after that it's one year in the amphora."

I love this wine, but to be truthful I love *all* wines.

Oscar "How many bottles do you make on average per year?"

Josko "Between 25 and 35,000 bottles."

Oscar "And do you intend to make more wine, buy more land, when you grow up?"

Josko "No. When I grow up, if I have the chance to, I'd like to sell one vineyard to buy another one. I should manage to work something out with one of my neighbors who's willing to sell me a piece of land that already contains a small slice that belongs to me. That way he can buy a piece of land that I now own that interests him."

Oscar "There, that's progress. There are some people who'd sell you nothing to keep you from improving. In this case your neighbor has done the right thing. Is your land spread out?"

Josko "Of course, but I do have some beautiful land."

Oscar "Do you think a woman can make wine as well as a man?"

Josko "Of course she can! I think a woman can even work the land. It's your head that tells you what to do. You don't need to go there with your hoe."

Oscar "And what about this young woman?" Naturally, I say this while his daughter is still there with us.

Josko "We'll see. I want to leave her time and room."

Oscar "You don't push her? So you don't think a son or daughter has to necessarily follow in their father's footsteps?"

Josko "No, I never even insisted with Miha."

Oscar "What's in your future, besides trying to make a great wine?"

Josko "If that were the only thing, there are some who might say I've already failed, but I don't feel like someone who's failed…"

Oscar "Of course not! So for as long as you live you'll try to make wine that's always even better?"

Josko "Yes. And I'll do so paying less and less attention to financial matters! Because if you dwell on the financial aspects your wine will be affected by it. Someone once brought me some wine and asked me what I thought of it. I said: 'It's the kind of wine a lecher would drink.'"

Oscar "A lecher?!"

Josko "Then he showed me the bottle and said: 'You're right, how did you know?' And I replied: 'You can tell from the wine!'"

Oscar "You mean you could tell from the wine that this person was a lecher? That's awesome!" I turn back toward his daughter. "Did you vote last time around Jana?"

Jana "No, since I've been of voting age I've only voted twice. I think that change has to come from the people. I do my best without hurting the people around me. When we learn not to hurt our neighbor then we'll have achieved the right ethics."

Oscar "And we'll be living in harmony: I really do everything in my power not to hurt my neighbor!"

Jana "However, I think we have the political system we deserve!"

Oscar "Let me suggest this sentence I found the other day about wanting to make money, it's something that Leo Longanesi wrote: 'They lived unhappily, because it cost less.' Do you like it?"

Josko's laughter is really noisy and it covers up the sound of everyone else's laughter. Shigeru's laugh is much more bashful; he understands perfectly, but is still on duty, so to speak. He still hasn't finished and this forces him to continue to observe a certain rigor that's only betrayed by the boyish look in his eyes… Shigeru's Japanese and the Japanese never laugh, they just smile.

Oscar "I'll add to that what my great friend Tonino Guerra used to say: 'Money moves people away from poetry.' He believed that a rich person could never be happy. In fact, at the beginning he didn't trust me because I was rich, but we eventually became good friends, although it took him ages to realize that there can be some exceptions."

We're almost at the end, our two hours together have flown by and no one feels like leaving. We share a few more thoughts on the greediness of some of the wealthy who will never stop their pursuit for more money, and for this reason are never satisfied. But I want to add some thoughts that I hold close to my heart. I want to explain what drives me to want more and more, to grow along with my companies. What drives me is my desire to create jobs, which are life's solution for so many people who can't or won't create business but have the right to find a pleasant work environment. I certainly think that working for Eataly is better than working on an assembly line. I try to give young people who are willing to work some hope, and this, to my mind, is the way to do politics today.

Oscar "This is how work is today: the bricklayer is out of work, the factory worker is out of work, a whole bunch of people with degrees are out of work. But have you seen any of the public offices cutting down on the number of clerks? The fact that we aren't capable of changing the ruling class is our own fault. Working for the state has in some cases become like welfare provision. The 3,000 forestry workers in Sicily are an example of this, and, as is often the case, we are incensed by these manifest absurdities that steal our country's future and competitiveness, but we do nothing to change this."

I don't talk about my working ethos at Eataly. I don't do so on purpose. I think that Josko plays an equally important role with his example. He is generous and willing to talk about his experience. He's infectious. All you young people out there, if you love the land, come to see Gravner. He'll make you want to become entrepreneurs. I don't say this out loud, but just as I am thinking this Josko and I look at each other. Could he be telepathic, too?

Luckily, **Shigeru** interrupts: "I'd like to talk about this Ribolla. The color is amber with red veins. The aroma is fruit soaked in alcohol and grass. It has a dry, powerful and sapid taste. It's important wine, but at the same time it's easy to drink. It's not easy to find both structure and drinkability in one wine. Amazingly, it's really good even after the Barolo."

And he doesn't spit this time either!

The Pendulum: If You Let It Get to You, You'll Go Crazy!

Our stay here must necessarily come to an end because our tight schedule means we still have a long way to go, another interview to do, and more driving after that. Before saying goodbye and leaving though, we can't miss the chance to visit Josko's wine cellar, the magical place where all his amphorae are kept, where the maternal wombs hatch his wines.

Oscar "Josko, explain the pendulum to me!"

Josko "The pendulum is something you can't let get to you too much, otherwise you'll go crazy. I take it out of the drawer two or three times a year to understand a few things. I'm convinced that the pendulum is right when I ask it questions about the amphorae. There are two ways to insulate an amphora: with beeswax or with tar. And when I was faced with this choice I instinctively answered: not tar, beeswax! But the pendulum chose tar, mineral tar, of course, not chemical tar."

Oscar "How does it work?"

Josko "You take the pendulum and you hold it over the amphora, or else over a person, or an object, and you ask for its positivity. If the pendulum swings counterclockwise, the answer is positive and that's fine, if instead it swings clockwise, the answer is negative and that's not good. Naturally, below the equator it's the opposite and the positivity is also proportional to the speed at which it swings. When I held it over the tar the pendulum practically went haywire. But you mustn't let it take over control, especially when you use it on people."

Oscar "Did you try it out on those people wearing ties and jackets who come to inspect you? Do you try it out on people in general?"

Josko "I tried it out to understand what they thought of me: positive/negative, and I did understand. But most importantly I tried it out on the cellar, and it gave me positive in every corner. But, as I said, I only take it out two or three times a year. No more than that!"

Oscar "The result can change from year to year?"

Josko "Of course."

We have this last conversation right inside the cellar with the amphorae: they're buried underground, with only the mouth sticking out, covered with wooden planks. It feels strange to be walking on wine! I never really care to, but this time I'm the one who wants a picture to be taken right here, with Josko, Shigeru and the amphorae. This place reminds me of a crypt, a sacred place. There are the amphorae, the old brick walls and a dusty chair. A beautiful blend of purity, tradition and respect.

Oscar "Do you have a favorite amphora here?"

Josko "No, they're all the same. One of them, the one that's covered, has a flaw... from the way it was made."

Oscar "Is there anyone else in Italy who makes wine in amphorae?"

Josko "I remember Miha here talking to some British journalists who had asked him the same question: 'no, we're the only ones,' he answered them in English. But I understood what he had said and I interrupted him: 'That's not true, Miha!' I told him. But he was right: 'having an amphora doesn't mean making wine in an amphora!' he corrected me. 'You know how it works, Papà: they keep the wine in barrels, barriques, steel and sometimes even in amphorae just to satisfy the demand of the whole market. Instead, we make all our wine in amphorae. It's different.'"

That's it! I loved everything about this man: but the thing that struck me the most was this combination of rational philosophy, superstition and nostalgia. Striking words that sum up complex ideas but addressed toward the heart of the matter, a return to nature's primary role, the rejection of useless conventions, a tough opinion on bureaucrats and red tape, and then the courage, high-standing, proud, infectious. Time, affected by his personal pain that's always there: "It happened the year Miha was born..." "Miha answered the British journalists..." And the farmer's attention to superstition. "It was a leap year, the year of our worst harvest..." And the amazing use of the pendulum that answers his questions and whose suggestions he follows. Meditation, observation and the capacity to be surprised by nature and chance: a truly rare combination that helped us to spend that time together pleasantly and constructively, and that took us back to life's genuine values. There are no bad years as such, because Nature gives us everything, and sometimes it has the right to take something back. I wonder, my heart broken: could that mean a son, too?

Notes for Wines Tasted with Josko Gravner
Shigeru Hayashi

Barolo Riserva 1978 Borgogno
Type red wine
Grapes 100% Nebbiolo
Vinification and fining at least 12–15 days of fermentation
followed by maceration; 4–5 years of maturation in large 60 hl
Slavonian oak barrels
Production area Piedmont

The color is still full-bodied red and ruby, with mild garnet and
orange hues. The aroma is violet, peach, white pepper and many
other spices that are hard to name, as well as chestnut and leather.
The taste is structured, with velvety tannins. Dry, balanced and
elegant.

I'd pair it with slowly-stewed braised meat, or with the famous
Japanese fillet of meat called *maezawa*, cooked on a griddle and
seasoned with salt and wasabi. And, why not, with cheese like Bitto
from Valtellina.

When we tasted this wine with Josko Gravner he exclaimed:
"This wine is alive!" Josko's right, this Barolo is like those women
who are almost forty but still look like young girls. If you're elegant,
you'll be young forever. And this wine is very elegant!

Barolo Riserva 1967 Borgogno
Type red wine
Grapes 100% Nebbiolo
Vinification and fining at least 15 days of fermentation followed
by submerged cap maceration; 4–5 years of maceration in large
60 hl Slavonian oak barrels
Production area Piedmont

Garnet color with orange hues. Ripe red fruit aroma, especially
prune. I can also smell spices, leather, pepper, licorice and iron.
The taste is well balanced and pleasant. Silky tannin, almost
smooth.

This wine is ideal with stewed beef cooked in Barolo, but it would
be perfect with baked fillet seasoned with white pepper, too.
I think it would take the stage with a cheese like aged Bra. Ideal
also as an after dinner meditation wine.

This is another remarkable wine that I'd like to drink with my
parents, my best friend or the woman of my life: this Barolo is like
a tonic for the mind and the spirit. Drink it whenever and in the
company of whomever you like, you'll be just as happy as I was!

Barolo Riserva 1961 Borgogno
Type red wine
Grapes 100% Nebbiolo
Vinification and fining 15 days of fermentation followed
by submerged cap maceration; at least 4 years of maturation
in large 60 hl Slavonian oak barrels
Production area Piedmont

The color is pale garnet red with orange hues. Aromas of incredible
fullness and intensity, with red fruit, pomegranate, dried rose,
aromatic herbs, tobacco, evident moss and licorice. Balsamic hints
on the finish. The taste is a burst of softness and elegance; the
tannins are extremely subtle, but they're still there. Eternal
aftertaste.

To be paired with stewed and braised meat cooked in Barolo.
Try it with barbecued tuna belly sushi dressed with soy sauce
and wasabi.

Anyone born the same year this wine was made is a lucky person.
We're beyond Barolo here, beyond wine, beyond everything.
We can really taste the *umami*, i.e. the "fifth flavor" here.
This is a soulful red wine.

Lune Riserva Teo Musso 2010 Baladin
Type Barley Wine beer
Made from Mulino Marino farro and barley grown directly
on the estate
Vinification and fining fined for a long time in barrels
and barriques inside the Cantina Baladin
Production area Piedmont

The color ranges from somewhat pale golden to amber. The aroma
is clearly apricots, then dried fruit, tobacco, honey, barley and
toasted notes. The taste is soft, suave, with delicate caramel
and date.

Pair with fish soup and artichokes, soup made with butter and
tomatoes, veal medallion cooked in lemon and soy sauce.
Hamburger with Japanese mustard is another perfect match.
I'd savor it after dinner, too, as a meditation wine... I mean,
a meditation beer.

The "legendary" Teo Musso decided to make a gift to the tradition
of great white wines, so he conceived of (and then produced) a beer
as though it were wine, aging it in the barriques where some of the
world's greatest wine selections had slept. Sipped blindfold, I might
even say it's wine!

Ribolla Gialla Anfora 2006 Gravner
Type white wine
Grapes 100% Ribolla
Vinification and fining in amphora for 7 months, with neither
the addition of yeasts nor temperature control; maturation in oak
barrels, bottling when the moon is on the wane, with no
clarification or filtration
Production area Friuli Venezia Giulia

Intense amber yellow color. The aroma is of aromatic herbs (sage,
oregano), ripe fruit such as apricot, peach and apple, then notes
of smoke, vanilla and graphite. The taste is sapid, full, round and
persistent.

Let's try it with grilled octopus sprinkled with salt and seven spices;
or with pasta in a vegetable sauce, risotto with porcini mushrooms,
smoked mackerel with a touch of Japanese mustard.
Ideal with bacon *shabu-shabu*, soy sauce and rice vinegar.

Where does wine come from? From the vines? From the land?
From man? In my view (in Josko's as well), this Ribolla comes
to us straight from the moon! A stellar white-that's-not-white;
once you drink it you're in harmony with the universe.

Marchesi Antinori: Piero Antinori
I Was Lucky to Experience the Forty-Five
Most Beautiful Years in the History of Wine

I'm Happy to Be a Marquis But I Don't Brag About It

"A really lovely bosom consists of the entire chest, culminating in two peaks whose roots spring from the ribs..."
(Cesare Pavese, *The Burning Brand*)

Comparing the hills of the Langa to those of Chianti... that's too easy! But here we are surrounded by the hills of Chianti Classico, in the midst of these huge slumbering breasts, and, of these, inside one in particular, in Bargino, in the wine cellar of Marchesi Antinori. Wine cellar or spaceship? It's hard to say, but it is a beautiful place, among the modern ones the most beautiful I've ever seen... The most beautiful wine cellar in the world! To build it Piero Antinori spent almost as much as we spent to buy all of Fontanafredda! The entrance is a horizontal slit that resembles an open mouth, access is via a spiral ramp like a wooden curl on a plane, the inside of a cathedral devoted to wine... where you might feel lost in the immense beauty here, or because of the complex logistics of the dimensions. You can find everything here: a reception desk with young, beautiful and efficient women, a splendid waiting room, meeting rooms, libraries, a restaurant, an amphitheater, row after endless row of steel vats, barriques, barrels, amphorae for oil, bottles... The whole cellar was dug out in the side of the hill, it has walls the color of earth, a tunnel connecting the various areas, a monumental staircase: everything is harmonious, peaceful, the choice of materials and the sinuousness of the lines are all natural.

182 Vino, I Love You

And all you can see from the outside is the unchanging shape of a truly beautiful bosom... Could I be obsessed? Maybe, like all Langaroli when they see hills, but here it's inescapable. This monumental work is even more beautiful than they told me it was.

In short, 90 million euros invested in wine! For the centuries to come, certainly not only for the glory of the Antinoris today.

We take an elevator to go down to the second floor and ask for Piero Antinori. We're politely told to have a seat, the Marquis will be right down. Lots of questions cross my mind, but in the meantime Piero Antinori joins us. Piero is a fine person. He was born in 1938, so he's seventy-five, but you can tell good wine has been good for him. He doesn't look a day older than sixty-five, and along with Angelo Gaja he's one of the most important Italians in the wine world: 150 million euros in revenue, an EBITDA (Earnings Before Interest, Taxes, Depreciation and Amortization) to arouse the envy of most people, and good, very good wines. How to combine business with pleasure. For this and for other reasons, we're probably talking about the most significant and complete journey you can possibly take in the history of Italian wine. These are big words but we're talking about a family that has been making and selling wine for the past 700 years, since 1300, that is, across this country's most beautiful centuries, across the ages that have made Italy's name a legend around the world... Unfortunately, today we're doing all we can to spoil the work done by our ancestors. But I'm an optimist. Another reason for my journey through wine is to bring to light the situation of people who, in different ways, but always in search of the perfect wine, design their future, which is never defeatist, never gregarious, always broad-ranging and largely innovative, but respectful of our great traditions.

We're talking about wine, but it's almost too easy to apply this approach to Italy in general, and to find surprising and inevitable analogies. "There's a great future in our past!" I think it was Ugo Tognazzi who said that in one of his movies. That's exactly how it is: after 5,000 or 6,000 harvests we're still trying to find the perfect wine, after many thousands of years around our seas we're still trying to find a form of civilization that will allow everyone to live in harmony and be happier. Piero Antinori certainly has lots of things to tell us and teach us. We just got here but I'm already fond of his Tuscan accent and the aristocratic eloquence of his pronunciation, so different from the broad vowels those of us from Piedmont use, and that give us such an inferiority complex when it comes to accents. At least Shigeru has an excuse.

Oscar "Why are you still working so hard at your age? Do you invest all the money you make in wine?"

Piero "First of all, when we started out seven years ago I was younger, but most of all I thought I would finish the job sooner. Then, because of a whole series of obstacles of a bureaucratic nature, external situations, caused by problems with the construction company, geological issues that called for further study and some important work to reinforce the hill, more time than we'd estimated went by, at least two or three years longer. Then came the crisis. Of course, if we'd known what was going to happen I don't know whether we'd have made such an investment."

Oscar "Did you feel the crisis?"

Piero "Well, of course I did! Especially psychologically, even though from a business standpoint we weren't hit too hard. We reacted well. There's a whole world around us."

Oscar "You're talking about 2008, so after Lehman Brothers? From that moment on we all felt like we were plummeting into another world! How much is exportation worth to you?"

Piero "When I got started in the business we were earning 80% in Italy and 20% abroad. Our goal was to turn these percentages around. Now we're at 70% exportation."

Oscar "So the L.B. affair was a real cause for concern?"

Piero "Yes. They were saying that the world would never be the same as we knew it to be, so this important unknown started gnawing its way into our reasoning, even though I've always been optimistic and I still am as concerns our sector, and not for emotional or sentimental reasons either. World production right now is at a standstill, if not actually decreasing, while consumption continues to grow. If it's true that in thirty years there will be another billion people willing to spend for goods that aren't strictly necessary, wine will be one of the most sought-after products. This, of course, will happen if we're good, both at producing and at communicating the value of our products. In the next thirty years we can continue to have fun the way we have been in the past thirty–forty years..."

Oscar "I always think about how we're 0.83% of the world population, and that out there there's a potential 99.17% of customers.

I invest a lot in wine too, and my opinion is the same as yours...
You're a Marquis! Do you like the fact that you're an aristocrat, or is
it something you don't give a damn about?"

I'm getting off the subject here, but nobility is an intriguing topic,
and in this case the visibility is twofold: very ancient nobility and very
high industrial productivity. I'd like to demonstrate, with Piero's
help, that he's an apparent contradiction. He doesn't come right out
and answer us, but he's gotten us sort of used to the peaceful flow of
his words, so we waited to catch his thought on the subject.

Piero "Of course, I feel some of the responsibility, because in the
past a noble title was the acknowledgment of merit. That said, however, just like my father, I'm very proud of our mercantile origins.
I afford more importance to our past as merchants in the ancient
Florentine Republic than in the title that came later. As for me personally, I'm prouder about what I've succeeded in doing and my
knighthood, my title as a Cavaliere del Lavoro della Repubblica (Order of Merit for Labor), than about the merits of my ancestors."

An interesting change of perspective: nobility as responsibility and not
as privilege and pride in one's merits here and now. Modesty maybe?
A feeling of guilt? I think about Gaja who refused a knighthood, and
Piero who's proud of it. "The world is beautiful because it's different,"
they say. Two very different approaches but there's beauty in both of
them. I prod him again: "How long has your family been around?"

Piero "We've been making wine for twenty-seven generations. The
twenty-seventh generation is that of my daughters."

Oscar "But I've been told that it's thanks to you, to the twenty-sixth
generation, that this winery has grown."

Piero "I was lucky, first, because I have a great passion for this activity,
and then because I've been able to work in the past forty-five years, a
period that has seen a real revolution in the world of Italian wine."

My Father Used to Say: "Work Is Not a Pastime"

Oscar "Did your father devote all his time to wine, the way you do?"
Piero "My father belonged to a generation that lived through two
wars, which took away a lot of his time, and then he became interested in public affairs, he was president of the Red Cross, president

of the Ente Turismo of Florence, for instance, even though he also had a true passion for wine."

Oscar "What was his name? Did you get along?"

Piero "His name was Niccolò. I did get along with him. I always had a very easy-going relationship with my father, even though I was a boy. What I mean by that is I have three daughters and I realize that it's easier for a father to get along with his daughters. However, my father always encouraged and stimulated me, he passed on to me his passion for his job. He was remarkably brave: I was just twenty-seven when he left me completely free to do what I wanted in the winery."

Oscar "He dropped it on you when you were just twenty-seven!" Sometimes I get carried away by my very direct language, and the slap on the wrist isn't long in coming.

Piero "He didn't *drop* it on me, he entrusted it to me! He said: 'Do whatever you think is right,' at the same time continuing to give me advice and guidance. I'm very grateful to him, even though all that responsibility kept me from living my life the way I could, the way a twenty-seven-year-old could have."

Oscar "Do you remember the company figures from back then?"

Piero "In those days we had 50 hectares of vineyard, now we have 2,000 altogether. We had two wine cellars, now we have about fifteen, also because we try to give each of our wineries a specific identity. Each winery has its own enologist and its own viticulturist; together they know every square inch of the place."

Oscar "And what about the turnover?" There's no other way for me to ask this question, and I need to understand the evolution of the Antinori family business through the figures that are typical of this winery.

Piero "Today, 150 million euros, when I started about 200–300 million lire."

Immediately my mind starts crunching numbers. From 150,000 to 150 million means multiplying by a thousand. I don't think that anyone in the wine business has done anything like that before. I'm talking about good, really fine wine, of course.

Oscar "So does all the credit for this turnaround in volumes go to you and you alone?"

Piero "The revenue has grown more than proportionally with respect to the number of bottles; in the past Chianti was mostly sold in one-liter or one-liter and 750-ml flasks, and in those days we also processed grapes for third parties. The real strategic decision, which we developed gradually, was only processing our own grapes. The peak was about twenty years ago. As I said before, I was lucky to be working during the right years."

Oscar "Were you able to grow so much because your father left you a pile of money, or because you reinvested your earnings?"

I know I'm showing my bad manners, but who cares! His smile of embarrassment and his prompt answer quickly follow: "Wineries aren't suited to set-ups that aren't family-run. The fact that it's a family business enables you to make long-term investments. A company with a joint-stock set-up could never justify, with short-run profitability, an investment such as this one. Another advantage to being a family business is that you never have to distribute dividends to partners. Since 1966, when I took over, I've never distributed dividends! Today this company's shares are in the hands of a trust, to which my daughters have transferred the property rights they already had. We're very pleased about this, because this way we're sure that for ninety-nine years this strong link between family and business will be maintained. Today things are going well, but you never know what might happen in the next two or three generations."

You need to have 700 years of family history behind you to be able to look forward to the next ninety-nine years! Forget the stock options for big managers who are rewarded even when the results of their work are disappointing and companies come out from under their management in a shambles. Top managers evaluated on the basis of a budget that's already the subject of negotiations, so that a person ends up being praised because he or she's lost less than what had been budgeted. Let's say that Piero Antinori's vision is simple and straightforward, the winery is the family estate and they all work to preserve it and make it grow, over the years or centuries. This is how a good family man thinks, no matter how big the estate is, and this is how politicians should think, who should see themselves as fathers and not as predators. But Piero's still talking about his trust, while I'm lost in my own thoughts.

Piero "The trust guarantees the union between the family and the business, which is something I want very much. After twenty-seven generations I wouldn't want disagreements or various other factors to cause the toy to break. In this sense I'm relatively unconcerned."

Oscar "Let's continue with our conversation after we taste this Verdicchio, the first one I brought over. A friend of mine, Fulvia Tombolini, makes it, and I have great respect for her because of the passion she puts into valorizing this splendid vineyard of the Castelli di Jesi, in the Marches. I really like it. What do you think?"

Piero "In my opinion, this is a very beautiful expression of Italian white wine: fresh, easy, pleasant, well balanced, not too much acidity, it can be drunk in large quantities. This Verdicchio is extremely pleasant, in the tradition of Orvieto, Soave. I've been accustomed to this type of wine ever since I was a child." Nice description.

I'm curious to hear what Shigeru has to say; synchronized, he launches his attack: "The aroma is fruit with a white pulp, like apple and pear. I can also smell wild herbs, and the taste is fresh and well balanced, dry. It ends with a bitter finish. It's the perfect wine that goes with a rich plate of grilled fish, fish risotto, but also with white meat cooked on stone and seasoned with salt and lemon. It's a delicate wine, so it needs to be paired with something delicate." Shigeru makes his impression, our host is charmed by him, I have to admit that hearing him and Piero talk about wine is very educational for me.

After the Verdicchio we go back to talking about the Antinori family. Piero has a sister and younger brother. His sister is dispensed with immediately as she showed no interest in the family winery. His brother's story is instead crossed by a whole series of events: first he goes to America to work with Antinori's import agent, then, convinced that Italian wine won't go far outside of Italy, he returns here in the late 1960s and in turn becomes an Italian importer of French wines and liqueurs. He abandons this road, too, to head into other managerial ventures, but then goes back to wine, bringing to fruition one of the family's estates and inventing Ornellaia. In this activity he distinguishes himself and is successful. Today he is again at the head of his own winery for which Azienda Antinori is minority stakeholder. So much for the history of the family, but what I'd like now is a little gossip, something about disagreements, differences of opinion. Let's see if they come out.

Oscar "How was your brother paid off?"

Piero "It was the early 1980s, my daughters were young and I didn't think they'd ever be interested in wine."

Oscar "Are you sorry you don't have sons?" (I'm struck by the fact that, in order to remember the year his first daughter was born, he refers to the year he received the winery from his father, which must have been a real emotional watershed in Piero Antinori's story.)

Piero "No, I was happy to have daughters, but I didn't think they'd ever get involved in the wine business. In those days women were interested in other things, whereas today you might say there are more women than men in the field of wine, in all the roles of the production chain in general. No doubt it was a difficult moment. I decided to let a British partner into the company, someone who was already our importer, and with this partner's financial backing I was able to pay off my brother. After seven/eight years of fruitful work this partner decided to sell, so we bought back the shares in several installments."

Oscar "Would you have preferred to carry on working with your brother?"

Piero "I would have liked to, on the condition that there weren't going to be any problems in our personal relations, which is something that might have happened. He and I pretty much complement each other, and this could have been a good thing."

Oscar "What's the Antinoris' relationship with numbers? I believe in the supremacy of math."

Piero "I'm really careful about business matters, too, even though I'm in love with my trade. My brother is excellent at marketing but he isn't as mindful of the balance sheet. In this situation, where you need to invest in research and quality, you have to have healthy, profit-oriented balance sheets."

Just listening to this family's story has been like walking on eggshells, but in the end we can see why the Antinori winery has ended up back in Piero's expert hands!

Oscar "Now, let's savor this Tocai. It's produced by Pierluigi Zamò, a brother of mine, so to speak: 60 hectares on the eastern hills of Friuli, 600,000 bottles. I bought 50% of his winery, Le Vigne di Zamò, in 2010. This is his very best wine, 100% Friulano, a vineyard with amazing exposure! I've brought you another white wine too, because after you drink it I want you to tell me why the French are better at making white wine than we are. So what do you think?"

Piero "I like it because it has personality. Tocai is a great vine that maintains its personality even outside the Friuli area, in California, for example, where I've had the opportunity to taste some excellent ones. It has an unmistakable taste. I believe that a great wine has to have great character."

Oscar "I'm asking you this question because you're the producer of one of the best white wines in Italy, Cervaro della Sala. Why do the French have a better reputation than us when it comes down to white wines?"

Piero "The French aren't generally better than us. They make some really great white wines in Burgundy, but, apart from a few niche products, you can't say the same for the other areas. Generally speaking, I think the credit goes to their environmental conditions, what they famously call 'terroir,' which means everything: soil, climate, and grape variety, the interaction between the vine and the environment, and man, who mustn't be forgotten."

Oscar "A few days ago Josko Gravner told us that the French talk a lot about terroir because they don't have one! What do you think?" Besides the laughter that Josko's words arouse every single time, Piero tells us that he thinks the French do have terroir, and lots of it at that. But then he makes the same points Josko made, saying that, unfortunately, Italy has only recently, for about the past forty years, begun to pay attention to the quality of the wine, whereas France has been investing in the value of wine for 150, and in all that time both their legislation and marketing have been oriented toward quality.

Oscar "Shigeru, are you ready to tell us what you think about this Friulano wine?"

Shigeru "Ready! I agree and say this wine has great character. It comes from vineyards that are sixty years old and this is its great merit. The mineral aspects are accentuated. You can smell the apple, wild herbs, the watered down honey and the ripe fruit. It's a sapid, flavorful wine, and very interesting when served with shellfish, grilled lobster, shrimp, pickled mackerel with mustard, but also with the *narasushi* we make in Tokyo."

Shigeru's intervention is often a good watershed moment between topics. After his description I always find it easy to turn the page and move on to other questions.

Oscar "When did your father die?"

Piero "In 1993, without being able to see our reacquisition of our British partner's shares, something that would have pleased him very much. My decision hadn't caused him any pain because he had understood my reasons for doing so, but he also knew it was a temporary situation. Unfortunately, he never got to see how it ended."

Oscar "What did you learn from your father?"

Piero "That work is not a pastime. He'd say: 'You mustn't take yourself too seriously, but work is serious!' And he'd also say: 'Profit isn't a company's only goal, it's proof of its efficiency and a guarantee of continuity.' And I agree with that."

Oscar "You bet! I even think that not earning any money isn't ethical because it doesn't allow you to pay workers' salaries and help the people who work with you to live well, but working only to make money is something small-minded, mean and unhappy people do. However, you're not attached to money."

Piero "My mother was a very generous person, she was intelligent, religious and for her whole life she always looked out for her neighbor. She taught me to think with my heart too. She died in her sleep the day of her ninety-ninth birthday after celebrating with the whole family."

Oscar "What were your hardest times?"

Piero "When I took over the company helm, in the late 1960s, in Tuscany we were going through hard times, because the era of sharecropping was coming to an end. A feudal way of managing estates. The owner would divide the fruits of the earth in percentages among his sharecroppers, without, however, risking anything during lean years. It was a form of joint-shareholding, but everyone in the sharecropper's family worked, including six-year-olds, and they were the ones who had to take all the risks. In those years a law was passed to abolish sharecropping and the landowners in the whole of Central Italy found themselves in a totally new situation, in which they needed to manage their land entrepreneurially, and for many it wasn't easy. A promiscuous culture was rampant in the sharecropping, everyone grew a little bit of everything: olives, vines, wheat, vegetables and they also bred livestock. The shift to direct management led the major landowners to specialize their production and to put all the vineyards together, which also caused a significant change in the landscape. Unfortunately, though, the right culture to manage this great change was missing. In those years the nurseries couldn't supply the right, good-quality vines. Tuscan viticulture was transformed in a decade, but the result was a disaster from a qualitative point of view! The quality of the wine had declined, and so did prices and Chianti's prestige as a consequence. This was the situation when I took over the business. In those years many of my friends who were in the wine business pulled out."

As Piero Antinori's gentle voice tells us these stories, I have my own thoughts: in moments of serious difficulty, the privilege of a person's birth becomes insignificant, while character and personal skills prevail. If others with the same privileges pulled out, and he, instead, achieved the results we can appreciate today, then it must have been this man's qualities that made the difference. This thought cheers me up because it would be frustrating to think that large fortunes depend solely on the privileges of one's birthrights (rather on randomness). A person's birthright can, of course, be helpful, but in this case it wasn't the crucial factor.

Piero "This first difficult period also encouraged me to travel around and see what others were doing: in France, in California. I hired an excellent French consultant, Émile Peynaud, who influenced me a lot, and with the help of our enologist Giacomo Tachis, we created Tignanello as a reaction to those hard times."

Here's a story from the Italy that counts, about people in their territories, told by an authoritative figure. It's a very interesting lesson, one that makes me think about the present. A law passed by the Republic, in its specific territorial manifestation, can generate negativity that isn't envisaged by the legislator if the change isn't suitably governed in all its manifestations. I'm thinking, for example, about people forced to retire early but who end up without a pension.

Piero "In the 1990s we had hard times as well, when I was forced to fall into heavy debt—and that wasn't the first time—in order to pay off the partners who were selling their stakes. On that occasion, Mediobanca helped us out, although somewhat reluctantly. We had to tighten our belts for several years. Then the situation went back to the way it had been before."

Oscar "Today you have one of the best EBITDA in Italy."

Piero "In our sector the ROE (return on equity) is structurally low because the fixed investments are very high, so you have to have a high EBITDA if you want to preserve management and continue to grow. The cellar we're in right now couldn't have been started up without earnings and—this is something I need to stress—without leaving them in the business."

Oscar "I'd like you to talk to me about your daughters, and I'd like you to do so while tasting Barolo Vigna La Rosa 2008 produced by Fontanafredda; 2008 was the year of our first full harvest. Do you like Nebbiolo?"

Piero "I like it, but I especially like it when it comes from the right positions. There are two kinds of vines: the ones that are easy to understand and produce, and the hard ones. Nebbiolo belongs to the latter kind. I like this one in particular because it comes from a marvelous vineyard, La Rosa, in Serralunga. *Wine Spectator* gave you a very high score."

Oscar "This vineyard is the one that gets all the awards. I prefer Lazzarito, but in the end they awarded La Rosa."

Piero "Nebbiolo is a wine that has to be understood, it's a transparent wine, not a 'black' one."

Oscar "Are you referring to Amarone?" (I try to shake him up with a drop of venom but all I get is a thin smile.)

Piero "No, I'm talking about Italian wines, or even Californian wines, which had their moment of glory, but have now been completely surpassed."

Oscar "Those so-called wines with an 'international profile.'"

Piero "I'm talking about those monumental wines that can even reach 15 degrees proof, super concentrated."

Shigeru is nodding vigorously.

Piero "Nebbiolo is a wine with a great personality, which is what we were saying about Tocai; it's wine that gives you hedonistic pleasure, but intellectual pleasure, too. Lastly, red wine has to have aging potential, all qualities that Nebbiolo possesses, so it's a great wine. Even a large-scale painting will give you aesthetic pleasure, but then you have to know more about the author, his or her story. The same goes for wine."

Oscar "Like making love to a beautiful woman, whose physical and intellectual features you need to know very well to get the height of pleasure. The Creator, a sly fellow, made it so that pleasure, actually the orgasm, can be found in two acts that guarantee the continuation of the species: food and love. Just as the pleasure of being with a woman is great when you know her well, and even greater when you love her, the same happens with wine: you can even love a great wine!"

Shigeru finds the right moment to speak up and tell us about this Barolo from his point of view. He describes it as having the aroma of violets and roses, white pepper, licorice, leather, and he says the taste is sapid and velvety with regular tannins. He says it's a great wine for aging, and we agree with him. Not only would he pair it with traditional braised beef stewed in Barolo, but also with a good assortment of pan-fried meats seasoned only with black pepper and Japanese mustard. And at the end he tells us that you need to savor it in small sips, ideal for conversing with friends about touchy... and cheerful subjects. Great job, Shigeru! The fact that certain wines might also be served for certain types of conversations is really interesting.

Oscar "Piero, while we drink this Barolo, talk to us about your daughters. When did you first realize they'd make it?"

Piero "What year was the methanol scandal?"

It was 1986. There! For Antinori the events of his life are marked by the history of wine, and this is unquestionably his most salient characteristic. Even his family memories are linked to events having to do with wine.

Piero "In 1986 I toured Canada with some other people in the business. There was also someone from Fontanafredda. I took my daughter Albiera, who was almost twenty, with me. She was born in 1966. The year I got married the winery was handed over to me, my first daughter born, and it was also the year of the Florence flood. In 1986 I was chairman of Federvini and just as I had reached the midpoint of my tour they called me from Italy to inform me of the methanol scandal. Since I had to go back to Italy right away I told my daughter to 'go on without me...' kind of like when you toss a kid into the water so they'll somehow learn to swim. That was the acid test that convinced her to go into this business. My other daughters followed their sister's example; their enthusiasm grew and now all three of them are working for the winery. They're great at it!"

Oscar "How did you fit them in?"

Piero "Albiera is mainly involved in communication, from start to finish, which means marketing, packaging, etc. But she's also vice president, so that, although she's not operative, she's very informed about and present in the important decisions. She personally supervised, along with the architects, the building of this cellar."

Oscar "Would she come to you with decisions she'd already made herself?"

Piero "Almost made…"

Fantastic, "almost made." Angelo Gaja comes to mind again, when he said "Daughters accept our advice more easily." These two giants of Italian wine live surrounded by women and do so happily.

As Long as I'm Enjoying Myself I'll Keep on Working

Oscar "But you didn't follow in your father's footsteps."

Piero "No, I didn't do what he did, basically because I enjoy doing this work and I still really like it. Why would I ever want to quit? Although I've delegated a lot. Especially to my right-hand man, Renzo Cotarella, with whom I have long chats every single day about strategy. He's an excellent enologist, but he's also a great manager and we get along very well. He's been with me for thirty-five years."

That's amazing, they still use the formal "lei" form of address when they speak!

Oscar "What's your second daughter's name?"

Piero "Allegra was born in 1971, the year of Tignanello."

Oscar "Strange names…"

Piero "Albiera, don't ask me why, is a family name. Allegra is the name of one of my nieces who was very close to my wife during her pregnancy. My third daughter's name is Alessia; she was born in 1976. I don't remember why we chose that name. My second daughter is less active in the winery right now because she has two small children to look after, but she's still in charge of PR and the restaurant side, and since she's an outstanding communicator, she's available for tastings or important visits. Alessia is an enologist."

Oscar "Can we find some event that corresponds to Alessia's birth?"

Piero "No, I can't think of any. She studied at the Wine Academy, a beautiful experience as an enologist, and then she wanted to gain experience in sales. She spent a few years in China, in charge of our work in that neck of the woods, and then she did the same in New York. Now she's married and lives in Rome. She oversees that market, but also a small winery, the Tenuta di Fiorano, which my daughters inherited from their maternal grandfather. Are you familiar with the Fiorano brand? She wants to somehow recreate the legend of Fiorano wine, which my father-in-law had to abandon when he fell ill."

We Have the Most Beautiful Job in the World

Oscar "Do you consider the fact that your daughters chose to follow in your footsteps to be a personal achievement?"

Piero "For me it's the height of personal satisfaction, but I'm not surprised, because this line of work is so fascinating and so beautiful that I'm astonished when a person who would have the chance to go into the business instead chooses to do something else."

Oscar "It's one of the most beautiful jobs in the world. I always think that!"

Piero "Absolutely! The product is marvelous, you live surrounded by vineyards, and if you like to travel you have the chance to do so, the international winemaking community is extraordinary."

Oscar "I started late because I come from another world, that of electrical appliances and electronics based on research, but I've noticed that the cultural level of the *vignerons* is very high. I meet people who read, who know all about politics, who philosophize. It's wine that makes you curious, it makes you think. This is a sector that's brimming with beauty. You're right: anyone who can go into the business and then doesn't is a fool!"

Piero "It's a wonderful world from a human point of view, and in terms of the landscape. The best wines always come from beautiful places."

Oscar "Let's move on to the next wine, but before we do, can you tell me who you voted for in the most recent General Elections?"

Piero "I voted for Monti, I had no doubts, given the competition."

Oscar "I know Monti. I respect him. In the past he offered me a place as chief candidate in Piedmont. But I couldn't accept. You know my opinion. But it did please me. Do you still think well of him?"

Piero "I think he made a few mistakes, probably owing to his lack of experience in politics. He was attacked by everyone, and some of the attacks he was the victim of were rather unfair. The disappointing electoral results he had might also depend on the fact that he isn't a communicator, something you have to be in politics. He's not like Renzi! And he has a professorial attitude that can be kind of off-putting. But you must admit he's a very serious person, and in to-day's Italian political scenario that's something that can't be over-looked, and this is why he deserves our trust!"

Oscar "Before we talk about Gaja's Barbaresco, I want to talk about the past some more. You were around when Italy experienced its great boom, and its great crises, the ones in the 1990s, the crisis of the Craxi government, the past twenty years. What do you think of this country today?"

Piero "My father taught me to love this country. He was in love with it, and that's why he devoted himself to public affairs. I think Italy could be an outstanding country because of all the potential it has. My words might seem banal because so many people say the same thing, but that's the way it is. Italian history, culture, beauty and even its creativity, its good taste. Italy has all these gifts. No other country has them in equal measure and all together. So it makes you angry to see this crisis. I don't know whether I should be pessimistic or opti-mistic about Italy's future. I've always been an optimist, but now the level of the crisis, in the short-term, makes me less so. After we hit rock bottom we should be able to start up again, but we don't know when that's going to happen because the problems are structural. We probably haven't hit rock bottom yet, and this is a detriment to the peace of this society. There are too many impediments to change. We can't manage to do anything new in social, political, bureau-cratic terms."

Oscar "And how do you see the world of business?"

Piero "There is some extraordinary potential that has yet to be ex-pressed. We have to redirect our resources toward the sectors that have a future and abandon the other sectors that no longer have a future, such as heavy industry, for instance."

Oscar "So we should invest in our calling."

Piero "Of course. Food production, tourism, which is a gold mine that we don't know how to exploit, high-level craftsmanship. Italy has lived beyond its means and this has created expectations. There's nothing worse than creating expectations and then disappointing them. And then there are the younger generations, who are often more interested in their rights than their duties."

Oscar "So you see the world of the young as a problem?"

Piero "They're not the problem, but objectively their situation is difficult, because right now there's very little work and for many of them it's hard to form the right attitude."

Oscar "How are your sales in Italy going?"

Piero "They're flat. We're holding up. We're satisfied. Outside of Italy we're growing instead."

Oscar "What do you think about young people? About their minds? Do they or don't they want to work?"

Piero "It's hard to say. What's important is that they mustn't give up. This uncertainty about the future is beginning to take its toll, but they must persevere, otherwise, as people who are simply resigned they'll get very little done."

Oscar "Is this the first time in your life that you're not optimistic?"

Piero "Yes, it is."

Oscar "We're on the fourth wine, Sorì Tildin 2004. Talk to me about this Barbaresco. It's produced by your friend Angelo Gaja. I brought it to you on purpose! Angelo is also a friend of mine..."

Piero "Sorì Tildin is a great wine, we're in the realm of the legendary here. It's extremely intense and there's a complexity of flavors and aromas even though it's not a strong wine, which I wouldn't like it to be. It's like the Barolo from before. These are wines that have an extraordinary elegance, finesse, class. I believe that in the future we're going to be more and more successful at selling wines that are less alcoholic, but with more minerality, which is given by the land and the age of the vineyards, as Hayashi-san would say. A very important characteristic. I'm still moved when I see a vineyard that's a century old! And I think the ones here are at least sixty years old."

Oscar "Let's talk about the very expensive prices for these wines. This bottle costs the public 300 euros. The French, some of them, manage to beat us on this front too. What do you think? Is it right to pursue this policy of high prices at a time when wine consumption is spreading across the world?"

Piero "I think so. Actually, we need to increase the number of wines that can get very high prices, although in limited quantities. This would help us to increase the prestige of wine and sell other wines as well. Angelo's work (and I hope mine too, to some extent) opens the door to many small artisans of Italian wine in the world. We mustn't forget that."

The Perfect Wine Is a Dream that Never Comes True

Oscar "Have you been able to make your perfect wine, or are you still searching for it?"
Piero "The perfect wine is a dream that never comes true! You get close to it, but you never make it completely!"
Oscar "You're right, it's a utopia. The word comes from *eutopos*, the happy place you can never reach, but that makes you keep going. Shigeru, what do you think of this Barbaresco? Do you like it?"
Today Shigeru looks great, and also his description of this wine is so elegant that it satisfies everyone. He talks to us about intensity perceived by the nose and the mouth, about the flavors of leather, coffee, hay, mint and rosemary. He insists on ripe fruit, on "balsamic" pepper, on its minerality, while the taste is sapid, velvety, with just the right acidity. But before moving on to what he'd pair it with, he also tells us it's a "sexy" wine because it has the kind of personality that you have to know how to approach from the right side. In the kitchen it's ideal with grilled rib eye steak, eel seasoned with black pepper (a fabulous Japanese dish!) and beef stew. It's almost lunchtime and at this point I'm really dreaming of a great rib eye steak eaten in some trattoria surrounded by these splendid hills. Piero invites us to lunch but we can't stay. We have to rush off to see his cousin in Bolgheri, Marquis Incisa della Rocchetta, the inventor of Sassicaia. There's bound to be lots of good wine today, but I think we're going to have to skip the trattoria. I'd rather talk to Piero a while longer.
Oscar "Piero, all that's left for us to drink is your wine, but first let's talk about the future. Actually, as Shigeru suggests, I'd like to combine our talk about the future with your Solaia, because I think it's the right wine for this topic."
But before going into the subject Piero talks about the people who

have helped his wines make a forward leap in terms of quality. He talks about Émile Peynaud, whom he met at the University of Bordeaux, a great wine figure, a consultant to the great French *vignerons* and to Tachis, another historic enologist from his cellars, but not just that. Two people who have changed his life, and the business. Technically speaking, Tignanello was born from their encounter, wine that's about 85% Sangiovese and the rest Cabernet. And then Veronelli got involved and inspired the sales strategy: that is, to sell table wine at a higher price than the others. In the meantime Renzo Cotarella has joined us, the real number two at the Antinori winery, a formidable wine expert. He must have smelled the aroma of the Sorì Tildin. He pours himself a glass, but they force him to try La Rosa 2008 as well. I don't want to miss Cotarella's compliments.

Piero "So Tignanello became our biggest seller and it was a real turning point. Today we produce 25–30,000 twelve-bottle crates and it can get about 70 euros per bottle."

Oscar "After Tignanello, Solaia was born, is that correct?"

Piero "In 1978. That year we had too much Cabernet for the demand for Tignanello, so we decided to vinify it separately. At the beginning it was 100% Cabernet, today it's 80% Cabernet and 20% Sangiovese. This is the most important wine produced by my winery. And it's also the first Italian wine, in 2000, to conquer the peak of *Wine Spectator*'s top one hundred wines. The following year we won again with Ornellaia, with no other Italian wines in the list. The name comes from the Solaia farmstead, obviously because it had good exposure to the sun."

Oscar "Is Solaia also the offshoot of Peynaud and Tachis?"

Piero "Of course."

Oscar "How do you see the future of wine? Will it be in the Far East: China, India?"

Piero "China will definitely become a great importer of wine. It's hard to say when that'll happen. We have to aim for China, no doubt, without overlooking the other very important markets such as the United States, though, which has become the country with the highest wine consumption in the world: something that no one could have predicted a decade ago. Italians have a solid, enviable position in the United States but they can still move forward."

Oscar "Our future is definitely the world market, but I see the French ready to fight again and give us a hard time."

Piero "We have to be very careful not to be caught off guard."

Oscar "Do you want to grow some more? Will you buy some other wineries?"

Piero "We still have to recoup the big investments already made and above all we want to grow in terms of quality rather than quantity. So we need to increase the average price just slightly in order to bring to fruition all the things we've done with the land."

Oscar "Southern Italy?"

Piero "We've invested in Puglia: there's a great potential there that still hasn't managed to emerge. The opposite of Sicily and Campania, which have instead already come through. But Puglia's potential is probably even greater."

Oscar "This year we're opening an Eataly in Bari. Eight thousand square meters at the Fiera del Levante. I'm going to dedicate it to the East, the 'Levant.' The Tigris and the Euphrates, where agriculture was born. But don't let me talk about Eataly, otherwise I'll never stop. Your personal future? What will you do? Do you plan to run off with a thirty-year-old?" I'm provoking him, but this time he smiles mildly.

Piero "I want to keep on working with this winery, which is a lot of fun."

Oscar "As the boss?"

Piero "As the spiritual leader. My role is to establish the stylistic direction of the wines, which the ownership can't delegate to anyone else. I want to have the last word on this. Practically on all the wines."

Oscar "So you think you know what the public wants better than anyone else? What's your earliest recollection of the scent of a wine?"

Piero "The war had ended, the Germans were leaving. My father was called urgently to the wine cellars of San Casciano, which had been machine-gunned by the Germans. He took me with him. I was six years old and I remember being able to smell the cellar when we were still two kilometers away. The smell, that smell was something I was familiar with already, but the circumstance left a deep impression on me. Then, of course, I could tell from my father's face that something serious had happened."

Here's the poetry: the madness of war goes so far as to riddle the barrels in a cellar with holes, but the nose of a six-year-old smells the wine and he is forever marked by a passion.

"Flowers bloom from manure," sang Italy's greatest songwriter ever. We have to go because it's late and because Piero, literally pulled by the jacket by Cotarella, has some foreign customers who want to meet him. I invite Shigeru to describe the last wine, Solaia Antinori 2009, and I invite Simona to drink it, at least this one. There are opportunities that can't be missed! Shigeru says it's herbaceous, with a hint of red fruit, very delicate, gentle tannins but excellent persistence in terms of taste. It's wine with a certain consistency, he says, and perhaps he wanted to say body, or structure. To him, Solaia is an international wine whose Italian provenance is understood all the same. He would pair it with stewed sirloin steak dressed with soy sauce and mustard, as well as with lamb seasoned with green peppercorns. And this is proof once more of how well-versed my Japanese friend is when it comes to our food and wine tradition. I would never have thought of lamb. Since we're in Tuscany I would have mentioned the typical Florentine porterhouse steak.

When Shigeru finishes speaking we say goodbye, leaving behind this surprising spaceship-like wine cellar that has really excited us. Listening to Piero has been very educational, and I realize that we've positioned another important piece in the complex mosaic of the great wines of Italy. I get into the car thinking about Pavese: as long as there is passion, we shall never cease to discover the world.

Notes for Wines Tasted with Piero Antinori
Shigeru Hayashi

Verdicchio dei Castelli di Jesi Classico Superiore 2011 Fulvia Tombolini
Type white wine
Grapes 100% Verdicchio
Vinification and fining cold maceration in steel, several months in bottles
Production area Marches

Light straw color. Delicate, fresh aroma with pleasant notes of peach and pear. The finish features medicinal herbs and hints of minerals. Dry and well-balanced taste.

Ideally paired with fish appetizers, also raw. I'd like to savor it with broth, or seafood pasta and risotto. The truth is it has just the right structure to be savored with a whole meal.

I remember when, in the 1980s, I was the director at the Suntory, Milan: on the wine list the only whites we had were Gavi, Arneis and generic Chardonnays. There were no Verdicchios, and that was a pity! This wine is famous in the world today also thanks to Tombolini, who is a member of the Vino Libero group as well. Good job, Fulvia!

Friulano Vigne 50 anni 2008 Le Vigne di Zamò
Type white wine
Grapes 100% Friulano
Vinification and fining partial cold maceration for 48 hours,
10 months of fining on the lees
Production area Friuli Venezia Giulia

Intense golden yellow color. You can smell the apple, wild herbs,
watered down honey and ripe fruit. Very complex. The taste
is sapid, delicious, with a very interesting return of mineral notes
(flint).

Pair with grilled shellfish, fish baked in salt with a touch of soy
sauce. I see it perfect with mackerel served with Japanese mustard,
or with lemon-flavored veal medallions.

Pierluigi has to change the name of his wine, because the vineyards
have grown, and now they're 60, no longer just 50!
I hardly ever say which white wine is my favorite, probably because
I don't know. But if I had to choose one, I'd choose this Tocai
(you can't call it that anymore, there are some things about Italians
I don't understand).

Barolo La Rosa 2008 Fontanafredda
Type red wine
Grapes 100% Nebbiolo
Vinification and fining long, traditional maceration, 24 months
in wood, short period (French oak barrique), long period
(Slavonian oak barrels).
Production area Piedmont

Intense ruby red color with garnet hues. Initial violet and dried rose
aromas, followed by spices, tobacco, red fruit and a hint of vanilla.
As for taste, the fruit is clearly noticeable, mature, soft and
balanced tannins. What I'm saying is it's a great sapid red wine.

I'd pair it with red meats, especially roasts. Braised in Barolo comes out tops, for sure! But I'd also drink it with aged cheese, such as Castelmagno. Or else with a special friend. Or maybe by myself!

I've slept down below the La Rosa vineyard many times in Fontanafredda: you feel like you're in the heart of the history of Barolo, because that's where the most famous Italian wine was born, a long, long time ago! Barolo is red wine that's not easy to produce and even harder to understand. But you don't always have to be moved to be able to understand something.

Langhe Nebbiolo Sorì Tildin 2004 Gaja

Type red wine
Grapes 95% Nebbiolo, 5% Barbera
Vinification and fining 12 months in barriques, 12 months in large barrels, last phase of fining in bottles
Production area Piedmont

Intense ruby color. Complex aromas emerge: black cherry, citron, sweet spices and balsamic edges. The fruit is compact and rigorous. The taste is vertical, sapid, full, a rare embrace between strength and elegance. The finish is very long (actually, it never finishes!)

Pair with grilled rib eye steak dressed with Dijon mustard, beef stew, or stewed eel with tomato, olive oil and Japanese mustard. I think it's fantastic with Parmigiano Reggiano aged 60 months.

It's like boxing: the first sip is a knock-out! A wine that's like a novel, to be read more than spoken. Gaja's wines can't be described, they can only be enjoyed. All those who have the good luck to taste them understand why he's "King."

Solaia 2009 Marchesi Antinori
Type red wine
Grapes 75% Cabernet Sauvignon, 20% Sangiovese, 5% Cabernet
Franc
Vinification and fining fermentation and maceration in conical oak
fermenters, 18 months of fining in French and Hungarian oak kegs
Production area Tuscany

Intense ruby red color with purplish hues. Very broad and complex
aroma: I recognize red fruit (cherry, red currants), pink
peppercorn, aromatic herbs, cocoa, coffee and licorice. The taste
is explosive, strong and round, but also elegant, refined, velvety
and soft. Very long and harmonious finish.

Pair with roast lamb seasoned with green peppercorn, pan-fried
Kobe-beef with sesame sauce, aged cheeses such as taleggio and
spicy gorgonzola.

How can you forget the first Italian wine to make the top of the
Wine Spectator list! It was the year 2000, but since then Solaia has
remained legendary. The ideal wine to be offered to the Japanese
Prime Minister on the occasion of his next official visit to Italy:
I have to remember to do that.

Sassicaia: Niccolò Incisa della Rocchetta
I Live in the Hope of Finding Another Ribot

"As long as there is passion, we shall not cease to discover the world."
(Cesare Pavese, *The Burning Brand*)

We're still in Tuscany. But on the side bordering on the sea. We start out from where we ended with Antinori: it's a small piece of fun to play around the sense of the passion for life.

After seeing Antinori's Bargino cellar, the one at the San Guido estate in Bolgheri really resembles a small house. But the first thing I want to do is quote the words of a great wine journalist about Sassicaia: "Finally a wine whose contents are superior to the container!" We're talking about the most glamorous Italian wine in the world! We're about to meet another Marquis, Niccolò Incisa della Rocchetta. Bolgheri is a famous name, at least for my generation, because at school we had to learn by heart the story of the "The cypresses that slender and lofty to Bolgheri run from San Guido two-columned to the town as on a race-course figures tall…" The Incisa della Rocchettas are also very famous, but they belong to another social group, that of the lovers of horse racing. Everyone is familiar with the name Ribot. The landscape is fabulous, just like in Carducci's description. There's a double row of cypresses, olive trees and vineyards, and it goes all the way down toward the water. The wine cellar, as I was saying, seems small as compared with the immensity of Sassicaia. "Five years ago I built this new wing, although for half a century the headquarters of our cellar was there…" The Marquis points to an even smaller, but delightful, construction, with something British and something

French about it, but very much in line with the Incisa della Rocchettas, globetrotting nobility. As soon as we go inside the large reception room appears before our eyes in all its splendor. A lovely combination of modernity in steel and glass, with shades of gray, rustic wood, wicker chairs and wooden benches. The crystal glass walls look outwards toward a wide path, needless to say, of cypresses, while inwards they overlook another type of wide path, rows of barriques for as far as the eye can see: 800 of them. A spectacular view.

Niccolò was born in 1936. His mother was Tuscan-American and his father Piedmontese. He, just like the Pope, came from Monferrato, in Piedmont. Rocchetta Tanaro is a small town with a population of 1,400, in the province of Asti. Mario, the name of Sassicaia and Niccolò's father, was a prominent figure, for reasons that I will explain later. Niccolò is a gentleman: he has a beautiful, sincere and captivating face. He speaks slowly and with measure, in a monotone, I think because he's shy. I've always thought that shyness is the fruit of intelligence, respect and earnestness. Today we'll have a chance to see that this is true.

I tell the Marquis the reason for our chat, the four-wine gimmick plus one for tasting, the project for a book that should, with wine as a pretext, paint a fresco of our Italy. My hope is to piece together a mosaic that isn't just a collage of more or less colorful pieces, but an overall vision. The idea is to try to understand where we come from and where we're headed. It's a hope, a dream. I'm not completely sure I'll succeed in the end. But making the attempt is already exciting in itself. Definitely useful to all three of us, but the readers should also be able to dig out at least a few ideas that will encourage them to think about themselves. I lay on the table all the names of the cellars visited so far, as well as the ones we still have to visit, in order to visualize the context. Niccolò listens to me carefully. I'm flattered that a special person like him is showing us that he thinks our visit is important.

Until the Seventies Making Wine Was a Hobby

Oscar "What percentage of wine do you export?"
Niccolò "About 60%."
Oscar "When did you start dealing with this winery?"

Niccolò "In the late 1960s. Until then wine was produced in very few bottles and strictly for family consumption. My father was very jealous of it. In fact, when I suggested selling it via the Antinoris he worried because he was afraid the wine would be undermined."

Oscar "What did your father, Mario Incisa, do?"

Niccolò "He had a degree in Agricultural Sciences, he loved agriculture, but he mostly dealt with breeding race horses. For him wine was a hobby. He was Piedmontese from Rocchetta Tanaro, but he came to live in Bolgheri when he married my mother."

Oscar "Did he speak Piedmontese dialect?"

Niccolò "Not much, because he spent a lot of time in Rome. He was born in Rome, his mother was Roman, my grandfather was from Rocchetta. Wine was never the family's main occupation, but it was always a passion. In the nineteenth century, one of our great-uncles had distinguished himself for a very large collection of descriptions of vinestocks, and in Rocchetta Tanaro he had a nursery with more than thirty varieties of vine clones that he had imported from France. His correspondence with the French nursery owners was published, and it attracted the interest of those in the business. Actually, the family continued to produce wine for its own sake. It was in the mid-1960s when we began to give it to a few restaurant owners so that people could try it out. It was already called Sassicaia."

The Marquis catches his breath while Shigeru prepares the wines for the tasting. Niccolò looks at him curiously. He's probably noticed that between a Barolo and a Spumante there's a Lambrusco. A Lambrusco in the home of Sassicaia, but because he is a nobleman he's careful not to react.

Oscar "Where are the vineyards?"

Niccolò "Sassicaia was and is our estate farthest from the sea. Can you see those hills under the mountains?—he points to the glass pane between us and the view. Because in those days it was believed that red wine would not have benefited from the saltiness and the south-westerly gusts of *libeccio* wind, so it was mostly the white grape that was cultivated close to the sea. The image of Tuscan wine back then was rather poor, and my father, as someone from Piedmont, refused to accept this. It was a huge challenge for him to show that Tuscans knew nothing about enology."

Oscar "Was the formula the same as it is now?"

Niccolò "Yes, it was prevalently Cabernet Sauvignon. The Cabernet grafts came from a vineyard owned by friends of my father near Pisa, who had always made wine that featured aromas that were completely new to him, different from those of Sangiovese. They couldn't come from France, because the war was on. In fact, the first vineyard was planted in 1944. The wine got its name Sassicaia from the farmstead, because of the stoniness of the land. From 1944 up to the 1960s my father continued to experiment with this wine until the result was even better than his best expectations. But he continued to make it only for the pleasure of his family and friends. When the bottles produced rose to several thousands in 1968, too many for a family to drink, we commissioned Antinori to bottle and distribute it."

Oscar "You and Piero Antinori are first cousins on your mothers' side?"

Niccolò "Yes, our mothers were sisters, both of them were from Bolgheri."

Oscar "You and Piero are almost the same age."

Niccolò "In fact we spent a lot of time together when we were young. We both spent a lot of time here in Bolgheri."

Oscar "How long did Antinori oversee the distribution of Sassicaia?"

Niccolò "Until the early 1980s, in the meantime Tignanello and Solaia had come out, and it was no longer a good thing to distribute these wines together."

Oscar "Tell me some more about your father. What year was he born?"

Niccolò "In 1899 and he died in 1983. He was a fantastic man and a great pioneer. One of the first in Italy to espouse environmentalist theories. He practically founded the Italian WWF along with Fulco Pratesi. Let's say that he was very much influenced in this by my mother who, although rather introverted, had always been an environmentalist. My father, instead, had been a hunter when he was young. In 1958 he founded the Rifugio Faunistico of Bolgheri, an oasis toward the sea. It's an obligatory passage for the migratory birds that head south, a very beautiful place!"

Oscar "You were around twenty. Did you follow your father's occupations?"

Niccolò "Certainly. There were three of us: I had a brother who lived in England for a long time and was involved in race horses, while my sister lived here in Bolgheri and followed the wine activity as well as that of the horses."

Oscar "So you inherited this passion for wine from your father."

Niccolò "It came upon me gradually. My father was an enthusiast and a collector. In those days he drank French wines, Bordeaux and Burgundy. Then we lived in Switzerland after the war, I myself studied in Switzerland and French wine was drunk there."

Oscar "Your father oversaw the winery to the very end, to the age of eighty, is that right?"

Niccolò "Yes, and I collaborated with him from about 1970 as his right-hand man. We would argue because our personalities were so different. He was much more of a visionary, I instead had my feet planted on the ground, but we compensated for each other well."

Oscar "Were there skirmishes between you?"

Niccolò "In those days he was especially concerned that large volumes would spoil the quality of the wine. In those years the Antinoris had sent their enologist, Giacomo Tachis, here, who then proved to be the best possible watchman for the quality of our wine. Both of them said that we had to be careful not to ruin what nature made spontaneously."

Oscar "How did you separate from the Antinoris?"

Niccolò "Gradually, but in complete agreement, untraumatically. In 1981 we started to bottle and export on our own, still leaving them in charge of distribution in Italy. Then, as of 1985, which incidentally was the year Sassicaia took off, we took everything back in hand."

Oscar "How many bottles were you making in the early 1980s?"

Niccolò "About 50,000. Now we make 220–230,000."

Oscar "Would your father be happy to see that you've known how to increase production without affecting the quality of your wine?"

Niccolò "It was something that worried him. He'd say: 'Because of you Sassicaia will end up like…' I'm not going to say the name of the wine out of respect. We talked about it a lot. My brother and sister weren't directly involved. They'd given me this great demonstration of faith."

Oscar "And what about distribution?"

Niccolò "I've always gone to professionals: in Italy, at Meregalli, which still deals with it, we have local importers in each country."

Oscar "Did you get married in the meantime?"

Niccolò "Yes, in the mid-1970s. I have a daughter who gives me a hand, especially now that I get around less. She takes care of the presentations and events."

Oscar "So the future lies in the family."

Niccolò "You have to remember that there are my brother's and sister's children too. At present no one works in the wine trade full-time. My daughter deals with it in part, and a nephew, my brother's son who lives in the United States, did, too. This nephew is now producing a Pinot Nero in Patagonia on his own."

Oscar "The Incisas are real globetrotters!"

We're about to taste the first wine, Cabochon 2008 from Monte Rossa, a Franciacorta. That's an area on Lake Iseo where Italian sparkling wine made using the traditional method has been highly successful over the past two decades.

Oscar "Cabochon is 80% Chardonnay and 20% Pinot Nero. A wine that aspires to be likened to the great Champagnes. Emanuele Rabotti is responsible for making it. He has known how to give a major turn-around to the quality of Monte Rossa for many years now. He's very ambitious, he tends to his vineyards as though they were a garden, and his cellar is equipped with the best technology, but without forgoing tradition. In 2009 I bought 33.3% of Monte Rossa and I'm proud of it. Every time I open a bottle of Cabochon I'm in seventh heaven. What do you think of it?"

Niccolò "I like it, I really do. The bubbles pleasantly fill my mouth and my nose, but they make it harder to recognize the vines."

Oscar "For many years Emanuele has depended on the advice of Pascal Vautier, a great *maître de cave* from Reims, who is now also helping Fontanafredda for Alta Langa. Instead, for your wines, who does the tasting, who decides on the style?"

Niccolò "Until 2009 Tachis was with us; after that we hired a very competent enologist, Graziana Grassini, and we do the tasting to-gether. Our director also takes part, a man who, in addition to his other qualities, also has a fine palate. For us it's crucial to analyze the wine well, and always guarantee the same standard of quality."

Oscar "How many people work here?"

Niccolò "In the cellar from eight to twenty, depending on the time of year and the production phase; on the land itself about thirty, but we have a total of 150 employees who also see to the horses and the traditional agriculture."

Oscar "How many hectares?"

Niccolò "In all, including the woodland, 2,500, but 75 of vineyard with the Sassicaia DOC, plus another 10 for the other wines. All in all, with the vineyards we lease, we work about 120 hectares."

Oscar "Which grapes do you use for the Sassicaia?"

Niccolò "80% minimum of Cabernet Sauvignon."

Oscar "Since when have you stopped selling it as table wine?"

Niccolò "Since 1994."

Oscar "Amazing! The most expensive Italian wine used to be sold as mere table wine!"

I am known for my intolerance of bureaucracy, especially rules and regulations that decide how tall the letters on the labels should be, what can and can't be written, at times laws amid great controversy. I got a 55,000 euro fine because I wrote that my Già is a fresh, young wine. I have often been tempted to downgrade certain DOCGs to the rank of table wine. To take my mind off these things I ask Shigeru to describe the Cabochon.

Shigeru "This wine is golden yellow in color. The aroma is vanilla, toasted bread and spices. Pear and hay, too. The taste is broad and structured. Harmonious and balanced like a mature woman. It's excellent as an apéritif, with a combination of appetizers, freshwater fish such as trout 'alla ghiotta' with black truffle, or Catalan-style lobster. It's also ideal with Pugliese *burrata*."

My Father Left Me with Two Occupations: Wine and Horses, but Horses Continue to Be My Foremost Passion!

The Marquis has obviously never seen Shigeru at work. I notice that he peers at him with curiosity. He sticks his nose back inside the glass, tastes the wine again and smiles.

Oscar "It's time to talk about horses, do you feel like it?"

Of course he does! And Niccolò is off.

Niccolò Our stable was founded in the late nineteenth century (1898–1899) by Federico Tesio, also a native of Piedmont, who is still considered to be the greatest horse breeder to have ever lived. The first stable was on Lake Maggiore, in Dormello. We still have a small piece of property around there, but that area has become a continuous line of supermarkets and shopping centers. The mayor even wanted to expropriate a piece of land from us so that he could build a rotary and erect yet another shopping mall!"

You have to imagine the Marquis's indignation from the syntax of his sentences because you can't understand how he feels just from his voice. We've become used to not missing a single word of what he says: these pearls of wisdom come out one after another but they aren't accompanied by any emphasis or an accent.

Niccolò "That mayor was obsessed. He wanted to bring in Eataly, and build warehouse after warehouse..." he smiles.

I, instead, do reply with emphasis: "Eataly is never located in non-places! One of Eataly's missions is to breathe new life, through conservative remodeling, into places that have been forgotten. In Milan it's going to be the old Smeraldo theater, in Florence the old bookstore on via Martelli close to the Cathedral, and in Bari a wing of the Fiera del Levante. There's no way I'd build one inside a shopping mall! It would be like selling Sassicaia in a discount store! Now let's go back to horses. Which do you love the most, wine or horses?" This is the mother of all questions.

Niccolò "They're two different things..."

The Marquis tries to wriggle out of answering this one, but I've got him in a corner and I insist: "Is it better to see your horse win a race or be awarded ninety-eight points for Sassicaia by the *Wine Spectator*?"

Niccolò "I get a bigger rush of blood to the head from horses! A few days ago a horse breeder from Mongolia came by, a place with three million inhabitants and three million horses. He came here because he knew Tesio's name: he kissed the earth where Tesio worked! This should give you some idea of the image of these stables in the world."

Oscar "Where do you keep your horses and how many do you have?"

Niccolò "Some here and some on Lake Maggiore, in Dormello. Today we have ninety horses altogether, including fillies and colts and horses that are already racing."

Oscar "I assume the goal is to breed race horses that will win. Do you make or lose money on it?"

Niccolò "It depends on how things go. Until the late 1980s the stable was self-funded, from the 1990s onwards this has become harder to do because of the competition. For example, the Arab emirs pay whatever is necessary to be sure they get the best horses. Before the war there was a horse here called Nearco. Well, even today, 70% of the horses that win have that champion's pedigree."

Oscar "Did Ribot have that pedigree too?"

Niccolò "No, Ribot had a different pedigree. Ribot was legendary, the greatest champion of all time (we're talking about the 1950s). Everyone remembers the horse, even those who were born after its time. At the start of this century the magazine *Panorama* launched a survey about the most famous Italians in the world and Ribot came out fifteenth."

Oscar "A horse!"

Niccolò "The *Gazzetta dello Sport* also conducted a survey on the most famous Italian sports figures in the world and Ribot got third place, even ahead of some of the most famous soccer players. Yuri Chechi won first place."

Ribot was the Marquis's great love when he was twenty, and it seems to me that as he talks about him he can see him and hear the sound of his hooves. A burdensome ghost like that of his father, but without any of the usual Freudian problems!

Oscar "Did you buy the horse, or was it homebred? Did you realize right away that it was going to be a champion?"

Niccolò "Homebred, the offspring of a brood mare that until then had given birth to some rather disappointing horses, so this came as a real surprise."

Oscar "Was your father in charge of the stable in the 1950s?"

Niccolò "Yes, and before him it was Tesio who, not having any heirs, had welcomed my father and mother who wanted a stable. That was 1930. Tesio died in 1954, so he never saw Ribot! After Tesio died my father took over the stable and he deserves credit for having bought some great brood mares. Most of the good results we had are thanks to horses my father bought. Until the 1970s wine was a hobby and horses was our main business. We were earning money with it at the time because we had Ribot, and when a horse like that becomes a stud you earn money."

Oscar "Was Ribot's pedigree good too?"

Niccolò "Not as good as Nearco's. If Nearco's pedigree makes up 70% of the winning horses, Ribot's makes up 5%."

Oscar "From my childhood days I remember a horse named Tornese."

Niccolò "Yes, he was a trotter." He peers at me the way he did before when he saw the bottle of Lambrusco.

Oscar "How do you make money with horses?"

Niccolò "A few years ago there was a horse in England that became a stud and he was evaluated as being worth 80 million euros. A horse like that can make 100,000 euros per mount, and cover 100–150 mares per year. That's 15 million euros per year. But such events are exceptional."

Oscar "It seems that when it comes to horses, more than wine, luck plays an important role. Is that right?"

Niccolò "Well, by now Sassicaia is always of the same high quality, while to get a good horse it's not enough to invest in the mount; a good stallion and an excellent brood mare don't necessarily produce a horse that's just as good. It's not mathematical, and in any case a horse is fragile, it can get hurt."

Oscar "It's a bet you make. So the world of horses revolves around the world of risk-taking. By the way, do you bet? I mean, do you gamble on the races?"

Niccolò "No. For fear of bad luck. If I were to go to a country where we don't have any of our horses then maybe I'd do some betting."

Oscar "What do you think of gambling in general? Why has gambling grown so much in Italy?"

Niccolò "Until ten–fifteen years ago the only bets that were made were on soccer and horses. Nowadays in Italy betting on horses has dropped because the bookmakers' have been opened up to all types of bets, without any compensation for horse racing, which was done in France instead. Ten years ago ten billion euros were spent in Italy, half on the Football Pools and half on horse racing. The amount spent for betting on horses has practically been halved, while several billion euros are spent overall for gambling."

The truth of the matter is that the revenue from gambling in all its forms, on-land and online, legal and illegal in Italy today is close to 100 billion euros. A huge amount, equal to what we spend on food (110 billion euros). One day, toward the end of 2012, I bought an advertising page in each of the major newspapers and wrote: "WE ITALIANS SPEND ON GAMBLING AS MUCH AS WE DO FOR FOOD. HAVE WE GONE CRAZY? COME ON, LET'S STOP IT AND EAT BETTER INSTEAD! Signed, Eataly." Lottomatica hired a lawyer to write me a letter.

Gambling is a disease of the soul, much more serious than certain diseases of the body, and the State should not be party to it. In the days of betting on horses and soccer, as well as on rubber ball from where I come from, you could catch sight of the relationship between cause (the result of a game) and effect (victory or defeat), because you could in some way see your skill (that of predicting the winner) rewarded. Even in the presence of a conflict between the passions. How can you predict that your favorite team or beloved horse will lose only to make money from a winning prediction? It really has become a kind of madness because it's the gambling that brings billions of euros to the State coffers (and to those of the organized crime syndicates) and you can't see the connection. You're prey to chance: many invest apparently little in a lottery, or a scratchcard, or a slot machine, in the hope of earning a lot or a great deal with respect to the investment. It is totally anti-educational for a Republic that claims to be founded on work. Pure vice that subtracts resources from families, quality food, children, schools, sports, reading, music, healthy fun, or even from productive investments, to redirect them toward putting unlikely hopes in a game that's unfair in any case. It's part of a gradual separation from real values, replaced by virtual values, by the imagined multiplication of money circulating by virtue of the emphasis on betting. Not to mention the bets placed in the financial world. Swaps and derivatives of various kinds have caused huge damage.

Idleness is the real father of this vice. Idleness that also stems from the dearth of jobs.

Niccolò "Right now we're forced to finance the horses with the wine proceeds."

Oscar "You won't give up on horses?"

Niccolò "No, I won't. Also because I have a duty toward everyone I know. An Australian who came to see us said that for a horse lover coming here is like going to the Mecca for a Muslim. The name of our horses' breed is Dormello-Olgiata, named after the historical locations of our estates: Dormello on Lake Maggiore and Olgiata near Rome (we no longer have this estate). Horse racing is going through a recession in Italy alone. In the rest of the world it's still very successful, even in Japan, for instance."

Oscar "What's the revenue for wine, and what is it for horses?"

Niccolò "Twenty-two million euros for wine. For horses it's hard to work out. It varies considerably from year to year depending on how our colts perform."

In Horse Racing You Thrive on Hope

Oscar "Who else in your family deals in horses?"

Niccolò "For now, no one else does, apart from my three-year-old granddaughter!"

Oscar "Wow: three years old! What was the last great satisfaction you got from horses?"

Niccolò "Right now we have some horses that are racing in France, I'm expecting good results from them."

Oscar "Let's go on to the second wine: this is a Timorasso. It's a pretty rare vine, typical of the Tortonese area, close to Alessandria and launched by a phenomenon who goes by the name of Walter Massa. He sells it all over the world, at a high price, although not as high as your Sassicaia. This is a 2009 vintage, from his most important cru called Sterpi. It's a white wine that has become a fad in the past five–six years, but its story goes way back. Shigeru, do you want to tell us what you think?"

Shigeru "Deep yellow color, with greenish hues. There's a whiff of honey and dried fruit. The aroma is flint, hay, and it's very mineral. It has a sapid, soft taste. It's elegant and persistent. It can be served with shellfish, fish soup with tomato and mushroom, but also baked fillet of sea bream with green olive pâté or medium-aged Tuscan pecorino cheese."

I add that Walter gave it that name because there used to be underbrush where the vineyard is located now, and he was the one who made a great effort to start growing Timorasso again. I don't need to insist much to see that the Marquis likes it, even though he wasn't familiar with it. I only spend a few extra words to promote the re-launching of these autochthonous vines and I get my palate ready for the Barolo. Although before tasting the Barolo we try a Lambrusco. A Lambrusco in the home of Sassicaia. An apparent contradiction!

Oscar "Let's go back to talking about the wine market. After the crisis in 2008 we all got really scared and thought we were about to enter another world. What's your take on the wine market? What do you see as being the future of Sassicaia? Will you increase the quantity?"

Niccolò "No, I won't. I believe we've gone as far as we can in terms of quantity. It's better to make a bottle less than a bottle more of what the market wants."

I suddenly realize how absurd the situation is: we're talking about the future of Sassicaia while drinking Lambrusco. We're practically at two extremes. A medium-sized Lambrusco winery produces at least 5 million (yes, I said million!) bottles. It's a pleasant wine, suited to rinsing your mouth while eating cold cuts. It's a big export, keeping the prices down, of course. But just like Sassicaia it's an Italian product and Italy is also great for its capacity to embrace extremes with the utmost aplomb and elegance.

Oscar "Until now you've always worked in a situation where demand has always been greater than supply, and the credit undoubtedly goes to you. Has it always been like this?"

Niccolò "With Sassicaia it has. Whenever we harvest, first we look at the demand and then we decide how much to assign to each country or importer, but we're forced to keep them all on a diet, so to speak, careful not to make them get mad and to avoid a parallel market run by people who buy to sell in other countries."

Oscar "Average retail price?"

Niccolò "In wine shops 140 euros, in restaurants 180–200. The prices are similar across the markets, except for Brazil where it's much more expensive because of the excise duties levied on it."

Oscar "And what about the Far East?"

Niccolò "Our Indian importer sells it in the Maldives. China has boomed over the past three years, to some extent also because the French have gone over the top with their wine prices. But pricing policies, when you're talking about rather limited quantities, are very sensitive."

Oscar "Practically 600 bottles of Sassicaia are uncorked every single day in the world. If it's true that at least a billion new consumers will soon be on the market for these fine wines then you have to understand that you're talking about very small volumes." I say this while drinking the Lambrusco. The one I brought is a Chiarli Premium Honorable 2011, and right away I'm dreaming of sinking a knife into a nice chunk of Parmigiano Reggiano. Lambrusco seems to be a wine made especially for Emilian cuisine, poor, but with generous flavors. I don't need to ask Shigeru what he thinks of it, he's ready to step in.

Shigeru "First of all, I have to say that there are different types of Lambrusco. This is a Lambrusco from Sorbara. It's produced in the province of Modena, in about a dozen specific towns. It has to have at least 60% of Lambrusco from Sorbara, while for the rest Lambrusco Salamino can be used. In this case it's a high-quality Lambrusco with 100% Sorbara vine. Chiarli is the producer. The company goes way back, founded in 1860. The color is a lovely cherry red. The aroma is red fruit, strawberry, candy and candied fruit. The taste is sapid and aromatic and it has a nice clean feel. It's excellent with cold cuts in general and it goes very well with Parma prosciutto and mortadella, or with boiled meats with fruit compote."

He didn't mention Parmigiano, I definitely would have.

Oscar "After the Lambrusco let's go to the Barolo and talk about other things because, as Shigeru often tells us, wines are also meant to go with certain subjects. So you were born in 1936 like Berlusconi. What's your opinion of the last two decades of Italian politics?"

Niccolò "I think there's a lot of confusion. Many people have lost their heads. In any other country someone like Berlusconi, the subject of harsh criticism and attacks by the public, would already have been removed from politics, and among other things it's hard to understand why he insists on being part of the political world. He's an excellent businessman. He should go back to his businesses. Someone like him, who loves life, would be able to do so without being in the limelight all the time."

Oscar "Right, but maybe being in the limelight is the only thing that excites him. Maybe he can't have fun if people aren't watching him! Do you think that this political class is capable of representing Italian beauty and creativity in the world?"

Niccolò "Our image has really declined in the past decade. It's hard for me to voice an opinion."

Oscar "I too think that from the postwar period to the late 1980s politicians were more courteous, and that they tried to do something for their country. Now I have the impression that when faced with a problem the first thing they worry about is how they're going to look."

The Marquis and I practically said these last words together.

Oscar "We need a change. Do you vote?"

Niccolò "I didn't vote in the last two elections. But that's because I'm a Swiss citizen, even though I live in Italy."

Oscar "What were your father's political ideas?"

Niccolò "He wasn't interested. In jest, he'd say he was a pre-revolutionary Frenchman. But they were both, my mother too, mindful of social problems. In San Guido they founded the first full-time and free elementary school in Italy. And the children would get there on a bus that went around to their doorsteps to pick them up."

Oscar "They were quite Left-wing, but not Communist, is that right?"

Niccolò "They were people who knew how to take the initiative in the name of the community. If people were more concerned about others we wouldn't need so many institutions to guarantee everyone's well-being. I learned a lot from my father and mother and in this period of recession our company tends to safeguard jobs, also guaranteeing a bigger workforce than is strictly necessary. The school was closed when the town opened its own in Castagneto Carducci."

The Marquis is marvelously "light" even when dealing with serious topics. I admire people like this. The lightness you find in Calvino, that music of the soul that puts you in harmony with the world.

I'm Not a Big Fan of the New Barrique

Oscar "Now let's talk about this Barolo, Casa E. di Mirafiore Riserva 2004, which is produced by Fontanafredda, a winery I bought in 2008. This Barolo has our highest label, created by Count Emanuele Alberto di Mirafiore in 1858. 100% Nebbiolo, naturally, refined in medium-sized barrels. In Langa there's this open debate about barriques and large barrels."

Niccolò "I remember a wine that came out a few years ago with a label that read 'No barrique, No Berlusconi.'"

Bartolo Mascarello, the philosopher of Barolo. How I enjoy the fact that the Marquis remembers!

Oscar "Exactly! Mascarello took sides against the barrique method. Instead your wine is all refined in those small 220-liter barrels. How many years does a barrique last?"

Niccolò "We use 30% new wood: out of 800 barriques there are always 240 with new wood. At our winery the barriques last three years and then they use them for other wines. Personally, I'm not a big fan of the new barrique. In France there are schools of thought that support the idea that barriques can even be used for as long as ten years. The meaning behind the barrique is based on the size and the fact that the wood brings the wine out, especially in cases like Cabernet Sauvignon which also has some aggressive tannins."

At this point I ask a question not so much because I actually want to learn something, but because I want to hear how the Marquis will shell out his thoughts, word after word, pearl after pearl, to tell us how Sassicaia was born.

Oscar "How do you make Sassicaia?"

Niccolò "We harvest in September, then the grapes ferment and in November the wine is made in barriques. After three months we decant, then we do two more decants, and finally we bottle it. Altogether it stays in the barrique for two years. After these two years we assemble it in vats and then bottle it. Before putting it on the market we keep it in bottles for four months. The buyer should then keep it in the cellar another three-four-five years."

There you are: the answer can seem simple to some, more complicated to others. But the answer is plain, clean, with nothing glamorous or snobbish about it.

Oscar "How many harvests have you done?"

Niccolò "Thirty-one since 1982."

Oscar "Do you remember one vintage in particular?"

Niccolò "Perhaps my favorite vintage is 1988. Eight has always been our lucky number! They were all good: 1968, 1978, 1988, 1998 and even 2008." I think that for every horse breeder superstition is a must. "Our most famous vintage, in which Sassicaia was described as the wine of the century, was 1985, which, however, was not one of our classics. That year a wine that was more suited to the palates of the New World came out."

Oscar "Barriques for the Sassicaia, medium-sized barrels that hold up to 2–3,000 liters for our Barolo. In the historical cellar of Fontanafredda, which we didn't touch, you can see that the original barrels from 1878 for Barolo were 2–3,000 liters and we, for this Barolo,

222 Vino, I Love You

kept this methodology. The philosophy is completely natural, no forcing, there are no pumps and everything happens by gravitational force, the fermentations last as long as nature wants them to." I'm proud, but this time I don't overdo things. The Marquis's lightweight tones have influenced me too.

Niccolò relishes this wine, to my great pride and joy, and pours himself another glass, while Shigeru, right on time, says: "Intense garnet red color. The aroma is of rose, white pepper, vanilla, licorice, and leather and minerals, too. The taste is warm, dry, sapid and aromatic. It has soft, velvety tannins. It's best served with fontina fondue, wild boar stew with black pepper and, of course, braised beef stewed in Barolo."

Oscar "The last wine we have to taste is one of yours. Which one do you choose?"

Niccolò "Let's try Sassicaia 2010."

As we listen to Shigeru the Marquis asks one of his assistants for the Sassicaia so that we can taste it and his second glass of Barolo is taken away. Over-zealousness that isn't "accepted" however: he rebels, mildly irked, and makes him bring it back! He may have liked the Barolo, but for me this little scene is almost orgasmic: it's a good thing I didn't miss it! Three cheers for Piedmont, Barolo, Fontanafredda, and most importantly for this passion that we all have in common! Wine, I love you!

Along with a bottle from 2010, bottles from 2008 and 2009 arrive as well. After what he told us I'm especially curious about the wine with 8 as the last digit. Let's see if it's just superstition! It's already in my glass and the aroma causes me to blurt out a "Wow, what an aroma!" With my enthusiasm I couldn't be more elegant!

I ask him to tell me something about the so-called Super Tuscan, wines, a term invented by Americans in the mid-1970s to identify Tuscan wines that were different from the region's traditions, using types of grapes that weren't autochthonous, such as Cabernet Sauvignon and Merlot. These wines didn't deserve the DOCG, and that's why they were called "table wines." The most expensive table wines in the world! In between Super Tuscans the Marquis reminds us that Sassicaia was released for the first time in 1968, then Tignanello in 1971, Solaia in 1978, and Ornellaia in 1985. And he tells us about others that came after them.

We go over the major wineries in Italy and go back to talking about the Antinoris (but there are others like them) who have been making wine for dozens of generations. Quite the opposite from me: I change jobs every ten years! But it's with great pride that I talk about my children who seem to be putting an end to their father's habit, because all of them, three boys, have chosen to work for my company: two are at Eataly and one of them, an enologist, oversees the wineries. I can't talk about them without expressing my endless pride in being their father. I force myself to think that if I'd had three girls I would have found the way to be equally proud. On the other hand, for these interviews I have included several Ladies of Wine, who all followed in their fathers' footsteps and even did better than their fathers.

We drink the three Sassicaias in succession so that they're easier to compare.

Oscar "They're outstanding, and I think the 2009 is out of this world." Has anyone ever told the Marquis that his wine was out of this world? But he's never caught off-balance with us.

Niccolò "You're right. It's more structured. Even though everyone says that 2010 is more classical and that it matches our style better."

My Dream Is to Find Another Ribot!

Oscar "While we drink Sassicaia let's talk about the future. What are you going to be when you grow up?"

Niccolò "I think that for as long as you can make a contribution you have to move forward. I've seen lots of people who retired from their working life and suddenly broke down. I met an engineer who looked sixty-seventy years old and instead he was ninety. His secret was that he never quit working. I'm sure it's important to keep making a contribution for as long as you can."

Oscar "I agree with you completely! Do you still live with your first wife?"

Niccolò "No, I don't. I spent fifteen years with my first wife and I had my only daughter with her. I've been married to my second wife, who's slightly younger than me, for about twenty years."

Oscar "If your time is a hundred, how do you divide it?"

Niccolò "I see to the horses for about 50% of the time, and to the wine for the other 50%, but until a year ago I spent more time with the horses because I had a trainer whom I didn't trust completely. Now things are better with the horses, so I've gone back to dividing my time equally between the two activities."

Oscar "And what about your vacations?"

Niccolò "Well, they're important too. They help me think. We've been going to South America a lot lately because we took some horses there."

Oscar "Horses, even on your vacation! And what about your wife?"

Niccolò "She's even more of an enthusiast than I am!"

Oscar "And your daughter?"

Niccolò "She likes them, but only to a certain extent. The most enthusiastic is my three-year-old granddaughter. I hope to continue with this life for a while longer."

At this point the Marquis takes a rather long pause. His eyes are almost shut, he's trying to find the right words and I let him search for them. He's about to say something that means a lot to him, I can feel his thoughts swirling around inside his head.

Niccolò "My dream is to find another Ribot!"

I won't even try to describe his face; all the reader needs to know is that looking at him brings tears to my eyes. I could get up, bid farewell and leave because after these words there's nothing left to say. This is the utopia of a man who has created one of the world's greatest wines. This is his endless yearning, his main desire, his personal challenge and maybe even his reason for living. And the amazing thing is that, despite everything, a man can only do so much. And then I think of his three-year-old granddaughter who's crazy about horses. It must be for her that a horse like Ribot needs to be found. What a beautiful dream: good luck Marquis!

Sassicaia Is a Winning Horse

The utopia theme always comes back. Mind you, utopia which comes from *eu-topos*, that is, a happy place, not *ou-topos*, an impossible place. To be able to live life to the full you need to have a great dream: the Marquis's dream speaks of horses, not wine. Why? I'd be able to answer the question on my own, but it's the Marquis who reiterates it: "Sassicaia is a winning horse," and he says it with such simplicity that no one could ever think of him as being arrogant. We come out of our reciprocal commotion and go back to wine. We now have the legendary 2008 in the glass and, as I taste it, I'm at a loss for words. The Marquis can't resist and admits: "The 2008 vintage was special for us, for the horses and the wine!"

It's up to Shigeru to reign in our emotions. He's so focused on the wine, and maybe he didn't let himself get overwhelmed the way we did.

Shigeru "Well, I talk about 2010 because it's the wine the Marquis chose for tasting. The color is an intense ruby red with purplish reflections. The aroma is intense: ripe fruit, undergrowth, aromatic herbs. You can smell spices, minerals, tobacco, coffee and licorice. The taste is full, warm, intense, velvety and persistent. It's wine that can be served with grilled meat seasoned with olive oil, salt and pepper. But it's also excellent with Grana Padano, aged 48 months."

It's time to compare our feelings (I insist on using the word "feelings" because our reasoning seems to have little to do with it) about these three wines. Shigeru admits that he prefers the 2009, for me it's definitely the 2008, in the sense that if I had to choose this is the one I'd take to a desert island, and instead Simona likes the 2010. The Marquis won't say... all three of them are his children.

In the grand finale of this rather special visit we all move over to horse racing!

The Marquis says so explicitly: when I'm feeling depressed, the only thing that pulls me out of it are horses: "I like to watch them when they train and of course I enjoy going to the races. During the race I get a rush of that special adrenaline that makes miracles!"

Oscar "What was your greatest joy in life?"

Niccolò "When Ribot won his second Arc de Triomphe. But it was a success every time he raced: in his career he ran in sixteen races and notched up sixteen wins."

Ribot, the Marquis tells us, died of cancer when he was nineteen, in America, where he has a grave with a tombstone. He was the greatest racehorse of all time and he supported the stable for twenty years. We take one more look at the family photos, the picture of Ribot, of course, and the crate with the bottle of Sassicaia that traveled into outer space. We leave, ready to cross the Apennines, from the Tyrrhenian to the Adriatic, heading toward the Marches.

When I get back into the car with my two traveling companions I think about this gentleman who entertained us for two hours with information that was both intriguing and surprising, which once again gave vigor and substance to my theory of apparent contradictions.

The Marquis talked to us about a life spent trying to free himself of an oppressive father, in the Freudian sense, but the whole time emphasizing his family's traditions and his father's passions: wine and horses. Niccolò Incisa della Rocchetta divides his time between two activities: wine and horses that apparently contradict each other. We can actually find lots of similarities between the emotions of a winemaker and those of a horse breeder. The vineyard owes everything to its origins, the great vinestock, the best possible terroir. A horse depends on the choice of the stallion and the brood mare. Sometimes wine seems good and then it lets you down, or else it seems disappointing but then matures over the years. Horses can disappoint you or excite you in the same way. But both passions hide a utopia: another Ribot or the perfect wine! And utopia is a reason for living.

We've just met a man who apparently isn't interested in politics, but works to improve society and is very sensitive to the environment. In the end he showed us, perhaps unconsciously, another contradictory side: some superstition combined with lots of reasoning and modesty about his feelings.

All we can wish for him is that he and his granddaughter do manage to find another Ribot. While for Italy we hope for a harmonious development that will allow us to find our "perfect wines" year after year and the ability to sell them abroad. I'm optimistic! I'll bet everything I own that, besides wines, we'll be able to find brilliant paths in other fields of agriculture as well, in tourism, art, fashion, design, in the precision manufacturing industry. There's a lot that still needs to be done in the field of natural Italian vocations. This is why the future is marvelous.

Cesare Pavese's words convince me that this is so: "As long as there is passion, we shall not cease to discover the world," and... (I might add) improve it.

Notes for Wines Tasted with Niccolò Incisa della Rocchetta
Shigeru Hayashi

Franciacorta Brut Cabochon 2008 Monte Rossa
Type sparkling wine
Grapes 80% Chardonnay, 20% Pinot Nero
Vinification and fining fining in 250 l oak kegs between September
and February, fining in bottles for more than 40 months
Production area Lombardy

Elegant golden yellow color, very subtle and persistent perlage.
The aroma is vanilla, toasted bread and sweet yellow cream. Fruity
note (green pear) on the finish. The taste is broad, structured, soft.

Needless to say, a bubbly wine like this one is perfect with a meal,
though I would still suggest drinking it with a mixed freshwater fish
appetizer (it's magnificent with trout and black truffle).

I'm going to tell you something I know I shouldn't. In 2010 my
physician friend Myojo got married at… Eataly Tokyo
Daikanyama! A hundred twenty guests in Oscar's store and they
drank Cabochon that was opened with a sword, just like real
samurais! When Oscar found out he was very happy, so happy that
it was the first and the last sword wedding to be held at Eataly!

Sterpi 2009 Vigneti Massa
Type white wine
Grapes 100% Timorasso
Vinification and fining maceration at controlled temperature, rest *sur lie*, fining 12 months at least in bottles
Production area Piedmont

Bright straw color with green hues. Honey, dried fruit and fruit with white pulp aroma. Pleasant flint and graphite on the finish. Sapid and soft, mineral and persistent taste.

Let's pair it with shellfish, fish soup in tomatoes and mushrooms, baked sea bream fillet with green olive pâté. I think it would be perfect with medium-aged Tuscan pecorino.

Raise your hand if you were familiar with Timorasso grapes and wine ten years ago: no one was. Raise your hand if you're familiar with it now: lots of you. The credit goes to Walter Massa, who created a vineyard where "underbrush" (weeds) grew before, and saved this vineyard from extinction. The story is a beautiful one, the wine is even better. It comes out tops!

Lambrusco PM Horonable 2011 Cleto Chiarli
Type sparkling red
Grapes 100% Lambrusco from Sorbara
Vinification and fining *prise de mousse* via natural fermentation in bottles, followed by fining for 6 months
Production area Emilia Romagna

Pale ruby red color, similar to pink cherry. Red fuit, like strawberry, and black cherry aroma. Sapid and aromatic taste, it conveys linearity and preservability, and has a clean and long finish.

I suggest it should be eaten with all sorts of cold cuts, especially Parma prosciutto and mortadella. I'd also try it with seared lard with pink peppercorn. And no doubt with tortellini sprinkled with Parmigiano Reggiano!

When you taste this wine, you can't help wondering why Lambrusco isn't considered a great international wine. It's refined and enjoyable, like a woman who hides before letting you find her. If I had to choose which wine to drink on a daily basis, this is the one I'd go for!

Barolo Casa E. di Mirafiore Riserva 2004
Type red wine
Grapes 100% Nebbiolo
Vinification and fining after a long maceration phase the wine is fined for 3 years in medium- and large-sized (from 20 to 140 hl) barrels, and then for 2 more years in cement vats and in bottles.
Production area Piedmont

Intense garnet red color, the aroma releases hints of rose, white pepper, vanilla, licorice, leather and flint. Warm, dry, sapid taste with a mild fragrance. Soft and velvety, practically silky tannins.

Pairs perfectly with fontina fondue, wild boar stew with black pepper, braised and roast meats of all sorts, all types of aged cheese laced with herbs.
The King of wines, made in the cellars of a King, with the name of a King! We Japanese are very envious of a beautiful, important story like this one, and every time I arrive at Fontanafredda and I see the vineyards and the cellar with barrels as big as my whole house, I say that I've come to the most beautiful place in the world.

Bolgheri Sassicaia 2010 Tenuta San Guido

Type red wine
Grapes 85% Cabernet Sauvignon, 15% Cabernet Franc
Vinification and fining 2 weeks of maceration with the skins,
with pumping over and *délestages*; 24 months of maturation
in French oak barriques
Production area Tuscany

Intense ruby red color with purplish hues. The aroma is a triumph
of fruit, undergrowth and aromatic herbs, You can also smell
spices, pumice, tobacco, coffee and balsamic streaks. Full, warm,
velvety and persistent taste.

Pair with grilled or pan-fried meat made with soy sauce and wasabi.
Perfect with Grana Padano aged over 48 months. Great meditation
wine.

The year 1968 was an important one in the world also because it
saw the birth of Sassicaia. This is the coolest of all the Italian wines,
the one that paved the way for Super Tuscans, thereby creating
the legend of Tuscany. It's hard to believe that at the start it
was considered a mere "table wine." It was so far ahead that
it was beyond classification!

Villa Bucci: Ampelio Bucci
A Man as Gentle as His Hills

If it is true that the landscape shapes our style and influences our taste, in the case of Professor Ampelio Bucci it seems that even the gentle hills of Jesi have become a part of his nature. Ampelio is as gentle as his hills. The way he relates to others is marvelously gentle. Gentle are his words, his tone, his way of thinking. Very clever, even sharp, but above all gentle. Talking to him is like stretching out on a soft mattress, or stroking a soft pillow. Spending time with Professor Bucci makes you feel good.

Hop Back into the Car, I'm Taking You to See the Vineyard!

Oscar "Where are you taking us?"
Ampelio "To see some of my vineyards. We're right in the middle of the hills of the Castelli di Jesi and I'll bet you've never seen these places. Don't just look at the landscape. Look at the land: here the land is beautiful both inside and out. From the outside you can see why… inside it's beautiful because it's rich in limestone. And limestone is the basis for all the best white wines in the world!"
We're practically out of the car, but Ampelio Bucci—born in 1936, and known to all, in the world of wine, as the "Professor" (an economist and an expert in fashion and design, he teaches Entrepreneurship and Design Management at the IULM and Brera Academy in Milan)—makes us get right back inside. He says he wants to take us to see "the things" his father started to build. For five–six stops we're

almost forced to look at the vineyards, walk in between the rows, dig a little into the earth, admire the landscapes, remark on the abandonment of old farmsteads. Ampelio has been in the field of agriculture for the past fifty years, and involved in viticulture and olive-growing for the past twenty, but before being an agriculturer and a producer he's a man of culture.

To interview him we drove all the way to Ostra Vetere in the province of Ancona, which is the realm of Verdicchio, between Montecarotto and Serra de' Conti, in the heart of the DOC for Verdicchio dei Castelli di Jesi: twelve small towns towered over by their twelve castles. Verdicchio is number one here, but there's also Montepulciano and Sangiovese. Ampelio welcomes us at the Pongelli estate; he owns more than one.

I don't remember how, maybe it's because of my well-known curiosity about dynasties, but when we get back in the car we start talking about his father again…

Oscar "Did your father finish college?"

Ampelio "Of course he did! And he became a professor of Economics. After that he worked for Assicurazioni Generali."

Oscar "When was he born?"

Ampelio "In 1879."

Oscar "And he even got his degree: that was rare back then!"

Ampelio "He had an excellent mind. When he was fifty he married a woman who was twenty-seven and they had four children. He invested in land his entire life."

I drive and Ampelio tells us where to go. He tells me to be careful not to hit the pillars with the Madonnas, votive columns that over the centuries were built at the corners of the country roads. As we climb upwards, these roads grow steep and lead us straight into the vineyards. We see lots of those columns and our host soon tells us why.

Ampelio "For centuries, this area was crushed under the power of the Church, and this is why there are still lots of holy images everywhere. And like all the areas that were poorly treated by the Church, which was especially harsh here, there was an underground revolutionary ferment of people like my father. He never once in all his life set foot inside a church! All these peaceful dissidents organized their lives in spite of the Church. There were no loud protests, just an antagonistic political sentiment. Just think, when my father got married he had the priest come to his home so he wouldn't have to go to church. It caused quite a scandal in town!"

Oscar "He must have found a very open-minded priest..."

Ampelio "Well, all you had to do was give the priest a little money. And there's more: my father's name was Ampelio too, and my name, just like his, stems from the fact that there are no saints called Ampelio around here."

And besides that, I think to myself, Ampelio comes from the Greek word *ampelos*, which means vine. It can't be mere coincidence.

A few minutes later we arrive at a vineyard in the bordering town of Serra de' Conti, and we get out of the car. Ampelio tells us that he owns land in the valley and on the hill. He has vineyards on the hills, and wheat, olives and alternative crops in the valley. For a total of 370 hectares, of which "only" 31 are used to grow grapes, divided into five different vineyards. This vineyard resembles a garden: fifty-year-old vines, with Montepulciano and Sangiovese mixed in, the way it used to be done. I think about how hard it must be to separate the two vines during the harvest.

Today we're lucky enough to be in the company of a man who buys old vineyards because, as he puts it, "All you have to do is treat them the way you would old people. If you take care of them they'll still have lots to give. The roots of the vine take years to grow deep into the soil and if the roots aren't deep the wine will taste ordinary."

Oscar "Well, of course, people who don't have deep roots are ordinary, too."

Ampelio "You have to be crazy like me to buy old vineyards. But in a world where everything is the same being a little crazy is what makes you a winner. No one around here has vineyards as old as mine, no one uses old barrels like me, no one tends to the plants the way we do. After we bought it we re-staked the whole vineyard, and in the end it cost me twice as much as it would have than if I'd started from scratch. But this is what makes me happy! All these plants you see were scraped down one by one, we removed all the rot and then applied a product that heals the wood and closes up any scars. Now the plants are healthy again and they thank us for it."

Oscar "Doing viticulture like this is expensive! It almost sounds like you're doing it more for the vineyards than for the wine."

Ampelio "I'm not really sure why I do it, I've always followed my instinct. For example, the fact that I only used the traditional vine-stocks in this area, Verdicchio, Montepulciano and Sangiovese, when international ones were all the fashion. The fact that I multiplied the oldest clones of the oldest vineyard. That I insisted on using eighty-year old barrels to age Villa Bucci. That I produced a Verdicchio 'reserve' when the rules didn't even require it yet, and it was actually forbidden. And the fact that I work with Giorgio Grai and not a traditional enologist, in spite of the fact that we had a huge argument the first time we met. My instinct told me he was the right person for the job, even though I really felt like telling him to go to hell!"

Arcevia, Barbara, Ostra Vetere, Belvedere Ostrense are the towns that surround us on all sides. A sequence of gentle, colorful hills and fields cultivated with the rotational method that is still intelligently being used here. The hills in the Marches are different from the ones in Tuscany: they're rounder, kinder, sweeter... in a word gentle, just like the Professor who "crosses over" them as Romano Levi, of grappa fame, would say.

Oscar "How do you make your wine? Do you vinify these five vine-yards separately from each other?"

Ampelio "Of course I do! Then I put the product of each of the vine-yards, which I separate carefully, into the barrels. With Giorgio's help I carry out the final assemblage. That's the most delicate phase."

Oscar "Like when you make Champagne. You assemble the blends and make Villa Bucci Riserva cuvée."

Ampelio "Yes, and it's the most intriguing part of the work every year, especially for the white wines, which are more difficult than red ones. White wines require a very fine palate, you need to know how to recognize certain subtle finesses, the texture, all the aromas... Later I'm going to take you to the cellar so you can have fun making your own blend! But first I want to show you the house where I was born."

We go around the walls of Serra de' Conti, one of the most beautiful castles in Jesi, and still perfectly intact. Ampelio has mentioned Giorgio Grai, one of the greatest winemakers, twice already. People say lots of things about him, I have to remember to ask him to tell us more about this man.

Thinking Local, Acting Global

After reading that name on the hundreds of bottles I've drunk over the years, I can now say that the villa really does exist. And what a villa it is! He was lucky to have been born here.

At last I enter the garden of Villa Bucci, where it seems as though time has stopped. A cobbled path leads to the house and it's surrounded on either side by boxwood that's well tended to. The style of the house is both sober and elegant, and the garden is shaded by tall maritime pines. It's a place that makes you feel good. As we follow him on his guided tour of the garden I say: "How much Verdicchio is produced in the Marches?"

Ampelio "I have no idea!" He answers curtly, as if I'd asked him how many drops of water there are in the sea.

Oscar "If you asked me how much Barolo we produce in Langa, I'd be able to tell you."

Ampelio "It's not something I care about much… should I?" he winks maliciously.

I wonder, maybe he's just pretending… or maybe he's not. After all, he is a professor of Economics. Does he really not know? He offers us one of his most beautiful pearls without too many aulic preambles, almost as if to apologize for what he'd said before, as if he had guessed what I was thinking.

Ampelio "I realize I've always done the exact opposite of what I read in all those sacred texts on marketing. The gurus say you have to 'think global, act local.' But instead you have to do the exact opposite, especially in Italy. You have to 'think local and act global.' Because in Italy, wherever you are, all you have to do is go deep (like in the vineyards) to discover layers of history, culture, goodness and beauty."

He's a unique kind of academic, and I like him for it. What's more, he's right, damn it! Thinking local and acting global, that's the best strategy for wine!

I go back to the figures, this time the ones for his winery, and I ask him: "How are your 31 hectares divided up?"

Ampelio "I have 25 of Verdicchio and 6 of red, including Montepulciano and Sangiovese, which I blend together because Sangiovese, in this land of white wine, comes out sort of pale, and is perfect for toning down the aggressiveness of Montepulciano."

He vinifies separately and then he blends: he likes the work of the wine cellar. While we talk about vineyards, the quality of the land in the area around the Castelli, and his oldest vineyard, Riccardo, his eldest son, joins us. Ampelio introduces him to us as "the photographer." Riccardo is an architect, but to learn the art of photography for a long time he worked with Gabriele Basilico, one of Italy's greatest photographers, who recently passed away. Lately, to his father's great joy, he's been devoting some time to the family business. His other son, Roberto, is an engineer, and he works in the field of business intelligence for a hospital in Bologna. I have the feeling that Riccardo's presence here today isn't accidental. I think Ampelio deliberately asked him to come. Later on we'll discover that this is so, and the relationship between father and son will become one of the most intriguing topics of this encounter.

We get back in the car and head toward the cellar, where I will have to make my own blend. He suggested I do so as though it were a challenge and I don't want to give up on it now. I'd like to talk about Riccardo, but I don't go straight to the subject.

Oscar "Ampelio, what was your relationship with your father like?"

Ampelio "Very difficult." How could it have been any other way. This is our ninth interview and I'm getting used to stories about the difficult relationships these people in the wine business always seem to have with their fathers. And yet each story is different, it always has certain unique and very interesting features that help us to understand the transitions from one generation to the next.

Oscar "What about your children, do they have a difficult relationship with you?"

Ampelio "They did, but for different reasons. My relationship with my father was difficult because there were more than two generations between us, and he was so stubborn that sometimes he refused to listen to others. He was as stubborn as a mule! He died when I was twenty-two. When you're that young you get heated up about things quicker. Today my sons are mature men."

Oscar "So you worked with your father for a while?"

Ampelio "Not exactly. He worked for Generali insurance. In 1940, when he refused to join the Fascist Party, they fired him. He was sixty-one and like any true Marchigiano he didn't dispute the fact that they'd fired him. He just accepted it. That's the way we Buccis are. You call it gentleness. Maybe that's what it looks like on the outside. But actually sometimes what's eating us up inside isn't so gentle."

Oscar "Did you have enough time to learn certain things from your father?"

Ampelio "Luckily I did. I'm a priest-hater and a Left-winger, just like he was. But most importantly, just like he did, I interpret the value of work to the limits of madness."

Oscar "April 25, 1945, you were nine then, do you remember that day? Where were you?"

Ampelio "Yes, I do. We were living in Milan at the time and I remember the city being crowded with people. However, if this is what you want to know, my father didn't take us to see Mussolini's body in Piazzale Loreto. He thought it was too atrocious a sight to see. Violence in itself never makes much sense, wherever it comes from." There it is again, the gentleness that's always coming out. After exchanging a few words with his son Riccardo, I realize he's gentle too. The gentleness of the Buccis is passed down through the generations.

I'm Lucky to Live in the City and in the Country

As we reach the cellar Ampelio explains that in the 1950s sharecropping still existed in the Marches, and the companies that dealt with more organized and profitable cultures, such as silkworms, tobacco and animal breeding, were forced to close because of the advent of intensive farming and globalization. In those years the whole of Italy was going through a period of huge renewal, and everywhere there was a feeling of great suffering: having to close businesses that had always been there, to change one's way of working radically and organizing interpersonal relationships wasn't "pleasing—that's exactly how he put it—to anyone."

"With a degree in economics—he says smiling—I'm especially good at organizing things I don't like and managing the economic results of our winery." It's nice to meet someone who knows his own limits and doesn't take himself too seriously. Ampelio confesses that what he enjoys the most is making blends of wine in the cellar. We'd figured that one out already. But he says that after doing it for fifty years he's not as good at it as he'd like to be, it's a good thing there's Grai. What he is good at, instead, is organizing the company figures, but it's the part that warms his heart the least.

Once outside the cellar, Ampelio proudly points to Bruno, his chief cellarman. "That's Bruno over there. Bruno, when he's not down in the cellar, is always on his tractor!" The chief cellarman at Villa Bucci had never had a drop of wine and knew nothing about it until he was twenty-seven. Before that he'd worked in a mechanic's workshop. He learned under Ampelio's mentorship. He's a big, sort of mono-lithic guy with a grin. He's an Italian champion of "ruzzola," a very old game that's still played in the Marches and was played by the working classes in the late nineteenth century. The game is even mentioned in Galileo's *Dialogue Concerning the Two Chief World Systems*. The Italian province is fantastic precisely because these tra-ditions withstand the test of time, remaining unchanged over the years and making up an incredible kaleidoscope of stories to be told and to preserve. The game of *ruzzola* consists in tossing a disc about 15 centimeters in diameter, similar to a whole round of sheep's milk cheese (cheese was in fact used in the past), wrapped in twine that, after the disc has been thrown, stays in the players' hands. The per-son who throws the farthest wins. Strength and precision are needed. You can tell Bruno is very strong.

I look around. The Bucci cellar today is just as it was a long time ago, when it was only used to make the area's "bad wine." The kind that everyone made to sell wholesale without even bothering to bottle it. The cellar was built in the 1930s and it's located on a hilltop over-looking the vineyards and wheat fields. Those fields belong to Ampe-lio, who produces from 700 to 800 tons per year. Over the years, the cellar hasn't grown on the outside, despite the fact that it currently has to hold up to a huge amount of work in terms of volume. The radical change has taken place inside. About 130,000 bottles are now produced here every year, for a turnover of a million and a half euros. The eighty-year-old large oak barrels dominate beneath the curved vaults. All the vinification and fining happens right here, and it is here that Ampelio invites me to play with his wines. He gives me a glass and invites me to taste his Verdicchio 2012s, tapping some from all the barrels. He calls them by name, using the names of the vineyards which, as he told us before, he vinifies separately. In fact, all the wines are different. One by one I taste each of the vineyards.

One of the wines is more acidic, one is fatter, another one is longer, and there's one that's more fragrant. Life is a blend—I think to myself—and the better you are at blending things the more successful you'll end up being. I think about what you need for your kids, love and rigor. At work you need poetry and math. In life you have to combine honesty and shrewdness, informality and authoritativeness, self-irony and pride. If human virtues were to flow out of these barrels, the game of finding the perfect blend would never end. I find it natural to turn to Simona, the youngest among us, to say: "See Simona, don't ever be just one single predictable thing! Try to be made up of lots of different things. Predictable people are boring people!" Ampelio has understood my obsession with apparent contradictions perfectly, and adds his own thoughts: "One of my greatest fortunes is to be able to live my life between the city and the country. I need both places, it helps me to live better. In the country I can develop the farmer's attitude that tends to run deep, while in the city I have to travel fast and have to ability to simplify. This is what makes me complete."

In the meantime my mind wanders and I get lost surrounded by the barrels while Ampelio, always the good storyteller, goes back to entertaining Simona and Shigeru on the subject of the limestone in the soil, which he says he can taste in his wines. I listen to what they're saying in the background, and I disappear with Bruno whom I ask to tell me again what's inside the barrels of wine I like the best. Bruno follows me around patiently repeating the names to me. I taste them all over again, I like them, and drunk here in the cellar, where it's cool, they seem marvelous to me. In the end I make up my mind: my perfect cuvée of Verdicchio is 33% Villa vineyard, 33% Montefiore, and 33% Belluccio. If I add up the years these three vineyards have been around that makes a 120 years. I know this result has nothing to do with it, but I like to think it does. Without realizing it I chose the barrels that contain the wine that comes from the oldest vines. I thought they had a more mineral taste, I must have felt they had longer roots, as Ampelio would say. I blend them freely, pouring them from glass to glass, and I'm so satisfied with the results that I exclaim: "If you make 2,000 bottles of this cuvée for me I'll buy every single one of them! (I'm very excited). I've created a fantastic wine. Go on, taste it."

I can clearly see that Shigeru doesn't agree with me but, being Japanese, he doesn't tell me. Ampelio is the host here and he criticizes it unabashedly: "I find that it's a bit... delicate... what I mean is it doesn't have any balls."

Oscar "Really? Nooooo! It's delicious! And now I'm going to give it a name..."

Ampelio "I think it needs more character. I'd add at least 45% of the sharper of the three you chose."

Oscar "I see, you think it's too soft. Well, then, I'm going to call it 'The Soft Ampelio' and you'll see how I manage to sell it! Start thinking about the label."

Naturally, he says yes, but I've understood perfectly that he's not entirely convinced by my cuvée. It was only a game for me: I love life and I love to play games. I had as much fun as a kid would making "my" blend. It may be slightly soft, but with vineyards, that all together are a 120 years old, this wine could only have come out as subdued as an old wise man.

We have to leave. We have to go back to the Pongelli estate to taste the wines I've brought over. I wonder how I'll manage: because of the many and repeated wine-tastings I was forced to do to create my blend, it's only mid-morning and I'm already feeling rather tipsy.

Oscar "When did you decide to start making really good wine?"

Ampelio "In 1980. Until then the winemaking was needed for the Villa's upkeep: the garden needs tending to and requires the non-stop presence of two people to keep it in order both inside and outside. In those years I realized I had to find an enologist capable of making white wines. I went to the Alto Adige and met Giorgio Grai there. A legendary character! Just think that even today, at the age of eighty-two, he rides into Vinitaly on his bike! They introduced him to me as the only person capable of making a white wine that could last twenty years, and I realized he was just the person I needed. I can't say I learned how to make wine from him, but I can say that he taught me the importance of words: few, carefully chosen, simple. I still consider him to be a great master today." Without even coming right out and asking him to he's told me everything there is to know about Grai.

Oscar "And did you make all these decisions on your own? Have your sisters ever been interested in the country?"

Ampelio "Luckily, they haven't. This has made it easier for me to make decisions."

Oscar "But your relationship with them, today, what's that like?"

Ampelio "Good with both my sisters and their husbands."

Oscar "Who does the Villa Bucci cellar belong to?"

Ampelio "To all of us."

Oscar "How nice! And besides your sons, are there any other nieces or nephews who will keep the company going?"

Ampelio "Yes, there are. For all of them this winery could be a splendid opportunity."

I Don't Throw Anything Away

We're back where we first started out at the Pongelli estate. We left from here two hours ago for what was supposed to be a quick half-hour tour.

Riccardo, his son, is back with us. I tell him about my blend and get straight to the point. "Why didn't you come to the cellar?"

Riccardo "I had to take a few more pictures, I would have missed out on that particular light."

Oscar "Do you like making wine? I think your father is counting on you."

Riccardo "Yes, I think so. But I'm still not sure I'm going to go into this business."

Oscar "You're an adult now. Do you get along with your father?"

Riccardo "It's not easy." He says no more, but I get what he means. Ampelio told me that he was separated from his first wife early, when their two children were still young. And that they always lived with their mother, a wonderful mother who adored them and raised them lovingly, but without doing much to foster their relationship with their father. Then their mother died of a terrible illness and the boys became close to their father again. Clearly, it isn't easy.

Instead Claudia, Ampelio's niece, who deals with the bookkeeping, has no doubts at all about her future in wine. She's sweet and easy-going too, she likes her job. She gets along with Riccardo. They might be the right pair to run things, maybe along with their other cousins and brothers and sisters. The Buccis have a big family. The point is this: how much leeway is Professor Ampelio willing to give them? I'll continue to investigate.

Ampelio shows us the museum of farming equipment, old tractors, old vats... and he tells us that throughout his life he has always kept in mind the buzzwords "reuse, reduce, recycle." He proudly says: "I don't throw anything away." Old barrels, old vineyards, a museum of equipment. I observe our host closely: at first sight it looks like we're both dressed the same way, comfortable trousers and a light sweater. But actually there's something about Ampelio that reflects his conservative spirit to a tee. His sweater has been around for several vintages and goodness knows how many harvests, his trousers are sturdy and of a shade that doesn't change much after the long dusty walks in the country or the affectionate assaults of pet dogs and cats. His shoes are an amazing discovery. I hadn't noticed them until now. They're old loafers, whose color can no longer be distinguished, but still serve their original purpose. Why throw them out? Ampelio proudly tells us: "I've been wearing them for fifty-six years, I remember perfectly well that I bought them when I started studying at the university, I was twenty then."

Riccardo "You see? He's a tightwad!"

Oscar "No, he's not. It's an apparent contradiction. Your father deals with fashion, yet at the same time he's capable of wearing old clothing that's still in good condition with pride and style. I've always thought of him as being a very elegant man."

Shigeru watches, Simona is delighted. At that point, to avoid being too much on the side of Bucci the father, I say: "But I find the three buzzwords 'reuse, reduce and recycle' to be too limited. I'd suggest adding a fourth: 'revive.' If you don't revive you don't get anywhere."

Ampelio doesn't agree with me, he's more conse.vative. He acts in line with his ideas and he'd like his sons to act according to his input. But children often want to do things differently from their fathers, they want to do things their own way. It's time for me to plunge the knife in, so I say: "Your sons are the thing you love the most in the world. Let them do what they want. Let them make mistakes, but at least let them find their own path. Teach them your greatest quality, gentleness, and you'll see how grateful they'll be." "It's not easy..."

he replies. I know it's not easy. It's impossible to be a perfect father, just as it's impossible to make the perfect wine. But each day you keep trying to, don't you?

Oscar "Don't think it's any easier for me, I have three sons." And as I say these words I think that maybe it's harder for them, for my three sons. That's what I think, but I don't say it out loud.

A Fellowship of Conscious Drinkers, or Almost So

At last we're seated around a table for our tasting. Riccardo is sitting next to me and we feel good about it. We're in harmony.

Like every time we gather around the table, Shigeru's minutious, painstaking rites begin: the bottles are opened and they are arranged next to each other in the order in which we'll taste them, so that the labels are clearly visible to him and to the other guests. By now we're familiar with his rites, such as the way he adjusts the glasses, because hardly ever does Shigeru leave them the way they are on the table. And the fact that he always asks for some cold water and then takes a seat. When Shigeru sits down he closes himself off inside a bubble and appears to stop listening to the conversation, until it's time to describe the wines.

The first wine we drink is Monterotondo 2009 produced by Villa Sparina, a Cortese di Gavi from vines that are seventy years old, like the ones today's crew likes.

Ampelio is the first one to talk and he says it's "A wine with a great aroma, which tells you right away that it's a good wine. It has a mineral nature that I really like. But I'm convinced that the aroma is truly great."

Shigeru speaks up solemnly. The nose is pear, vanilla and citrus fruits. The mouthfeel is fat and rich, with an almost buttery flavor. Butter! I would never have thought of that, but now that I do think about it he's right. As usual he hits the nail on the head. Riccardo compares it to Bucci Riserva because, he says, it's a full-bodied, round wine. Back to Shigeru who even dares to compare it to a beautiful woman, slightly ostentatious and well made-up. He says it would go well with clam soup with butter, fresh Roman pecorino cheese, pasta with sardines and Japanese tempura seasoned with salt and lemon. My contribution is to sing the praises of the three Moccagattas, Stefano, Massimo and their sister Tiziana, the producers. Stefano is an old, genuine friend of mine. The Moccagattas are marketing geniuses. I tell them, among other things, about how they invented an amazing bottle and label. Their wines may be good, but their greatest quality is the fact that they're immediately and uniquely recognizable on the shelf.

We move on to the second wine, the one made by another great friend of mine: Mimmo Casillo. The Castel del Monte Chiancarosa 2011 rosé, made by his winery, Masseria San Magno, in Murgia. The vineyards are near Castel del Monte, for a one-of-a-kind panorama.

Mimmo shares the winery with his brothers Francesco and Pasquale. We're talking about the Casillos of durum wheat fame. They own countless mills and have a say at an international level as concerns the durum wheat market. Mimmo is the middle brother and he deals with the diversification. Which always aims for high quality food. Including wine. They use neither weed killers nor chemical fertilizers, and the amount of added sulfites is usually very low.

Ampelio again makes the first comment, saying that in this wine he tastes the elegance of the South, its pungent odors, that southern brashness that you forgive because it's synonymous with spontaneity and being attached to one's roots. This gets us talking about our South, that of the Mediterranean, of the past 3,000 or more years of history that you can still breathe there, and the dominations that came and went, cross-pollinating amazing territories and deep-rooted traditions.

Oscar "What do you think of the Northern League?" I'm an expert at the Pindaric flight.

Ampelio doesn't seem be thrown off and he shoots back: "As someone from Milan I can tell you I'm shocked by some of the characters in the League. But the idea is quite innovative and stimulating, even though there still isn't a truly Federalist formula that we can put into practice. Our country isn't ready, we can't separate from the South." With these words we digress a little. I ask Riccardo whom he voted for, whether he was influenced more by his mother or his father for his basic values. He hems and haws, tells me about his mother's illness, how the arguments and differences of opinion between his mother and father suddenly evaporated before her terminal illness.

We go back to the wine as if driven by the desire to return to the merry atmosphere that wine always creates.

Shigeru starts in again: "It's a rosé wine, but it would seem to be a young red wine. The nose is apricot, hay, pear. It has a fair amount of minerality and just the right amount of acidity. You can tell it has a red-grape base, in fact, it's made with Uva di Troia and some Montepulciano. I'd pair it with fish, but also with cold cuts, pizza margherita, ricotta made from sheep's milk seasoned with oil, salt, pepper and some cooked must. In Japan I'd drink it with seven-spice chicken kebabs." Kebabs again! I'm hungry, it's noon.

Ampelio "This rosé is so nice I'd drink it cool as an apéritif."

Riccardo "Let me add that I can taste a very aromatic note, maybe that's why my father would like to drink it as an apéritif." Good, I think everyone enjoyed it, but, let me say it again, I think it's a really good wine to drink, and so I do just that, emptying the glass into my mouth, naturally.

I'm gloating now, thinking about how I'm going to get him to drink the poorest wine from Langa, Dolcetto! In Langa, we were raised on bread, salami and Dolcetto, the table wine. The one I brought here today is a very special Dolcetto though, Vigna del Pilone Superiore 2010 produced by San Romano.

Oscar "Dolcetto is the name of the vine, because when you taste the grapes they're sweet, then you vinify them and the wine becomes dry. One of the best areas for Dolcetto grapes is Dogliani, which borders on Novello, Barolo, Monforte, the towns where Barolo is produced. In 1933, when a division was made to identify the original zones of the grapes used to produce Barolo, the town of Dogliani was left out. So Dolcetto instead of Nebbiolo was planted in Dogliani, on the land with the best southern exposure, and the wine they make is fantastic. Many years ago I bought the San Romano winery, which has a tower known as 'Il Pilone' at the very top of a beautiful hill, which rises high above the others. The vineyards get the sun on all sides." I speak of this place with great pride because I really like the location, the winery and the wine! I let them keep talking—who knows whether they'll be influenced by my self-praise—while I enjoy the Dolcetto, and dream about a couple of anchovies seasoned with basil and parsley: it would be a wonderful prelude to a lunch that won't be long in coming now. Ampelio has decided to take me to

Senigallia to see our friend Moreno Cedroni. He definitely isn't a tightwad! Moreno will make sure I get my anchovies!

Ampelio "The aroma is interesting and fruity, almost herbaceous. The flavor is acidic characterized by fresh, sharp tannins. I'm no expert, but maybe it needs a little more time. It tastes like wine that should be drunk while eating, possibly at lunchtime."

Oscar "Of course it does! To be drunk while eating anchovies on buttered bread, along with salami, and peppers: simple dishes. I agree! What do you think Shigeru?"

Shigeru "First of all, it has a nice intense purple color that's very clean and sharp. The aroma is violet, rose, dry red fruit and moss. The mouthfeel is warm and dry with soft tannins and just the right amount of acidity. I would pair it with cold cuts, Bra, but not the aged kind, pan-fried pork with *salsa verde* and with all those soft, fatty Piedmontese dishes that need to be balanced by an aggressive wine. This wine is a hard-working country woman: your everyday companion."

We've almost come to the end of our visit and as I taste the last two wines I want to talk about the future, the way I always do; just like the past, it's always a stimulating subject. "The present doesn't exist—I say—because as I say these words it's already past. What will happen soon is already the future. We've already talked about the past, so as we taste this Amarone let's talk about the future. Hear me out: Barolo makes 12 million bottles of which 68% are sold abroad. Amarone makes 17 million bottles of which 93% are sold abroad! The whole world is crazy about Amarone, and this 'wretched' wine is still growing. I've brought you some Amarone Valpolicella 2008 produced by Allegrini because I adore Marilisa Allegrini. So what I want to hear now are a few words on this Amarone and 200 on your future. Go for it!"

Ampelio "Well... this isn't your typical Amarone with its traditional fruit jam flavor."

Oscar "That's because Marilisa wanted it to be different! She knows how to look beyond things!"

Ampelio "She was right to weaken it. It's definitely more elegant. It has nothing to do with the kind of Amaraone the Germans like; while they know a lot about beer, they'd pair Amarone that tastes like jam with a fillet of sole! Don't ask me why everyone in the world likes it. Maybe for their cuisines..."

Oscar "Riccardo, what's your take on this?"

Riccardo "I'm not an expert, I've only drunk it a few times. It's definitely pleasing. Maybe, it's sort of hard to digest on an empty stomach. No one would drink it as an apéritif... at this time of day, before lunch, I prefer the Dolcetto we had before."

Oscar "Shigeru, tell us all about this Amarone, how would you describe it?"

Shigeru "I can see that none of you appreciate Amarone. Today it's possibly the most popular Italian wine in the world. And the reason for this is that it's a great wine. You ought to be more respectful of it."

That's exactly how he worded it, a modal verb followed by a comparative, incredible.

Shigeru "The color is typically very concentrated. As for aroma, vanilla, leather, dry fruit. The minerality that takes you back to the stones, the land, cocoa and coffee. It's persistent, but it's also delicate. I would pair it with braised meat, aged toma, or with a nice rare steak dressed with soy sauce and Japanese mustard. And if I were to compare it to a woman, this wine is a career woman, like the ones you meet in the Milan underground in the morning."

I wonder why Shigeru feels like talking about women today. It's strange, he's usually very reserved and discreet. Funny.

The wine made by Ampelio that we're about to taste is Villa Bucci Riserva 2004. But first, I insist, I want to talk about the future!

Ampelio "It's hard to talk about the future. My future is short, Ampelio Bucci's future, I mean. But it's also true that the future belongs to those who remain. And the future also belongs to these wines of ours, and I can't say what will happen to these wines over the next twenty years... you need time to understand, and I need more time to think about it."

It's easy to see that these days Ampelio is busy trying to design the future of Villa Bucci and doesn't want to show his hand of cards. Then there's his son, maybe he still doesn't know what he wants to do; how well I understand him.

Oscar "I had the great fortune of befriending Tonino Guerra in 2000, when he was eighty. He was the greatest scriptwriter and one of the most important poets of the twentieth century. He kept telling me how happy he was about his old age because he finally had time to reflect, think, meditate, laze about and observe. 'At my age even a sunset is marvelous' he'd say. He enjoyed the time he had!"

Ampelio "As long as your mind's still working you're fine. As long as you don't become an old show-off, and the secret is never to stop being brave. And the land helps you with this…" Ampelio is lost in his thoughts, I realize that maybe, if we were alone, it would be different. As I think about it I instinctively pour the last wine into my glass. I do so repeating a gesture that this morning I did over and over again. With a distracted twist of the wrist I hint at the movement one does to oxygenate the wine, I raise the glass to my mouth without smelling it and I drink. And then I drink again. What a wine this is! "You're a devil! Did you know that 2004 was this good? This is the last one but it wipes all the others out! How many bottles of Villa Bucci 2004 do you have?"

Ampelio "Maybe 1,500. But I'm not sure."

Oscar "So you'll sell me 200?"

Ampelio "Are you kidding, it costs a fortune. You can't afford it!" He winks at me and I play along, I try to bargain with him a little… while he goes back to the fact that what counts is the miracle of time, he goes back to the wine that makes itself, to the vintages that are all different. The mystery of wine and the miracle of nature. Walter Massa said it was "the balancing point above the madness." I think about it again and it seems even more true.

Ampelio "This 2004 is shinier and more brilliant than our new wine. It's the product of the stabilization that comes from the old barrels. A wine like this one is the result of mysterious factors, the most important of which is our hope…"

Oscar "It's a luminous wine. Shigeru, what do you think of it?"

Shigeru "The color ranges from straw to yellow. I can smell mineral salts and honey with vanilla, apricot, and it's herbaceous. Also toasted almonds with good sapidity. The body is just right and the acidity well balanced. The flavors are long and they stimulate your appetite. It's best drunk with shellfish, *acqua pazza*, fish stew, pork cutlets cooked in lemon juice and an assortment of grilled white meat."

I can't take it anymore. I'm starving. Ever since Ampelio mentioned we'd be having lunch at Moreno Cedroni's I haven't been able to think of anything else.

Oscar "Let's go, Ampelio. We'll talk about other things over lunch, things I won't write about. But, please, get two more bottles of Villa Bucci 2004, let's take them over to Moreno's."

Notes for Wines Tasted with Ampelio Bucci
Shigeru Hayashi

Gavi del Comune di Gavi Monterotondo 2009 Villa Sparina
Type white wine
Grapes 100% Cortese
Vinification and fining cryomaceration for 24 hours in stainless
steel; 4 months in barriques, 4 months of steel and 1 year in bottles
Production area Piedmont

Bright golden color with light green hues. The aroma features hints
of fruit (pear, citrus fruits) with a vanilla backdrop and interesting
hints of minerality. The taste is soft, sapid, endowed with body
but elegant and extremely enjoyable.

Pair with clam soup, pasta with sardines, fresh Romano pecorino.
I think it can be served with Japanese tempura sprinkled with salt
and lemon.

Maybe it's the most famous Gavi in the world, even if the
production of this selection is very limited and the wine isn't easy
to understand. But when are the most interesting things ever simple
as well? Just think of women! In any case, compliments go to the
Moccagatta family for having always believed in the quality of Gavi,
even when no one else did.

Castel del Monte Chiancarosa 2011 Agricola del Sole
Type rosé
Grapes Uva di Troia and some Montepulciano
Vinification and fining soft pressing of the grapes, fermentation
at controlled temperature, 5 months of fining in steel
Production area Puglia

Intense, bright cherry red color. The aroma is raspberry, cherry,
red currant, licorice and wild herbs. Dry taste, with hints
of saltiness and just the right amount of acidity.

I'd pair it with a fish stew or pizza, marinara-style. Excellent with
chicken kebabs seasoned with seven types of spices. The truth
of the matter is it goes down well with a full light meal.

One of the most delicious rosés I've ever tasted! Simply perfect.
In the summertime this is the only wine I ever want to drink,
and to think it comes from one of the most beautiful lands in
the world, at the foot of the magnificent castle of Frederick II,
who had others (modestly) refer to him, in Latin, as "Stupor Mundi."

Dolcetto di Dogliani Vigna del Pilone 2010 San Romano
Type red wine
Grapes 100% Dolcetto
Vinification and fining steel vats with control of the fermentation
temperature (25/30 °C). Wine extracted from must after 5/10 days.
Induced malolactic fermenation completed before winter. Fining
for 2 months in bottles
Production area Piedmont

Intense ruby color with purplish hues. Intense aromas: I can smell
prune, herbs, violet and hints of wine. Dry taste with soft tannins
and well-balanced alcohol.

I'd pair it with some mixed appetizers, pan-fried pork dressed with
salsa verde, cheese such as Bra or Asiago, better if it's aged.

Why do they call it Dolcetto when it's one of the bitterest wines in the world? I used to wonder about it all the time, and then I discovered that the grapes are sort of sweet, and for the first time ever I can say you Italians aren't so strange after all! The San Romano vineyards are gorgeous: they start from the riverbed and clamber up 700 meters. This wine is a hard-working country woman: your everyday companion.

Amarone della Valpolicella Classico 2008 Allegrini
Type red wine
Grapes Corvina, Corvinone, Rondinella, Oseleta
Vinification and fining grapes are dried under cover until December, pressing in January, maturation 18 months in barriques, then blended together and aged for an additional 7 months, followed by a minimum of 14 months' rest in bottles
Production area Veneto

Very intense ruby red color. Aromas of pulpy red fruit such as cherry, prune, and raisins. I can taste minerals and coffee, cocoa, clove. The mouthfeel is robust, but with velvety tannin. Splendid concentration of fruit.

Pair with meat braised in Amarone, steak dressed with soy sauce and Japanese mustard, any type of game, aged toma.

A spectacular wine to be drunk in the heart of winter in the company of the right person, sitting in front of the fireplace. Its 15.5 degrees proof might put you off, but you really don't feel them. Actually, the wine seems "suspended" in its grace and harmony. If I had to compare it to a woman, I'd say a career woman, like the ones you meet in the Milan underground in the morning.

Verdicchio dei Castelli di Jesi Classico Villa Bucci Riserva 2004
Type white wine
Grapes 100% Verdicchio
Vinification and fining at least 18 months in large Slavonian oak
barrels, followed by 1 year in bottle
Production area Marches

Light straw color. As for aroma, the fragrance of ripe fruit is
unveiled, as well as honey, vanilla, flint and sage. Sapid, balanced
and persistent taste. Good mineral finish.

To be paired with fish, shellfish and grilled lobster especially.
Excellent with white meats such as veal medallions cooked
in lemon or charcoaled chicken kebabs. It would be perfect with
Japanese cuisine: I'm thinking of tempura, but also sushi.

I have an idea for this white wine. I'm going to take it to Japan for
the next "Kawadoko." It's a celebratory dinner held on the banks
of the Kamogawa, the river that crosses Kyoto. There are always
lots of women there, and this wine is seductive, because it's strong,
elegant, but forthright. Just the way they like it!

Lungarotti: Teresa and Chiara
The Miracle of Complementariness

We are about to witness a miracle. The miracle of complementariness. Today we will discover the story of a couple, Giorgio and his wife Maria Grazia, so magically complementary that they were able to bring success to a winery, create museums and be active in the world of culture. This story, after Giorgio passed away, has lived on thanks to the miracle of complementariness that is perpetuated in his two daughters, Teresa and Chiara. So "equally" complementary between themselves they have ensured the continuation of that same success. Without this evident complementariness it would probably have been impossible to uphold this identity and achieve these results in such a special winery.

We're Half-Sisters, or "Demi-Soeurs," As They Say in French

Torgiano, province of Perugia. The 5,000 years of the history of wine are enclosed in the Wine Museum in Palazzo Graziani Baglioni: a museum rivaled by very few others in the world! Archeological findings, art objects and technical equipment for viticulture and vinification. Collections of medieval, Renaissance, Baroque and contemporary ceramics; antiquarian books, Italian "waffle" makers, engravings, contemporary sculptures and a section dedicated to the use of wine in medicine delve into the Dionysian legend and the occasions for drinking. To whom is all this due? To Giorgio Lungarotti and Maria Grazia Marchetti. He was the founder of the cellar, son of the landowners, with a degree in Agricultural Sciences from Perugia, and a bold experimenter in both the vineyard and the cellar. Alongside his work to recuperate and valorize autochthonous vines, his job was to select and adapt new varieties, according to and even anticipating enological trends. His wife, sixteen years younger, was an art historian. In 1974 they founded the Wine Museum. In 1987 they breathed life into the Fondazione Lungarotti, dedicated to the valorization of the great cultural heritage linked to Italian agriculture. In 2000, a year after Giorgio's passing, the Olive and Olive Oil Museum opened, which they had conceived and designed together. Giorgio died in 1999 after having been nominated Cavaliere del Lavoro (Order of Merit for Labor). And he truly deserved it: he was eighty-nine and getting ready to go to work! He left behind three marvelous women: his wife Maria Grazia, his daughter Chiara (he had become a father for the first time when he was sixty-one) and Teresa Severini, Maria Grazia's daughter from her previous marriage to the magistrate Luigi Severini. Ying and Yang, land and sky, male and female… Chiara and Teresa, half-sisters. One more determined, the other gentler: together the perfect pair. The utmost expression of complementariness.

The first of the sisters we meet is Teresa: she is one of the first female enologists in Italy, and someone who has created wines that bear her signature for the Lungarotti cellar. She's the mother of three children, founder of the association "Le Donne del Vino," and since 2011 she has been President of POST, Perugia's museum of science and technology. A beautiful woman the same age as me but (and I'm not just trying to pay her a compliment) who definitely looks much younger than fifty-nine. She's the one who takes us on a tour of the museum created, she says, "by my mother."

Oscar "Where is your mother?"

Teresa "At a meeting, she's giving a talk… otherwise she would have come here personally to show you around."

Oscar "When was she born?"

Teresa "1926, but she's incredibly dynamic, totally active at the Foundation!"

Oscar "Eighty-six and she's giving talks. She must be a toughie."

Teresa "Yes, she sets an example. Looking at her makes you feel like doing your very best, but in a natural way, just like her: with no obligation. I joined the business when I felt like it, no one expected me to."

Giorgio Lungarotti comes to mind again: he was the head of the company to the very end, so I ask: "You were forty-five when you took over the helm, when he died, is that correct?"

Teresa "I had already been working for the winery for many years, but when Giorgio—she calls him Giorgio and never "Father," of course—passed away, it was Chiara who became CEO. I was a liaison between Giorgio and my sister. He was a male chauvinist, but with Chiara and me he had to give in to the cold facts: it was either us or no one else in the family. So he always had lots of trust in us. He was stubborn by nature, but he was also a man who knew how to listen."

She describes Giorgio to us as someone who had the insight of a genius. He ended all the sharecropping contracts, like Gaja's father had, and gave his workers new jobs with salaried contracts. Teresa talks about his generosity, his desire to do business with no holds barred (from peaches to mink breeding!), about his practicality alongside the incredible inquisitiveness that encouraged him to travel around Europe so that he could understand the world of wine and learn more. "He and my mother were an exceptional couple: so different, so close and perfectly complementary: one of them flew, the other acted."

Oscar "You and Chiara have the same mother."

Teresa "Of course. We're half-sisters, *demi-soeurs*, as they say in French, which sounds even sweeter." Sweetness is Teresa's distinctive trait.

Oscar "How old was Giorgio when he married your mother?"

Teresa "Fifty-five. He was a prized bachelor: he'd never been married or lived with anyone. We were neighbors, his land bordering on ours. We were just good neighbors until he got to know my mother better; she was thirty-nine at the time and gorgeous... She'd been a widow for many years."

Oscar "So what happened? Did he court her?"

Teresa "I'd say yes, but very discreetly. At the time, with two small children—me and my older brother—my mother didn't have an easy life: she was a teacher, and at the same time she managed the farm on her own. But she was very curious and had lots of interests. Reserved and fascinating. Then Giorgio burst onto the scene and their love story was born. I never suffered because my mother always fueled the cult of my father. My brother Giuseppe followed in his footsteps and became a magistrate and Councilor of State."

Her voice dampens when she mentions her father. Teresa speaks naturally and her eyes are so beautifully bright that you feel comforted. I ask her to give us a "Cliff Notes" tour of the museum. I wish I hadn't used that expression: Cliff Notes. The Lungarotti wine museum is famous but, somewhat shamefully, I have to admit that when I was in high school those study aids for books like *The Betrothed* and *The Divine Comedy* came in real handy. She realizes we have very little time and accepts uncomplainingly. She loves talking about Giorgio's and her mother's work. Even today it's the inexhaustible drive of her mother's tireless work to expand and delve further into the study of wine, and it is her search to acquire new objects that makes the museum collections more precious and complete from year to year. The museum teaches us about history and the civilization of the vine and wine. It's a private museum, but there isn't a single Lungarotti bottle or label, no mention of the family cellar, no logo. We walk up and down through the twenty or so rooms of Palazzo Baglioni. The museum has about 18,000 visitors per year. I think the number is pretty low if we consider the uniqueness of this place, and the first thing that comes to mind is that it must be expensive for a family to manage a private heritage such as this one. In France it would no doubt have become an example of national pride publicized the world over. Here instead it's all thanks to the generosity and love of wine of two philanthropists.

Teresa is an expert guide and at every opportunity she shows how proud she is, and rightly so, of the objects housed in the museum. From Etruscan art to Gio Ponti to Jean Cocteau the tour begins and ends much too quickly for me not to feel like coming back again and taking it in more slowly. I'll come back for sure. And for now I just want to tell you, the reader, if you love wine, not to miss out on this wonderful place.

There was Nothing in Torgiano

Teresa "The cellar, the way you see it today, is the result of lots of enlargements and renovations, but it was actually started up in 1962. Here in Torgiano we don't even have a trattoria! Giorgio and Mamma were two amazing pioneers. They were so ahead of the times that some of their ideas weren't understood: such as the free wine tasting of the local wines... the only people who'd go were the old towns-people to have themselves a glass!"

Oscar "When did you start working for the winery?"

Teresa "In 1979."

Oscar "How many harvests have you done?"

Teresa "This year is the thirty-fourth."

While Teresa talks to us we reach the cellar where Chiara is waiting for us. Forty-two, an agronomist, the mother of a six-year-old boy. She lives in Torgiano (because that's where she works), but she sleeps—she uses the verb "sleep"—in Perugia where she has a house. I'm struck by the image of a woman totally dedicated to work who only associates the nighttime to her home, and I know this will come up again. She's the CEO of the various Gruppo Lungarotti wineries: the "Cantina Giorgio Lungarotti Srl," the Resort & Spa "Le Tre Va-selle," the Farms in Torgiano and Montefalco and "Scap Srl," the energy company founded in 1948. She has a degree in Agricultural Sciences, and a graduate degree in Viticulture. She feels "profoundly Umbrian," and as soon as she sees us she takes over the tour of the cellar. I look around: there are vineyards as far as the eye can see, all of which owned by them.

Oscar "How many hectares do you have?"

Chiara "In Montefalco we have 20 hectares, all around the cellar. Here in Torgiano we have 230, again all around here, and on Brufa hill—you can see the crest from here—we have our Rubesco vine-yards. Added to these are the lands where the Monticchio vineyard grows, it's our best cru, where Rubesco Riserva comes from.

Oscar "So you make 2 million bottles here?"

Chiara "Yes, last year maybe even a few more than that!"

Chiara is energetic both spiritually and physically. She leads us around the cellar at a good pace, so much so that even she's breath-less. She jokes about it and says she's in "great shape," while I go back to thinking over her words. She only goes home to sleep, no way does she find the time for sports or taking walks, or devoting time to herself, as some women say. I've already figured her out: she's like me, we take our work by the horns, we throw ourselves into our work, and if there isn't any work to do then we invent it! Teresa was very athletic when she was young: skiing, tennis and sailing. Chiara, too, I assume, must have done sports, but I have a hunch that for some time now she's set aside all vain ambition.

Oscar "Do you make more white or red wine?"

Chiara "Around Torgiano there's a slight prevalence of white grapes: Trebbiano, Grechetto, Vermentino, Chardonnay and Pinot Grigio. The red grapes grow on the hillside: Colorino, Canaiolo, Sangiovese, Cabernet Sauvignon, Syrah and Merlot."

Oscar "Listen, Chiara, your father was born in 1910 when the Fascists were in power, how did he react to that?"

Chiara "He minded his own business. Just think, he was even under house arrest because he hadn't gone to the meetings of the GUF, young Fascist university students. He was working and he didn't want to waste time. But after that he wasn't oblivious to politics, quite the opposite! He was the first Republican mayor of Torgiano, Partito Repubblicano Italiano (PRI), even though he hated making speeches. He did that for two years."

Oscar "So he was in politics too. You wouldn't believe how many vintners are involved in politics!"

As we speak I can't stop looking around. I see row after row of wooden barrels and I can't help asking which wines they're for.

Chiara "The large barrels are for Rubesco, which is a medium-bodied Sangiovese. We use the barriques for Rubesco Riserva, the others are for white wines."

Chiara is always the first to answer, she takes all the space she needs and dominates the scene. Teresa steps in every now and then, but always gently and only to finish off her sister's answers.

We also walk through the shade of the beautiful grottoes for refining the wine until the tour ends and we sit down around a table for the tasting.

I Used to Graze in His Office

Much more than half-sisters, I think to myself. Teresa and Chiara show their strength in the assertion of their similarities and in the need for their differences. They are the mirror image of each other, just as they are complete opposites. The feelings that bind them together are the stuff that endless relationships are made of. I think, for instance, about my parents and theirs, even though they are the "daughters" of a relationship that began late in life. They're neither stepsisters nor half-sisters. They're "ultra-sisters" because they choose each other every day. They don't have the exact same blood, but what does it matter after all? These are my thoughts while both of them fuss around the table to bring glasses for the water and the wine. I wonder if Shigeru can imagine what I'm feeling. Without waiting for my go-ahead he takes the space he needs to comment on the wine. I'm surprised, but I soon understand why. Shigeru—or Hayashi, as Chiara calls him, constantly addressing him—is an old acquaintance of the Lungarotti family. He knew Giorgio, and is also very familiar with Maria Grazia. Before we got to Torgiano, while I was driving, he entertained us with his description of the beauties of the museum, and you might say he was the one to "guide" us to our meeting with Teresa, who was waiting for us at the highway exit. He's been to Torgiano on numerous occasions and, by his own admission, he feels at home here.

Shigeru Hayashi, the Italian wine specialist, whom I've brought with me on this trip, also has a very interesting personal story, which easily explains why many of our producers know him well and have great respect for him. He was born in Shizuoka-ken, Japan, in 1954. He earned a degree in Business and Economics at the state university in 1978. In 1982 he was already in Milan working for Suntory Ltd., a company he'd been hired by right after graduating. From that moment on he would spend long periods of time in Italy, first as head of the Suntory restaurant in Milan, and then as chief representative for the same company.

His journeys back and forth between Italy and Japan have made him one of the finest connoisseurs of Italian food and wine. He has racked up a series of prizes in Italy as well as publications on themes closest to his heart: wine, food, tourist welcoming. Until 2005, the year he founded Soloitalia Co. Ltd. (Wine & Food Business Consulting) and headed it. Currently, he's president of Eataly Japan.

Actually, Shigeru has spent half of his working life making his many Italian customers get to know and appreciate Japanese cuisine, and the other half explaining the secrets of Italian wine and food to his fellow Japanese. There's no doubt about it: Shigeru is the perfect example of intercultural integration. But not just that, because his work has also been consolidated in real commercial ventures designed to spread

Italian products in Japan, which, also thanks to him, are now very popular and sought after.

An authentic, important story that I really like, and that makes me realize that during this trip each and every comment he makes is permeated with that ability to overcome ethnic and cultural barriers, and to introduce precious cross-pollinations by means of the wine-food pairings that are as bold as they are right on cue. The Lungarottis know this, and just like me they await his remarks with great interest. He speaks up and these are his words to the people listening to him: "Let's start with 2011 Sanct Valentin produced by San Michele Appiano, a Gewürztraminer." It's just like he's on stage! He says the color is straw with green hues. "The nose—he continues—is fresh fruit, like pear or apple. And you can smell wild herbs, flint, pepper and nutmeg." The taste is dry, sapid and perfectly aromatic like the best Gewürztraminers. "It should be paired with grilled dry-salted fish or even shellfish, mushroom salad, eel marinated in rice vinegar served with Japanese mustard. It can even be served as an apéritif." And I picture him bowing before the audience applauding him enthusiastically.

I jump right back in because I don't want to lose the attention of my two hosts.

Oscar "Chiara, how much time did you spend with your father? Did you manage to enjoy his company? He was old..."

Chiara "Yes, when I was very young I used to *graze* in his office or go with him to the country." When she uses the expression "to graze" we all burst out laughing, even Shigeru gets it, maybe because he knows what she means. Chiara uses the expression "to graze" to describe her earliest relationship with her father: the verb is generally used to say that one "tends to the animals" or takes the sheep out to pasture. What she means in this case is that her father nourished her with food, both material and spiritual. To educate. Chiara was educated by spending time close to her father when he was working in the office. It makes sense, now that I see her as she is today.

Chiara "My father had hoped I'd be a boy because I was born when he was getting on in years. It was his last chance, so to speak. Instead, he had to be content with another girl. Teresa was already seventeen by then."

Teresa, the sweet one, speaks up: "But he always had great respect for us."

Chiara "Ah yes, he was very proud of us. And he was proud of our mother, too! They did everything together. Trips to France, to understand the 'great masters' trade, which they took together. This also had a romantic side to it. They complemented each other and their differences of opinion were always constructive. He was more practical, she was more devoted to culture; mother's a stickler; father wanted to decide things fast." And the two of them go on about the moments in Chiara's childhood.

Oscar "From 1962 until today has the winery grown at a regular pace?"

Chiara "It has, more or less, also thanks to the exporting side that began at the tail end of the 1960s."

Oscar "So working for this winery was your first real work experience, right?"

Teresa "Yes! I cut my teeth working in the cellar. I started with the harvest of 1979: I'd work until ten o'clock at night, partly to learn, and partly to show everybody that I had what it took to do the job. On top of that, the presence of a woman in the cellar (and I was the first in ours) brought order to everything."

Oscar "How many bottles were you producing at the time?"

Teresa "In 1979 we were making about a million. There were very few people working in the cellar, all of whom had a lot of experience. Succeeding in carving out a place for myself even if some of my ideas were very new was like winning a bet!"

Oscar "How did production grow after that?"

Chiara "For about a dozen years, until the early 1990s, production hadn't grown. Then a series of innovations began. I brought my own too, especially in the country. We changed the layout of the vineyards and overhauled the pruning techniques. And we bought new land: since then we've doubled our production."

At this point I can't hold it back anymore and, turning to Teresa, I say the first thing that came to my mind when I met Chiara "She's Giorgio with a skirt on!" Teresa laughs sweetly, nodding in agreement. Shigeru agrees as well. Chiara, however, disagrees—ultimately confirming my impression: "Who me? No way! I'm sweet, gentle and compliant." She says so with a menacing look and a tone so peremptory that only the cheerfulness of her smiling eyes manages to soften her words. Yes, Chiara is definitely Giorgio Lungarotti.

The Taste We've Become Accustomed to Is Our "Madeleine"

Oscar "But did Giorgio, this special person whom the two of you absolutely adore, love you or the company more?"

I assumed they'd think about it for a while, and it would have been interesting to have if not two completely different answers, at least ones with different nuances. Instead, they answered right away and in unison: "He didn't make any distinction!" The fact that he didn't make any distinction means they were on the same level for him. But it also means that in his eyes, Teresa and Chiara were the company. Everything he did was actually for them, that's why he didn't distinguish between them and the company.

Second act: Shigeru takes the stage again to talk to us about the second wine: today he's his own man. He's playing a part he knows by heart, at the same time peeking at the script with his notes. He's a true performer and even his tone of voice today seems more self-assured and firm. He feels right at home, and a person who feels at home knows where he or she stands in the world, and finds a sort of inner peace, all to the advantage of his or her relationship with others. This is how Shigeru is today.

Shigeru "This wine is Arnus 2011, produced by the Cantine del Castello di Santa Vittoria in Alba. It's a Langhe Arneis. So at least 85% Arneis, the rest is Chardonnay. It's one of Oscar's wines. Intense straw color with light green reflections. The aroma is fruity, like pear, green apple, pineapple, and wild herbs, too. It has a dry, aromatic and sapid taste. The finish is very pleasing. It's a 'democratic' wine because it goes well with many occasions and many people. It pairs well with fish salad, Genoese pesto, Catalan-style lobster, mackerel pickled in rice vinegar with soy sauce. But this wine is also good as an apéritif or wine for the whole meal. We sell a lot of it in Japan."

Oscar "You're really on the ball today, Shigeru! Did you notice how quiet everyone was while you were speaking? The ladies were enthralled. Be honest, are you giving it all you've got because you know them?"

Shigeru smiles, but it's Chiara who speaks up to save him from his blushing: "No, Mr. Hayashi, for as long as I've known him, has always been very professional. He's one of the best wine tasters I know."

Oscar "I agree. That's why I brought him along. But today he seems to have outdone himself."

We go back to the subject of Lungarotti. "Which of you makes wine today? Do you have an enologist?" Teresa answers first, confirming the fact that they're two distinct people, but it's as if they were one because of the way they complete each other.

Teresa "The wine we make today is the result of the taste Giorgio got us used to. That taste of wine, which we clearly remember, is our *madeleine*."

Oscar "Of course, like Proust's *madeleine*! One of Proust's great insights was understanding that smell and taste play a key role in remembering and the recovery of memories. Taste and smell are the only two senses that are connected to the hippocampus, which is the center of long-term memory. So in the back of your mind is the memory of the flavor of Giorgio's wines, and this way you also manage to impress the style on today's wines, too. Right?"

Teresa "Yes, that's right. We're both technically specialized and have the skills that allow us to convey our personality to the wine. We're capable of coordinating the work of our team, and we know what to ask for and how to ask for it. In the cellar you have to know how to speak the right language. Our wine today is made with one eye on the past, the *madeleine*, and one on the future. Research and science help us a lot today."

Chiara "That's right. Giorgio's great insights still exist today because they are part of a dimension that's open to what's new."

Oscar "Giorgio never had any doubts about whether or not you'd succeed?"

Chiara "I'm not sure…"

Teresa "I'm not either. Maybe we should ask our mother."

Oscar "My impression is that he didn't. The two of you together are strong."

Chiara "Who knows. In any case, we never talked about it directly."

Oscar "These are things you just feel. As my friend Beppe Rinaldi says, you women don't need words, you have feelers!" Teresa smiles, sweetly as always.

Chiara "If you really want to understand how our father related to the future, I can tell you that a few years before he died he decided to plant a walnut grove. It takes thirty years for a walnut grove to be ready for cutting. He always carried on with his projects without thinking about his age."

Of course Giorgio Lungarotti wasn't thinking about his age. Not about his own. Instead, he was thinking about bequeathing a great company to the three women of his life. And that's what he did. The description of the relationship between Giorgio and Maria Grazia doesn't surprise me. We all know that the alchemy of a couple is unfathomable, and that it can create indestructible, strong and fruitful ties from every point of view, even when it's a question of sharing company choices. Giorgio deserves the most credit for having tried to envision these two women's capacities, totally and justifiably overcoming the male chauvinist beliefs of a lifetime. Affection definitely played a key role, but his choice was also determined by the ability of the two women to pick up signals and embody his teachings. A beautiful blend of heart and mind on both sides.

Better to Wear Your Coat Inside Out than Take Money Away from the Company

Oscar "You're both mothers. What are your children going to be when they grow up? Do you have high hopes for them?"

Teresa "You always nurture high hopes for your child. The most important thing is for your child to be a happy human being. I have three children. Francesco, the eldest, is already working for the company—marketing, communication and exports office. Gemma has a degree in Art History and now her dream is to get a Master's degree abroad. Giuditta is my youngest and she's just finished high school. I don't know what paths they plan to embark on, but if you're asking whether they're interested in wine the answer is yes, they are. To be able to talk to young people about wine you need to find exactly the right words. Training is indispensable. They need to drink their first glasses inside the family, and kids have to get used to seeing the wine bottle on the table. In Italy wine is part of our tradition, like pasta and pizza. And you know what they say: fruit tastes better when it's forbidden. So it mustn't be forbidden. Youngsters have to learn how to taste with their senses and their culture."

Oscar "You wrote a book about this, didn't you?"

Teresa "Yes, *L'uva nel bicchiere*. It's a topic that's close to my heart."

Oscar "And what about you, Chiara? What do you think about children?"

Chiara "I have a six-year-old son. What I learned from my father and want to teach my son is that in life you can never do without work and hard effort, in anything you do!"

There you are, just compare the two sisters' answers to the same question. You can appreciate how different but complementary these two women are.

We speak openly, digressing a little, too. Both Teresa and Chiara talk about how happy they are with their children and husbands. They are completely satisfied with their families. Only Chiara, a bit mischievously, adds: "My husband's going to read this book, too..." You bet!

I insist on Chiara's son: "Your son is still a little boy, but does he know what he wants to be when he grows up?"

Chiara "He can be whatever he wants... as long as it's Lungarotti!"

That's Chiara at her best, just like Ford who would tell his customers: "You can have this car in any color as long as it's black!"

We talk about wine sales in Italy. "What do you think of the fact that in every region in Italy people mostly drink the wine produced locally? In Piedmont people drink Piedmontese wines... Is it like that here, too?"

Chiara "Yes, we sell lots of wine in Umbria, and this pleases us. Although it's true that in our country there's very little curiosity about wines from other regions. We're not very present in the GDO (mass consumer retail sector)."

Oscar "Instead, I think the GDO could actually take on the role of better distributing wine from the different regions. And it could also help to bring ordinary people closer to quality wines. They should create more specialized wine shops, hire specialized staff. We producers could help the GDO as well. But in Italy, most producers, wine shops and restaurant owners have a snobbish attitude toward mass distribution. I think the crisis is going to get lots of people to change their minds. Maybe this crisis will help all of us to be a little less certain about what's right and what's wrong."

Chiara "Come on, it's not a question of what's right and what's wrong. But there are markets in which one channel excludes another, and others instead in which the two channels live in harmony side by side. In some countries we have excellent clients in the large-scale retail channel, in others we're only in the specialized channel." Clearly, I haven't convinced her.

I move on to the topic of growth. This is a question I always ask hoping to hear about great strategies, but more often than not the answers stray into another subject. The future and the past are combined for these producers whose aim is quality. Tradition and prospects get mixed up. So I ask: "Do you plan to work to increase the number of bottles you produce?"

Chiara "We learned from our father—(she should say "my" but instead she says "our")—to always plow back the profits. He preferred to wear his coat inside out than take money away from the company. And so do we!"

Teresa "We're Umbrian, Oscar. This is the land of Saint Francis. And just as Saint Francis preached, you need very little to live on, as long as you live joyfully and with enthusiasm."

Chiara "We bought the Montefalco estate after father's death. We chose to invest in Umbria so that we could always live closer to our land. We answered a beckoning call that flowed in our veins. We make 60–70,000 bottles per year there, but in the beginning it was a major investment." These two women are in love with the place they come from, and by acting the way they do they confirm the choices their father made. Two people like them, together, would be excellent administrators of the area: I can just see them in the role of mayor and I'm sure it would work.

Oscar "Did you vote?" In the meantime Shigeru has poured the Barbera produced by Brandini in all the glasses, but they both seem to be interested in another glass of Arnus: I'm glad they like it! They're much more interested in the Arnus than in my question. Teresa is the first to speak up: "I signed up for the primaries, but then I didn't go to vote. There were too many things that bothered me…"

Chiara "I cast a blank vote."

Again Shigeru makes a timely entrance to help us to get around a thorny subject.

Shigeru "It's time to taste the third wine. This is Barbera d'Alba Superiore Rocche del Santo 2011 produced by Brandini. Intense ruby color with purplish hues. The aroma is violet, berries, some cocoa, vanilla, and even some licorice. The mouthfeel is intense, soft and velvety. You can pair it with Piedmontese *panissa, bagna cauda* in winter, robiola cheese from Roccaverano. And also with *sukiyaki* with soy sauce and sake."

Oscar "You forgot to say it's organic wine, that it comes from the La Morra hills, and that it's delicious."

Shigeru "Oscar, you know I love Brandini, but I'm not as crazy about Barbera as you are." Shigeru is particularly authoritative and loquacious today.

The Elder Sisters of a Minor Region

Oscar "Does the current scenario scare you?"

Chiara "In terms of sales the Italian scenario worries me right now. I'm less concerned about other countries, because there's still some room for improvement. We need to roll up our sleeves and forge ahead."

Oscar "So how do you see the future? Are you always going to try to increase production?"

Chiara "My goal is to make wine that's better and better and to sell it all over the world, increasing the export quota, but without taking things too far."

Oscar "So you want to take Umbria out to the rest of the world."

Chiara "That's right. This region is a gemstone, for its landscape, history, culture and traditions. Making it known to the rest of the world through our wines is our contribution to getting the collateral tourism business off the ground."

Oscar "Of course, wine is a catalyst for the territory, just as food is. That's what Marshall McLuhan used to say."

Teresa "And for the visitors who come to see us, we have the museums of the Fondazione Lungarotti, our gift to Torgiano and Umbria."

Oscar "Is that your goal for the future?"

Teresa "Yes, to consolidate the efforts made and to continue the work begun by Giorgio and our mother."

They both want the same thing, that is, to provide new opportunities and drive to a region that's considered to be of lesser importance. They imagine their future as something that continues from the present. They'll do what they already do today, but with far more experience and energy. While talking about Umbria and the future we

come to the subject of energy saving. For the past few years, Lungarotti has been producing thermal energy from the pruning of the
vineyards that covers about 70% of the demand. This means the
company is almost self-sufficient in terms of the production of the
refrigerated water used to cool the musts during the vinification
phase, the production of steam used to sterilize the bottles, the production of sanitary hot water, and the air-conditioning of the spaces
during the summer. Chiara tells us about these things with her usual
enthusiasm, and you can tell that eco-sustainability and respect, coupled with saving, are values especially close to her heart.

Once again Shigeru sets the pace and serves as a deadweight when
our conversation takes us too high up or too far off track. He's already poured some nice red wine for everyone and he's ready to tell
us what he thinks about it. But what I want to do is get my two guests
to guess the name of this wine's producer. "It's produced by a woman who became a mother at the age of fifty-four. Tuscan bred and
born. Can you guess who she is?"

They play the game, thinking about who she might be, but they don't
toss out any names. Maybe they don't have enough clues. "She's famous, she's a rock music singer. She may even be the only Italian
female rock star. Come on, can't you get it?"

Teresa "Gianna Nannini?"

Oscar "Yes!"

Teresa "No way! She and I met during ski races on the Abetone, and
then we kept meeting at summer tennis camps. At the Abetone we
became friends. We wrote to each other for many years, she'd send
me the lyrics of her songs. A rebel, totally crazy, but adorable! She's
been to Torgiano several times, also because she's taken part in lots
of Perugia-Assisi peace marches, so she's stopped in here. I'm so
glad she's producing wine, she really wanted to! I think she was born
in 1954 like us: we're all united by a wine ring!"

Oscar "Shigeru too! I guess it means that those of us who were born
in 1954 like wine! I became a friend of Gianna thanks to wine. Recently, she was my guest at the Fondazione Mirafiore in Fontanafredda and she fell in love with the place."

Teresa "How nice, I'm so happy to be tasting her wine! It'll be an
excuse to get in touch with her again."

I like the idea I had, and this stroke of luck. I devote myself nose and palate to Gianna's wine, Rosso di Clausura 2009 produced by Certosa di Belriguardo.

At this point, **Shigeru** starts in: "In this wine you can taste the features of Tuscan Sangiovese dissolved by a small portion of Merlot. The color is bright ruby red with garnet hues. The aroma is violet, ripe prune, moss and wild herbs. It has a sapid taste with persistent minerality. It's round and it slips right down. I suggest pairing it with a pan-fried beef fillet with black pepper, or an assortment of grilled meat served with mustard and pink peppercorn. It would be just perfect with a Florentine porterhouse steak. This is the best red wine from Gianna Nannini's cellar. A beautiful expression of the Tuscan territory."

Oscar "Do you like it? Do you agree with Shigeru's description?"

Chiara "Yes, Mr. Shigeru is great at making pairings. I skipped lunch and hearing all this talk about food is making my mouth water."

Oscar "Have you already decided which of your wines we should taste? We've almost finished."

Teresa looks at Chiara as if she were the one to have to choose. Chiara already has something in mind and has someone bring in their red Torgiano Rubesco 2009.

I look at the label, which has the picture of a bas-relief: nice name, Rubesco. I say so and Teresa explains it to me: "Mother chose the name: 'rubescere' in Latin means to blush. She liked the idea of using an imaginative name that alludes to a drinker's blushed cheeks, but that's also the color of a healthy person's cheeks. A joyful meaning filled with promise."

Chiara "And Giorgio immediately filed the brand name." The ebbing and flowing of complementariness. We uncork the bottles and drink noisily while Shigeru concentrates in silence. He'll start talking when he's ready. In the meantime I taste it and evaluate it in my own simple way. "Delicious!"

Shigeru "This wine is made with Sangiovese and Canaiolo grapes, there's also 10% of Colorino. The color is intense ruby red with purplish hues. The aroma is clearly violet, berries, spices, coffee, cocoa. The taste is very complex and elegant, with a very pleasant balsamic finish. Silky and persistent. It's ideal with fillet seasoned with pepper and Japanese mustard. Pigeon with black truffles and beef roast with wasabi would also be good. This Rubesco is just like Giorgio Lungarotti: forthright and strong."

We've finished and have to go now. Sicily awaits us.
We linger just a bit longer with a few more words in the cellar's large courtyard. Shigeru and the Lungarotti sisters say goodbye to each other at length. They're very fond of each other.

Income and Generosity

I look at them and start thinking about the things I'm going to write about this encounter. Two in particular: complementariness and Umbria. And then a gigantic umbrella theme above everything else: their father Giorgio. Plus a series of thoughts in random order, hard to put down in words. When you look at Umbria on a map of Italy's regions it looks like it could be the country's belly button. It's a very beautiful land and this family that lovingly gives everything it has to the region fills me with tenderness and admiration. And I keep hearing Chiara's words in my mind. I'm going to call it the Lungarotti model. "Better to wear your coat inside out than take money away from the company."
The sisters talked to us about a male chauvinist who passed the winery on to his two "daughters." This is how I see it: Giorgio wanted to pass on the heritage and protect the name and the company. With such a powerful goal in mind, he easily overcame the male chauvinist bias that the culture of his day and age had taught him, and instead he looked at his daughters' qualities, forgetting, rightly so, their sex. And, even more powerfully, he also overcame blood ties; by loving Teresa as much as Chiara. This is an important lesson.
Generally speaking, I'd say that companies that produce wine from their land combine the positives from two important economic sectors: agriculture and processing. The attachment to the land comes from the farmer's spirit, and I use the word attachment according to the correct meaning of the term. In some cases it's also a kind of good sort of "greediness" that drives a person to have more and better. The person who works the land knows perfectly well that they have a "roofless" company, at the mercy of nature's designs; so that person teaches us not to spoil the good results of a season because you never know how the next one will turn out. Attention to efficiency, innovation, and the search for commercial outlets to optimize

distribution all stem from processing, whether artisanal or industrial. But the land heavily "deadweights" the transformation, which can't be delocalized, because wine is made where the grapes are picked. So "local" production, but "global" distribution. The height of virtue for our country, as Ampelio Bucci taught us. The Lungarotti sisters have given me some great ideas, but then again I could say the same for all my visits. No doubt I'm going to find the same values in the South. Wine production promotes the development of the territory, because it creates job opportunities, and because, such as in this case, it spreads the area's culture and history. This can even happen thanks to a private museum, as well as to numerous cultural events. But it also promotes exports because when you have millions of bottles to sell and you live in a country that's going through a crisis, you start traveling all over the world; if necessary, you race around just to be able to sell, and you go looking for money wherever there is some.

I'm also amused by the rethinking of the word "delocalization" when it comes to wine: here, you delocalize when you buy a vineyard or a parcel of land just a few miles away, or even on another hill, to cover another zone in your region and make a different wine. Some people build a dedicated cellar for each vineyard, so they're sure to give the wine the attention it deserves. This is completely different from the delocalization of traditional industry, which produces where labor costs less, leaving the Italian workforce jobless.

From these simple observations you can also understand the reason why many of our hosts have worked hard (they themselves or their relatives) at public affairs, too. The winemaker knows how to look far into the future and this should explicitly be the main characteristic of the public administrator. I was hoping to find proof for one of my insights: people who have done more harvests have a better understanding about how the world works. And I definitely have.

In short: I've met wine producers capable of making money, who find it natural and necessary to act virtuously. I really love this romantic characteristic, matched with a much more concrete one, knowing how to balance the books. I like the sincere generosity that stems from the ability to earn a livelihood on one's own, thanks to one's own creativity. I like the courage that's intrinsic to winemaking. Wine, I love you.

Notes for Wines Tasted with Teresa Severini
and Chiara Lungarotti
Shigeru Hayashi

Alto Adige Gewürztraminer Sanct Valentin 2011
San Michele Appiano
Type white wine
Grapes 100% Gewürztraminer
Vinification and fining fermentation and fining in barriques and
tonneaux (1/3 new 2/3 used) for 11 months, then 6 months in steel
Production area Alto Adige

Straw color with green hues. The aroma brings out pear and apple,
followed by wild herbs, flint, pepper and nutmeg. Dry, sapid taste,
with a delicately bitter aftertaste.

To be paired with grilled dry-salted fish, mushroom salad, pickled
eel with Japanese mustard. This white wine is the perfect apéritif.

If I had learned German, I would have gone to make wine
in Alto Adige and my model would have been the wine cellar
of San Michele Appiano. Don't ask me which of their wines
is the best, they're all super. The wine we tasted during our trip
is actually the most typical of all, actually, it might even be
"the perfect white wine," which can also be appreciated by people
who don't normally drink.

Roero Arneis Arnus 2011 Castello di Santa Vittoria
Type white wine
Grapes 100% Arneis
Vinification and fining vinification in steel with prolonged
fermentation (15 days) at a low temperature; long fining *sur lie*
Production area Piedmont

Intense straw color with pale green hues. Burst of pear, green
apple, pineapple and wild herb bouquet. Dry, slightly aromatic,
sapid taste.

Pair with fish salad tossed with Genoese pesto, Catalan-style
lobster, mackerel cooked with rice vinegar and a touch of soy
sauce. Perfect as an apéritif or as a white table wine.

A very particular Arneis, not very typical, but very complex and
robust. It reminds me of when the samurais want to challenge an
exceptionally strong warrior: they can either win or lose. The same
bet is at stake when making the best Arneis, and I think it's about
to be won.

Barbera d'Alba Superiore Rocche del Santo 2011 Brandini
Type red wine
Grapes 100% Barbera
Vinification and fining in steel at a controlled temperature, short
fining process in bottles
Production area Piedmont

Intense ruby red color with purplish hues. Aromas are pleasant
with evident violet, mixed berries, black cherry and a hint of
licorice. Intense red, soft and velvety taste. Very enjoyable.

Pair with Piedmontese *panissa* (rice and beans), *bagna cauda*
(hot olive oil, butter, garlic and anchovy dip) and other traditional
recipes from the region. I'd like to taste it with robiola cheese from
Roccaverano.

A sip of this wine immediately calls for... another sip of the same wine! Truly a well-made Barbera, very enjoyable, one that I'd take to Okinawa, to the seaside, in the summer, so that I could enjoy a nice day off.

Rosso di Clausura 2009 Certosa di Belriguardo
Type red wine
Grapes Sangiovese and some Merlot
Vinification and fining after fermentation at controlled temperature, long fining in small wooden kegs
Production area Tuscany

Intense ruby red color with garnet hues. Violet, ripe prune, moss and wild herbs aroma. A hint of coffee on the finish. Sapid taste with body, and persistent minerality. Velvety wine, round and smooth.

Pair with pan-fried beef fillet seasoned with black pepper, or with grilled meat dressed with mustard and pink peppercorn. Naturally, it's perfect with Fiorentina porterhouse steak! Try it with Parmigiano Reggiano aged at least 48 months.

I like wines that were made by singers and other artists, because I always find that they've transmitted something about their art to the wine itself! This is the top red wine at Gianni Nannini's cellar: I like them both very much (the red wine that's tops, and Gianna Nannini, too!). A wine that's "beautiful and *not* impossible!" as Gianna might sing.

Rosso di Torgiano Rubesco 2009 Lungarotti
Type red wine
Grapes 70% Sangiovese, 20% Canaiolo, 10% Colorino
Vinification and fining maceration for 15 days in steel, 1 year
of fining in barrels, 1 year in bottles
Production area Umbria

Ruby red color with purplish hues. The aroma is of violet, wild
herbs, pepper, tobacco and red preserves. Fresh, enjoyable, velvety
taste. Balanced finish.

Pair with porterhouse steak or Piedmontese-style assortment
of fried meat. Excellent with risotto made with liver and red wine.

A wine for joy and celebration, also for loving, given the origin
of the word "rubescere," to blush. So remember this wine
when you want to court someone: the wine will blush for you,
and you'll be able to confidently win over the person you've had
your eye on!

Donnafugata: José Rallo
Wine Song

Woman in Flight

What a pleasant surprise it is to learn that Donnafugata doesn't mean "the woman who fled," but rather "woman in flight." Completely different, and much better. First, it's a tribute to our host José Rallo, the undisputed lady of the house here, who has spent her entire lifetime fleeing from the shadows that try to obscure Sicily's beauties. Then, it's an attribute referred to the present and not the past. So it's perfect for describing the breath of modernity and innovation that pervades the heart and mind of women who raise questions about themselves. It's also a proactive expression: it implies movement, passion, change. Lastly, "in flight" can also mean flight in a forward direction, not running away from something but running ahead of it. Like cyclists who pedal more and surge forward, forcing others to pursue them, thus triggering the miraculous effect of spurring them on. So that those who are in flight in this sense will be the first to arrive. And among this group of first comers, there will be one person who arrives before the rest. I'm aware of the fact that I've spent a whole lifetime in flight. I just love playing the part of the "uomofugato," the man in flight. I haven't always been the first to cross the finish line, but no matter, you can't always be a winner. The important thing is to always try to be in flight.
But also "in flight" in relation to my interview, because no sooner do we arrive than José Rallo takes over, accompanying us on a stroll through the Marsala estate, to help us to familiarize with the atmo-

sphere of this land and with the beauties of this particular location, which is incredibly cool despite the latitude, bright, but with a special light, new for those who rush down here from the North and aren't familiar with the wild herbs and plants of these places. "Kennst du das Land, wo die Zitronen bluehn?" (Do you know the land where the lemon trees bloom?). Goethe had much more than just this to say about Italy, but the line fits right in because on the plants here we see lemons as large as citrons together with the blossoms (fruits and blossoms growing together? Where we come from, never.) These words come to mind because on the bookshelf close to my bed there's a relatively old copy of *Italian Journey*. There's so much to learn from that book. We should really start looking more closely at our landscapes, our squares, our works of art, the way he did. But when I left off reading my book, Goethe was still in Veneto. I'm going to have to read many more pages before I get to the part that will tell me how he saw Sicily.

José Rallo is a splendid woman with the somatic features so typical of dark-haired Sicilian women, the kind of beauty you see in movies, whom you can easily imagine in a café with Inspector Montalbano, whose home is right here in Sicily. Even if you listen to her without looking at her you know she's smiling as she speaks, and that she is frantically pursuing a ton of ideas that she wants to share with us. It's clear to me from the outset that I'm not going to have a hard time taking the past, present and future of this house away with me.

José "Let's make a pit stop right away!"

Oscar "A pit stop? We're in Sicily and you're telling us about pit stops?"

José "In honor of Ferrari, which just won a race!"

A pit stop to prepare the wines for our tasting. Two whites, one sparkling wine, a Barolo and a wine from José's cellar. And then the tour. First (what a coincidence, I swear I hadn't seen it before), we stop to comment on Goethe's words written in big letters on the entrance to Donnafugata.

"Without Sicily, Italy leaves no image in the soul. Sicily is the key to everything." There's my answer. Goethe's eyes started rolling when he saw Sicily for the first time. It's easy to understand how proud one might be about a tribute of this kind, and how one might want to make it public on the door to their home!

José "This cellar, which was created for Marsala, has existed since 1851. It was founded by a Rallo, who was inspired by the English, who did so much for the wine business. I'm the fifth generation of Rallos in this cellar, together with my brother, Antonio, with whom I jointly share the role of CEO. Those were my father's wishes."

Oscar "A father with modern ideas, who didn't favor his son. Do you get along?"

José "More or less."

Oscar "Does that mean no?"

José "We're complementary, but we get along very well. Especially when we find ourselves having to deal with hard times, like now, in this crisis."

Oscar "You sell too much wine in Italy. You need to export more. Just keep thinking that more than 99% of the citizens of the world live outside of Italy. And that they look at us with envy."

We Once Had an Italy That Was Bursting at the Seams!

José "Despite the fact that my father encouraged us to export more, we had too much of a demand here in Italy. Donnafugata was born in 1983 and at the beginning we were selling 70% of what we produced in Sicily."

Oscar "So in 1983 you dropped the Marsala and shifted to wine?"

José "In 1974 my mother, Gabriella, inherited from her father the Contessa Entellina vineyard, which had to be restructured. From that moment on she, who was also an English teacher, devoted her time to viticulture, and this eventually became her greatest passion. At the age of thirty-two she started traveling the world. California, Australia, she surrounded herself with consultants and agronomists. As soon as she could quit teaching she built a revolutionary winery, with autochthonous and international vines."

Oscar "Were you here, too?"

José "No, I was in flight—that's right!—I was nineteen and the whole of Sicily was just too small for me. Women were whistled at on the streets, chased after by men on motorbikes. No one ever mentioned the Mafia, everyone depended on 'raccomandazioni,' personal references, to find a future for themselves. In the middle of all this

I was seeking my independence. I said goodbye to everyone and went to Pisa with a scholarship to study at the Scuola Superiore di Sant'Anna. I left in great harmony with my parents."
Oscar "They were modern. 1983 was the start of Donnafugata's new production, and you left for Pisa. So *you're* the woman in flight?"
The sound of José's laughter is strong and musical as she tries to get around my compliment, and then she explains: "Actually, I had always thought of my mother in flight from her past occupation. She, my *mother*, is the woman in flight."
Oscar "Who chose this name? I think it's a stroke of genius."
José "They did, the two of them together, my father and my mother. They wanted an inspiring name, so the *Gattopardo* came to mind, one of the most translated Italian novels ever, and also because of the movie, of course. Donnafugata is the name of the summer residence of the Prince of Salina and his family. It's a catchy name, because it contains the word 'donna,' i.e. woman, which always attracts interest and curiosity."
Oscar "It's a beautiful name; they were smart to choose it. But while you were in flight, did you know you'd eventually go back to winemaking?"
José "Well, in the meantime, for three years I worked really hard. I had studied at a classical lyceum, so there were lots of hurdles for me in studying Business and Economics. Then when I got to the fourth year I quit to go back to my passions: tennis, jazz, books. But most importantly, I didn't think I'd ever go back to Sicily."
Oscar "And then what happened?"
José "I came back because I fell in love with a Sicilian. One summer I was here on vacation and, while I was at a concert, I saw this guy playing the drums in a group. I went up on stage and offered him a bottle of Donnafugata. The flowers blossomed, and we got married. We're happy together and we have two children."
Oscar "Usually it's the men who offer a bottle—you did the exact opposite."
José "Actually, I was interested in their female singer, who represented everything I wanted to be. I wanted to ask her for advice, suggestions about how to become like her. I needed an excuse to talk to her, and in the end that excuse turned out to be my future husband."
Oscar "So in 1983, thanks to the fusion between two factors, the vineyard and the skills your mother honed, together with your father's experience, this new company was born."

José "Then in 1989 my father decided to stop producing Marsala completely."

Oscar "There's room on the market today for a great Marsala."

José "You're right. But there aren't any vineyards to make it. Pantelleria is another story, a nice one. In 1989 my mother and father went to the island for a short vacation. The second day, after going out for a stroll, my father had already managed to lease a vineyard and a cellar. He'd become a producer in Pantelleria. Now we make a very special wine there, which gives us a lot of satisfaction."

We're now standing under several paintings where Sicily is depicted as being completely golden. Peering out from behind it is a golden sun, and there's a woman with baskets filled with grapes, and Pantelleria, also golden, in a corner. It reminds you of something a child might draw.

Oscar "Who made these paintings?"

José "Stefano Vitale, a graphic artist and illustrator for children's books. He also designed most of our labels." We're having this conversation as we walk around the cellar, from the old part to the new one. José is eager to show us around, you should see her: she talks with her hands, smiles, but above all she talks. She speaks with a beautiful, musical voice, modulated and carefully controlled. I'd been told she's an exceptional singer, especially jazz and Brazilian music. I decide I'll ask her to sing, I want to hear what she sounds like. So I start preparing my strategy. Accompanied by her voice we can envision her family's story, we can "see" the conversations between her mother and father, we can guess the dialectics of such a dynamic and innovative group.

Communication, the essential role of communication. Today we use the word "marketing," which in the world of wine isn't suited to describing what you have to do to sell your own wines well, at the right price. All the things you have to do to get others to understand the concept of the intangible values enclosed in a bottle of excellent wine! It's all about enlightened families, brilliant insights, important turn-arounds impressed on entire wine regions, changes that have taken place in the drinking culture thanks to a few men and women "in flight" from the devastation produced by non-culture, mass production, the sheer interest in moneymaking. In flight toward tradition, toward respect, toward genuineness, toward truth. In flight from the short-term perspective, and with an eye that's long-sighted in time and space and turned toward the future, but the past, too. We've been making wine for five or six millennia and we're still trying to find the perfect wine. We make wine for a small percentage of the world population: there are six billion people out there who in the decades to come will approach the wine culture, and they'll be coming to us Italians to try to discover quality, history… in a word, beauty.

That's what we're working for. That's the message that comes from these great families, and I'll add my own, even though I'm a late-comer and have just a few harvests to my credit. Here's the essence of the intangible value that we need to add to the wine so that we can uphold the value of quality and make it known to others.

Now we're in the heart of the cellars. The original one dates from 1851; it's undergone lots of work since then, demanded by the new types of wine produced. One hundred thousand bottles were produced here in 1983. Since 1986, after the methanol scandal, the company grew until it achieved today's numbers: 270 hectares of vineyards, both owned and leased, at Contessina Entellina in Sicily, then another 68 hectares in Pantelleria. For an average turnover of 2 million euros and 300,000 bottles. The wine that sells the most is Anthilia: an autochthonous vine, Catarratto (minimum 50%) blended with other international grape varieties. But this zone has other vines, too, such as Ansonica, Nero d'Avola and Grillo.

Oscar "Do you make Grillo?"

José "Yes, only recently, and it's a very Sicilian wine. We call it Sur-Sur, like the cricket in Ancient Arabic, and we describe it as being a 'gourmet picnic' wine, meaning a picnic where you use real glasses."

We're visiting an important cellar characterized by traditional architecture, with large cement and steel vats. But what especially impresses me is the new underground *barriquerie*, a sort of immense mosque with a long series of arches held up by columns, in which hundreds of barriques lie.

For Ten Years I Sang These Notes Inside

The cellar is very big, we have to walk for a long time, and what strikes me most of all is the cleanliness and order. I just can't help

but make my usual sly remark: "It's like being in the North of Italy."
This is what I always say whenever I land in Bari and find the streets
leading into the city clean, and the flowerbeds neat and tidy. I tell my
Pugliese partners that this is why I chose Bari for the only Eataly located in the South. And every time they tell me to go to hell, and
remind me about all the great qualities Southern Italians have. So I
digress, asking about the wines produced. The white wines include
Anthilia, SurSur, Chiarandà. The reds are Angheli, Tancredi, Mille e
Una Notte... Stop! As soon as I mention Mille e Una Notte, José
stops dead in her tracks and bursts into a jazz ballad. And to think
that I'd been trying to figure out for the past hour how to ask her to
do just that, to sing. We're right in the middle of the *barricaia*, above
a suspended footbridge that seems to have been built deliberately for
the performance. José's marvelous voice is helped by the fantastic
acoustics in this place, which at this point causes us to wonder
whether it was designed for wine or for her beautiful voice. A song
that she'd heard sung once by a jazz singer who was a guest of the
cellar during a special event. A song that it took her a whole decade
to find. A song born around a goblet of Mille e Una Notte and dedicated to the forefather of the cellar. Because it speaks of mature men
and good wine, both destined in time to reveal new and intriguing
qualities. José sings, she sings the whole marvelous song and as we
listen to her I wonder whether she had planned this performance, or
whether the idea just suddenly came to her. I hope the latter is true,
and I pay myself the compliment of thinking that José is showing us
how much she appreciates our company. We continue along the way
and run into a remarkable photograph. Young Ferdinando, José's
son, a picture taken when he wasn't even a year old, cradled in a
bunch of freshly picked Nero d'Avola grapes. As naked as the day he
was born. A great picture with a great idea behind it: "vita," life, and
"vite," the vine, all in one. I know there are problems publishing
pictures of children in some countries, but I really think you should
see this particular picture in this book.
José proudly tells us that both of her children, a boy and a girl, are
planning to follow in their uncle's and mother's footsteps.
A woman in flight. An entrepreneur who's also a mother, and who
now, still youthful, turns her gaze toward the sixth generation of
Rallos... whose name won't be Rallo anymore, but no matter.

My Mother Taught Me to Smile

The stories she tells us about the years of her youth emphasize the modern education she received, thanks to her parents' open-mindedness: when she was just eight years old they sent her off to the United States to understand the greatness of a people who start every sentence with the word "maybe," and of course to learn English. In the meantime, the old Marsala cellar was given a makeover, the cultures, the vines, the methods and organization changed. José broadened her horizons in terms of school and sports, as well as thanks to her new relationships and encounters.

Oscar "What did you learn from your mother?"

José "To smile, always, wherever and with whomever."

Oscar "Smiling makes you feel good, but it also helps you sell! And what did your father teach you?"

José "I wish I had learned his strength and determination. He knew how to set long-term goals for himself, and then pursue them. But conquering those kinds of qualities takes time, more time than learning how to smile."

Oscar "Is your father the boss?"

José "Of course he is. He's the company leader, but since 2012 he's taken a step back and given my brother and me more freedom. As I told you before, we've become the CEOs here."

Oscar "Forgive me for this next question, it's something I ask all the 'sons and daughters of...' Who does your father love more, you two or the company?"

José "He loves us more, no doubt about it!"

Oscar "The answer's not so obvious. I'm not talking about your situation in particular, but in general. There are parents who answer that they love their kids more, but you can see they don't really. They never give up, they're always at work, they criticize, they keep repeating the words, 'Back in my day...' How did you feel when he stepped down? Do you like being able to act independently?"

José "At the beginning I felt lost. I went from a sectorial kind of responsibility, marketing and management control, to a more general responsibility. From that moment on I had to learn to keep my eyes on the whole company all the time, and make decisions based on priorities."

Oscar "How have you and your brother shared what you need to do?"
José "Routinely, we've kept to our old roles: marketing for me, production for him. But together we deal with sales and management control."
Oscar "Who decides the prices? For example, when you have to decide how to position a new wine, who decides?"
José "We decide together. I tend to be more of an optimist, he's more of a realist."
Oscar "The moment when you establish the price list is magical. There are those who start from costs, and others who instead start from the price they want to get in relation to the values they hope to convey."

My Father Is the Most Feminist Man I've Ever Met

We've just sat down around a nice table for the tasting when the first thing José says is that her father is the most feminist man she's ever met.
Oscar "I find it hard to believe. A Sicilian. Is that possible?"
José "He's always believed a lot in women's qualities: first of all in those of his wife, then in his daughter's and his two collaborators'. The first people he hired were always women. He has a special relationship with my brother, an incredibly loving one. They go around arm in arm and seem like two young brothers, but he's always shown he has lots of confidence in me."
We go back to the story of the "woman in flight" I have before me. She left Sicily in 1983 and came back after seven years during which she studied and worked in Pisa. In 1990 she managed to marry her Sicilian, who in the meantime had never left the island and had no intention of doing so. So she decided to dedicate herself to the only Sicilian company that interested her: her mother and father's.
Oscar "Why did you want to get married?"
José "It's a model that's part of my upbringing. I wanted to gain fulfillment through marriage."
Oscar "Did you want kids?"
José "Yes. And I was also looking for a man with whom to share important interests, such as music, traveling. My husband and I have a lot in common."

Oscar "Maybe you even fell in love with him. You never mentioned love…"

José "What do you mean by that? I told you I fell in love with him when he was on stage playing!"

I'm chuckling to myself because I managed to get her goat, but she sort of deserves it because she's gotten me accustomed to using very direct language. Whenever we talk about her private feelings she beats around the bush, so I have fun giving her a pinch. Then she tells me about her brother who chose the winery right away, preferring a major that would be of use to the business, Agricultural Sciences (in Palermo, proof that around here it's the women who are in flight). Anyway, it's their father who decides who does what. The vineyard and cellar are for her brother, management control for José. And on this theme she pulls out the linguistic repertoire of business schools, the language used by consultants. With one basic difference. It's the management control of the "owner." This is another contradiction: the property is self-managed instead of being handed over to a third party. This means creating a controller who feels moved when he or she counts the number of bottles as they grow from year to year, experiences admiration and recognition in analyzing the profitability of a company that has always made money, thanks to a *padre-padrone*, an authoritative father (I say this with a positive meaning this time), who took off like a rocket. Because only seven years had gone by since the invention of Donnafugata and he'd succeeded in putting a million bottles on the market!

As you can well imagine this piece of news excites me. So much for the much acclaimed (and often excessively praised) slowness of this trade. I love speed. I know that when it comes to wine it's impossible to be as fast as industry or retail. Here we're dealing with the land, agriculture takes time, it has its seasons. However, the fabulous story of Donnafugata proves that you can still add a little speed and a little rhythm to the winemaker's trade, too.

And speaking of pit stops, here's the first wine for our tasting. It's the 2011 Riviera Ligure di Ponente Braie reserve produced by the Durin family. I deliberately chose a Ligurian white wine. A vine cultivated and a wine produced on the other shore of the Tyrrhenian, a thousand kilometers north.

I take the opportunity to tell everyone how I chose the forty-eight wines by the same number of vintners that aren't part of the twelve I'm visiting. The product has to answer to the trilogy of Carlo Petrini, the founder of Slow Food: it has to be good, clean and right, they're the basics, but I add to this that the producer has to be a good person, someone of quality. I'm convinced that the intangible values of the people who plan them are then transmitted to the wines themselves, and that these values can be tasted, turned into a sensation that can't be classified, but that can clearly be identified.

Oscar "Do you like this Pigato?"

José "Very intriguing! Very fresh aroma. It has a long taste! It's a wine that comes from the sea." Bingo.

Shigeru steps in: "Straw color with golden hues. The aroma is filled with yellow fruit, such as peach and apricot. And it's also very mineral. It has a sapid, soft, full taste. I'd pair it with *cappon magro* the way they make it in Liguria, veal medallions in a lemon sauce, fresh cheese like Tuscan pecorino. I'd also like to drink it while eating fish sushi sprinkled with salt and lemon, or raw sea urchin with wasabi."

Oscar "Good, Shigeru, Ligurian *cappon magro* is a great, but little-known dish! How do you know about it? You know everything! José, while we get ready to taste Villa Bucci Riserva, talk to me about Sicily. Talk to me about the contrast you felt between these wonderful landscapes that move you to tears, and the people. What didn't you like?"

José "I thought Sicilians were too resigned in regard to politics and the jobs that didn't exist. And women here weren't appreciated as they should have been. Then there was the problem of the Mafia and the struggle to defeat it. A problem that was ignored, almost swept under the carpet."

Oscar "Let's get an idea of the time frame."

José "From 1990 to 1994 I lived in Palermo and you know what happened during those years. Then I experienced the years of civil rebellion and I was proud to be there. That's when I made up my mind to stay, out of pride, more than because of the interests of the family business."

Oscar "Did you rediscover your pride in your land?"

José "Yes, because the Sicilian people had finally revolted. Whenever I came back from my trips, Sicily seemed more beautiful than ever."

Oscar "However, resignation, bad politics and very little work still exist today. What's more, you're a bottomless pit that absorbs endless resources."

José "That's because of the excessive state aid, but something has changed. Lots of new companies have started up, in the field of quality food production and in the tourism sector, even in high-tech. Today women can organize both family and work. In the past ten years women's liberation has made important strides but I still don't think it's gone far enough."

I try to understand how frustrating it must be for a Sicilian woman like José. With her personal story, with her everyday comparison between a modern and innovative family and the situation of this island, which is still lagging so far behind. There are natural beauties here that are perhaps unrivaled, architectural riches that are unique in their stylistic and historical connotation. A rich and fascinating story that stems from the meeting between and the cross-pollination of the most refined ancient civilizations, and, to finish, a climate that's designed to make life and happiness triumph. But there's also the legacy of a way of conceiving the organization of a community according to a style that's not exactly democratic. Despite this island's lucky combination of beautiful things, a place that's unique in the world, a society capable of disseminating the quality of life, pleasure and respect still hasn't been completely developed. Unfortunately, in certain cases here society has rebelled against its weakest sons and daughters, leaving some heartless people considerable opportunities to carry out evil deeds.

It's hard to say something that hasn't already been said about organized crime and its capacity to spread into every aspect of life and work. But I want to bring my optimistic approach to things here, too. José says that there have been signs of ferment for the past few years, new companies, new opportunities for work and equity. Honest politics has to grab onto this hope, however weak it may be. It has to lift its eyes toward a dream, toward utopia, and begin to clothe it in concreteness. It can be done, and a piece of the road to do so has already been paved. Some honest citizens, politicians, too, have already started to do it.

Like for many winemakers in other regions, Sicily has also known how to go beyond the mediocre wines produced over decades of detachment from the land, traditions, know-how, and in fewer than forty years successful companies capable of competing with the world have flourished.

Day after day we have to plan a virtuous and totally innovative road that, I'm sure, can make Italy whole again, including Sicily, a leader, without being afraid of taking up the challenge. Ten years of hard work and courage on the part of all of us, accompanied by some good politics, might be enough. In the end we would find ourselves in a country that's very different, but at the same time very stimulating and enjoyable. We really could offer everyone the same opportunity for a better quality of life. And in this family from Marsala there's certainly no shortage of hard work and courage.

The Villa Bucci Verdicchio we're drinking is 2008 vintage, it's a good way of showing what a man who feels the call of his roots can do, someone who returns, without abandoning a personal success story, to his village in the hills of Jesi to produce the finest Italian white wines. I'm talking about Ampelio Bucci, whom we visited earlier. You can just imagine how I go on and on about Ampelio's gentleness, which José listens to with great interest. So together we taste his 2008 wine. Shigeru says the color is light straw with "pale greenish" hues. It has a ripe fruit aroma, like apricot and pear, as well as sage, orange blossoms, aromatic herbs, stone and mineral. The taste is sapid, full, round and very mineral: it's a very elegant wine that he thinks would be ideal with mussel soup with garlic and butter, grilled lobster dressed with soy sauce and rice vinegar, supreme tempura plate, and, in order not to miss out on anything, a tuna tartare and mango with wasabi. I tease him because the dishes he pairs with this Verdicchio are expensive and for the privileged few. But that's not so true either. When it comes to food you have to train people to make well-rounded considerations: there are some commonly eaten pre-packaged dishes that cost more than many specialities with quality ingredients if they're cooked at home. We at Eataly have taken very seriously our job of educating young people so that they nourish themselves thoughtfully, avoiding off-season products, learning to read labels and ingredients carefully, forgoing costly and useless packaging, and avoiding waste. In our small world of food, we're trying to prepare the population that in the future will be able to courageously act as a guide for the great changes that Italy is expecting.

José Sings and Shows Her Business Model to Others

Oscar "Do you really feel like working your ass off for this Sicily? Also in terms of political commitment I mean." Whatever way you look at it, this is the most important of all the questions today. And at this point the conversation opens up. José wants to keep singing her song to Sicilians who study and work. But she doesn't want to get involved in politics in the active sense of the term. She wants to show her business model to others, to show them there's a way.

José "I've improved at public speaking thanks to my singing." That's easy to believe. Public speaking is as hard as singing, perhaps even more so. Because you have to be in complete control of the message you want to get across.

José represents all those Italians who are disgusted by our shameful political scene and she doesn't want to get involved. She, like many others, probably cast a protest vote at the General Elections, sending a negative message. I'm not surprised, I found myself facing the same dilemma. I felt like a "stranger in my own land" before a party, a so-called progressive one, that I sometimes have a hard time recognizing and from which I'm not hearing real words about change.

José chose to start from the bottom: she sings her song and tries to bring with her people with good will, but she doesn't trust petty, short-sighted politicians. You can do politics in lots of different ways. We entrepreneurs do politics by creating jobs and behavior models.

The morning creeps toward lunchtime and it's starting to get hot. I enjoy pouring the 2006 Perlé Ferrari into my glass, and I'm sure that José will appreciate this gift, too. It's no accident that I kept it for her, a woman.

Shigeru "Straw color with golden hues. Fine and intense aroma. There's a whiff of green apple, breadcrust and spices. It has a fresh, sapid and persistent taste. It can be enjoyed as an apéritif or paired with appetizers like melon and prosciutto or chicken liver on toast. It would also go well with buffalo mozzarella with anchovies and cherry tomatoes garnished with lemon leaves. In Japan it would be ideal with fried fish bones, with a pinch of salt."

The pairings seem endless and actually trigger a storm: he mentions, among other things, smoked Norwegian salmon with sheep's milk ricotta.

José bursts out with a: "No way! Salmon with sheep's milk ricotta?!" But in the end Shigeru wins, with no need to shout, because he's incapable of doing so, and without taking back what he said. He actually raises the stakes, amazing us with "fried fish bones." *Noblesse oblige.* In this case we have to acknowledge the supremacy of Japanese cuisine. Even José withdraws and mortifies her beautiful voice that could easily overcome Shigeru's measured and monotone one. But our host once again takes over the scene by suggesting a musical combination: Bollani playing Gershwin. I give myself a pat on the back for having put together this rare blend of people, for having chosen Shigeru, for having come to Sicily. I don't think I've made any mistakes, because the value lies in the differences and in the apparent contradictions. Shigeru and José have very little in common, but around this table they have given proof of the opportunities offered by integration and discussion. If you're good then I'll copy you so that I can at least be as good as you, but if I have the chance to I'll "take flight" and overtake you. I wish that Matteo, Marcello, Camilla and Alessandro Lunelli, the cousins who run that great company that goes by the name of Ferrari, could be seated here with us now. When they were still very young, they inherited the most important Classical Method sparkling wine cellar in Italy. An inheritance that's not easy to manage. But they have been very good at doing so. This Perlé 2006 is proof of that.

I Have Never Given Out Dividends!

That was her firm answer to my question.
Oscar "Why's that?"
José "Because the company has to depend on its own assets to expand, and not just on money lent by third parties."
Oscar "But why are you still doing so little work abroad?"
José "My plan is to go to China, but in the past we were so successful in Italy that maybe we overlooked the export market somewhat."
Oscar "Now you're going to drink the king of wines, Barolo. A Barolo Pio Cesare, Ornato 2008. Pio Boffa, Cesare's son, is a friend of mine, and someone my own age. He, too, has to deal with a very difficult legacy. But he's succeeded in carrying forward an important

label and with great skill. We hardly get to see each other because he's always abroad. Now there's someone who does a lot of exporting, I'm not sure exactly how much, but definitely more than half of his output. This is a great Barolo, a rare cru: Ornato. It's also a vintage that came out really well in Langa. What would you pair with a Barolo?"

José "A Chopin nocturne!"

Oscar "Good job, that would be perfect! Let's talk some more about your plan to internationalize."

José "I want to go to China. I'd like to take three Italian wines there. Bollicine, Piemonte and Sicilia. I'd like to coach someone, possibly someone who's Chinese, and in two–three years' time get some nice export flow going from Italy. We might even be able to get the banks to finance the internationalization costs, not just the machinery and the cellars."

Oscar "Are you considering the sociopolitical situation of the country you want to export to? I see China as being the epitome of the worst aspects of Communism and Capitalism and I have an issue with that. I'll probably open, but not directly, with a franchising idea."

For the first time Shigeru speaks out without directly being asked to. This is a matter that means a lot to him, too.

Shigeru "I quite agree!" I'm sure you do, I think to myself. The Japanese aren't crazy about the Chinese, to put it mildly. Centuries and centuries of wars… and now they've even stolen a lot of their work. "Do you want to hear what I have to say about the Barolo? You can tell this wine has great structure. The color is an intense ruby red. The aroma is rose, tobacco, licorice, minerals and tar. Leather too, but not too much. It has a warm taste, full of ripe fruit with soft concentrated tannins. It can be paired with a Piedmontese dish such as stewed hare, or beef stew with wasabi, bra 'ciuc' and aged toma."

Sicily Is a Continent of Wines

We're about to move on to the wine chosen by José, which means our visit is coming to an end. But there's still something I need to understand about this land. "Are you happy about Sicilian wines?"

José "Very much so! Sicily is a continent of wines. I'm happy about the quality and the research. I'm not happy about the quantity yet. There are only a few of us producing and very few of us bottling. Only 40% of the wine produced in Sicily ends up in a bottle. The rest of it is sold unbottled and mainly goes to the North, where it has always gone. The collateral business is scarce too. We're still forced to get our corks, bottles, labels, boxes, from outside suppliers. What's more, we producers need to learn how to form networks so that we can deal with the difficulty of acting upon faraway markets." What José has to say about the need to act system-wise is right, and it's also true that we Italians aren't inclined to work in groups. We have to do some really hard work on these drawbacks because they make us miss out on so many opportunities. And we also need strong and anti-model solutions, otherwise it'll take too long to change our ingrained bad habits.

I've almost come to the end of my journey. The picture of Sicily that emerges from José's words (I'd even go so far as to say from her song at this point) is more stimulating than ever. When Sicily is capable of valorizing and bottling all the wine it manages to produce right here, then we'll have fulfilled our goal. In this dream situation, Sicily has its most formidable partner in the world: nature. In this dream the producers "in flight" don't bother anyone, they don't pollute, they don't worsen the quality of the life of the people who work there, probably actually improving it. They don't damage the natural and artistic beauties. In this dream they will truly make Sicily's gross domestic product grow and they'll sell ever-increasing amounts in the world. This dream, brought to a national level, can be the guiding spirit for other productive sectors in the same situation as viticulture, sectors that have great potential that should be exploited. Food and agriculture in general, but tourism, too, as well as design, fashion and Italian art, both antique and contemporary, in all its forms. And now for the grand finale. A few explosive questions and some amusing answers.

Oscar "Do you want your winery to grow in the years to come?"

José "Not too much, but maybe I'd like to diversify, using our brand, developing other art forms: textiles, for instance."

Oscar "When you're at home, are you a housewife?"

José "No, but I'm a mother. I have someone help me in the house. My husband decides on the menus and someone else takes care of that."

Oscar "And now for the devil's proposition: a great American impresario offers you a fabulous tour as a solo singer, but asks you not to think about wine for a year. Would you accept?"

José "Yes, I would, but only if I could bring my husband, a musician, along with me. I'd do it and I even have a name for myself already: Donnafugata!"

Oscar "Do you really think someone could get you to forget your wines? I don't think so! How many harvests have you done in your life?"

José "Twenty-three. Every single year from 1990 to 2013. Not many, but they've all been significant. And we did our 2012 harvest in live streaming from Contessa Entellina. The night of August 10 we broadcast our harvesting of the Chardonnay grape in the moonlight live. I'll never forget it!"

José's right to be proud of her winery, and she answers off the bat when I ask her to choose her wine for the tasting: "Ben Ryé!" A child of the wind blowing on a magical island: Pantelleria. I only regret drinking it without a buttress for my stomach, most people would choose a Sicilian dessert with a fresh ricotta base. I'd instead prefer some cheese laced with herbs or even a fat fresh liver cooked in a pan. As Shigeru describes it, I start daydreaming.

Shigeru "This 2010 is an extremely complex year! It's made with Zibibbo grapes (white Muscat grapes from Alessandria) and I remember when I tasted it directly off the vine a few years ago in Pantelleria. The color is bright gold with amber hues. The aroma has the scent of ripe fruit such as apricot, peaches, dried figs and candied citrus fruit. You can smell honey and minerals. The taste is delicate, aromatic, but very fresh. I'd drink a wine like this by myself, as a meditation wine."

We really do have to go now. We walk across the sun-drenched clearing in front of the winery and say goodbye to each other. We take with us the memory of half a day in crescendo: we started out with a woman who welcomed us with the mild but perfectly justifiable attitude of a "donnafugata" career woman, someone who controls her Sicilian accent and throws a few English business terms in when she speaks. But we end with a Sicilian woman who says goodbye to us warmly, who very nonchalantly lets the language of this island flow, with a sophisticated and romantic musical intermezzo in between. What can I say? The past and future of this winery are clear to me. As I leave I like to think that the story of this family's courage can be a good omen and an example for all those who feel like setting out in business.

Notes for Wines Tasted with José Rallo
Shigeru Hayashi

Riviera Ligure di Ponente Braie 2011 Durin
Type white wine
Grapes 100% Pigato
Vinification and fining cold maceration, only steel, several months
of fining in bottles
Production area Liguria

Straw color with golden hues. Vast aroma with evident fruit (peach,
pear). I can also taste honey, herbs and a pinch of saltiness. Sapid,
soft, full and juicy taste.

Pair with *cappon magro* (Ligurian salad with a fish and vegetables
base), veal medallions cooked in lemon, raw sea urchin with
wasabi, fish sushi sprinkled with salt and lemon. I'd like to see what
it's like with a fresh cheese, like Tuscan pecorino.

Pigato, Vermentino, "one face one race": that's what Italians say,
right? And indeed the family is the same. I've been told that Pigato,
in Ligurian dialect, means "Mediterranean maquis": this wine is a
creature of the sea, the wind and the sun. Could this be why I like it
so much and never tire of drinking it?

**Verdicchio dei Castelli di Jesi Classico Villa Bucci
Riserva 2008**
Type white wine
Grapes 100% Verdicchio
Vinification and fining at least 18 months in large Slavonian oak
barrels, followed by 1 year in bottles
Production area Marches

Straw color with green hues. Aromas of ripe fruit such as apricot
and pear. I can also taste sage, orange blossom, stones and other
minerals. Sapid, full and round taste. Very elegant.

To be paired with mussel soup with garlic and butter, or else
with grilled lobster and soy sauce. I think it would be great with
a supreme tempura mix.

Ampelio Bucci is a friend, I enjoy repeating it! He used to come
to my restaurant in Milan in the 1980s. He was interested in
everything, he was inquisitive. He wanted to get to know Japanese
cuisine, and the Japanese market. Now I can pay him back
for his friendship by telling everyone that Villa Bucci Riserva
is definitely one of my very favorite wines!

Trento Brut Perlé 2006 Ferrari
Type Classical Method sparkling wine
Grapes 100% Chardonnay
Vinification and fining at least 5 years on yeasts selected in their
own cultures
Production area Trentino

Straw color with golden hues. Rich, neat and persistent perlage.
Subtle, intense aroma with hints of green apple, breadcrust and
spices. Sumptuous, soft, almost butter taste, pleasantly tasty
and very long.

It can be served as an apéritif, but also with an appetizer. I think it's ideal with "fried fish bones," and a pinch of salt. With buffalo mozzarella, anchovies and cherry tomatoes garnished with lemon leaves it would be excellent. Now that I think of it, it's the perfect wine for a meal!

If I had to choose between a Ferrari and Ferrari, I'd choose Ferrari (to have with me in a Ferrari!). To me, it's one of the 2–3 Italian wineries that can hold their own against Champagne, no doubt about that. It would have been to the liking of the Kyoto samurai when they celebrated the cherry blossoms and invited their illustrious friends over.

Barolo Ornato 2008 Pio Cesare

Type red wine
Grapes 100% Nebbiolo
Vinification and fining maceration for 15 days, maturation in French wooden barrels for 38 months (70% new barriques, 30% 25 hl oak barrels)
Production area Piedmont

Intense ruby red color with garnet hues. Rose, tobacco, licorice bouquet. Light leather on the finish. The palate is warm, full, with soft but at the same time dense tannins. Structured, persistent and harmonious.

Match with strong Piedmontese dishes, such as stewed hare. Excellent with beef stew cooked in wasabi. I'd drink it with two-year-old "ciuc" Bra cheese, and aged toma.

For four generations, this cellar has produced wine in the historic center of "Alba Pompeia," using grapes from the best Langa vineyards. In particular, Barolo Ornato arriving from Serralunga, which, according to some (and Oscar is included!), produces the best Barolo of the whole designation.

Passito di Pantelleria Ben Ryé 2010 Donnafugata
Type straw wine
Grapes 100% Zibibbo (Moscato d'Alessandria)
Vinification and fining 30 days of drying in the sun, 7 months
of fining in a steel vat, 12 months in bottles
Production area Sicily

Bright golden color with amber hues. The aroma is apricot, dried
fruit (especially figs), honey and raisins. Hints of candied fruit
on the finish. The taste is sweet, but not excessively so, very well
balanced between sweetness and acidity. Soft, round, very long.

Meditation wine par excellence. But savor it with Sicilian pastry
too, cannoli and cassata. My dream is to try it with sushi
and sashimi one day: I think it would be a marvelous match!

I remember when, many years ago, I went to Pantelleria with
Antonio Rallo for the first time. What struck me the most was
the wind, relentless and very strong. This wine is the offspring
of the wind and sun, and when you pour it into the glass it's like
drinking the light and warmth of the Mediterranean. A miracle!

Planeta: Francesca and Alessio Planeta
Good Wine Is Made in Beautiful Places

Let's Try to Redeem Our Land

We started out in heaven and have ended up in heaven once more. This time we're welcomed by the unrepeatable Eden that is Sicily. It's the afternoon, in springtime, and we're bathed in the golden light of the sun as it starts to set. We're on the shores of Lake Arancio, in Belice, which brings back terrible memories about the usual mismanagement of natural disasters. But today everything seems to have been forgotten here. The landscape is of the kind that gets under your skin, inside your nose, into your heart. Your eyes are important but they're not enough to fully enjoy what you see.
On our way here we saw horses running free, their blond manes tossed in the wind. White horses running. I imagined that one of them was the white horse in the Vidal shower gel ad. The best endorsement in the history of advertising. It never gets old, it doesn't do anything it shouldn't, it doesn't cost much and it's gorgeous. I tell my two partners what I'm thinking. It really does feel like we're inside a dream, or an ad for Vidal.
In the background, on the hilltops, there are wind turbines. Horses and wind: driving forces in both cases, and always nature that generates, that gives you everything, but that sometimes takes things back. Wind turbines are a controversial subject. Some say they spoil the landscape, that they're not worth the bother. I don't know enough to be able to express an opinion about their economic advantages. As for their impact, I think that young Italian architects should be hired

to solve the problem. Italian wind turbines should be different. I'd make them the color of clouds and the sky. In Sicily nature is filled with wonders, and even in art and literature Sicily is second to none. It has, however, lost control over its most refined product: human beings. Luckily they come in a very small percentage of specimens, who have nonetheless managed to rob many others of their harmony, well-being, and quality of life. And there are always those who, like the Planetas, say "let's try to redeem our land." That's another reason why I chose to visit them, so that we can see how to do this together. We're at the Ulmo estate in Sambuca, Sicily. Two cousins, whom I am familiar with, welcome us: Francesca and Alessio Planeta. They accompany us to the table. "Would you like some pasta?"

Can you think of a more Italian way of welcoming a guest? Can you think of an easier way to chat and talk about the meaning of life? We sit down at the table and start to broach the topics that interest me, eating and drinking, naturally out in the open air, in the cool shade of a pergola, in the middle of a sun-drenched courtyard.

Here "we" is king. But the "we" of these two cousins who love each other has several meanings: it's used to refer to the group of owners (fifteen cousins), to the plural leadership entrusted to three of the fifteen, to the six who play different roles in the management, but also to the generations that are involved and that still consult each other (at least two). Lastly, it's a "We Sicilians" filled with pride and self-satisfaction for the successes achieved in the last twenty-eight years of work. The pasta is delicious, tossed with vegetables and seasoned with mint, the salad is chock-full of genuine flavors, and the strawberries were picked in the garden. The wine is made right here, and it's great. This is the Italy I love.

The story of the Planeta winery is that of the happy insight of a patriarch, the grandfather of this family, and of Francesca's father, Diego, who was born in 1940 and became a legend.

Francesca is what you might call a "turn-on." Blond with blue eyes, she tells us that her mother is English. She's wearing boots today. I say, jokingly, that she's being flirtatious, that she wants to wow a group of Norwegian clients who've been trailing her since ten o'clock this morning. She doesn't wear makeup, her hair is disheveled, she talks slowly, with a hint of a Sicilian accent. Her cousin's accent is stronger.

My Grandfather Was a Sicilian Baron

Alessio tells us that his grandfather was a Sicilian baron. He says so
without emphasis, but not because he's being falsely modest. However, he does add that: "He was a special kind of baron: he was in the
farming business here in Sambuca." We listen to his description of
his grandfather. A "modern" agriculturer, at a time when Sicily was
at the mercy of banditry, the country wasn't safe, there was a lot
poverty, and malaria was rife. In the early twentieth century, Alessio's grandfather founded a cooperative winery called Settesoli, in
Menfi, which today counts 2,000 members and has 6,000 hectares of
vineyards. In these parts farming works.
Alessio may be more talkative than Francesca, but you can tell she
totally agrees with what her cousin, who is the first to talk to us about
Diego, is saying. Today Settesoli is a giant that exports wine all over
the world. But their grandfather, i.e. Diego's father, had devised a
wholly different plan for the family. Rather than divide the estate
among the children, seven in all, three boys and four girls, he combined them all in a single, large joint-stock company.
Until the mid-1980s the family was a partner of Settesoli, but when
the third generation, fifteen brothers and sisters and cousins, including Alessio and Francesca, had grown up, it left the cooperative and
starting making wine on its own. The plan worked, and continues to
work today, because this is really an old-fashioned family. They're
always together, sharing joys and sorrows, holidays and vacations.
I'm pondering on the different modes of family cooperation we've
come across on our journey. Everywhere we've been we've seen that
the forebear makes choices based on the values of his household,
and on the qualities demonstrated by his descendants. Each of these
solutions operates in a distinct manner thanks to the science, the
knowledge and the conscience of the head of the family. In these
success stories there's always an ancestor who had the gift of socio-
economic, but especially anthropological farsightedness. I think
companies start from a product. The entrepreneur has to know perfectly well what the aim of his project is, he has to give it a shape,
substance and value to be shared with his travel companions. But
once the purpose of the business has been determined, the entrepreneur also has to know how to evaluate the people who work with

him, or else go looking for them one by one, because the survival of a business depends on the people who work there.

This is also true for family businesses. The ones that have been successful all had a leader who found the right formula and then chose his successors from within the family, combining all the roles to a tee. All the others have simply disappeared.

Sicily Was Light Years Away from the Market

Alessio "The Planeta project was created in 1985, wholeheartedly encouraged by Diego. It began by planting 50 hectares of vineyards around here. A few years later the three of us had completed our education: Francesca had majored in Media Studies, my brother in Business and Economics, while I'd studied Agricultural Sciences, and we were ready to join the company. You might recall that in 1980 Sicily was at the height of its productive phase: 10 million hectoliters of wine, 180,000 hectares of vineyard, but it was light years away from the market. All the wine was given to the cooperative wineries, which then sold it in casks and distilled whatever was left over. Very few companies sold their own wine directly to the buyer. In 1986 with the methanol scandal consumption dropped and the process that had led winemakers to produce for cooperative wineries came to an end. I was born in 1966, she was born in 1971. In those years, under Diego's guidance we created this great experimental field."

Oscar "Diego sounds like he was a real cool guy!"

"He still is!" they exclaim in unison.

They were born cousins but they became like brothers and sisters. The merit goes to their good nature, but unquestionably also to Diego's charisma, the generosity of their siblings, the fact that they all shared a great idea.

So it all begins with this grandfather, an impeccable member of the military, clearly uncontaminated by the Mafia, hailing from a territory that has always been devoted to agriculture and viticulture, but "far away from the market."

As early as the nineteenth century Sicily had 330,000 hectares of vineyards. In the first half of the twentieth century there was a lot of

Sicilian wine, but it was anonymous and it had no history. After the methanol scandal, when Italy touched rock bottom in terms of ineptitude, the wine volume decreased drastically. In the meantime Diego had completed his education. They describe him as being a daredevil, expelled from schools for bad behavior, an impassioned traveler, with very little money to spend, but capable of mingling with the high society, his rich cosmopolitan and international friends. In Spain he met an English woman and they married. At this point in the story we start to glimpse the concept of "great heritage, very little income, so very little cash flow." On the other hand, before and right after the Second World War, the rich and the poor were brought up in the same way: you didn't leave anything on your plate, you never threw bread away, you wore out your clothing and shoes before buying anything new. The rich and the poor were distinguished on the basis of their heritage, not their wallet.

Alessio "In 1985 Diego was ready. He founded this big new family business, and got Francesca and all us cousins involved. He was elected President of the Istituto Regionale della Vite e del Vino, and he started to redirect the public subsidies he was granted toward research and innovation, summoning famous scholars such as Giacomo Tachis, an enologist, and Attilio Scienza to Sicily."

Oscar "Giacomo Tachis and Attilio Scienza truly wrote the history of Italian wine. Many excellent producers have mentioned their names to us."

Alessio "That's true. So the Settesoli cooperative grew into a giant making 500,000 hectoliters of wine for 6,000 hectares of vineyard, without considering the other food activities. This is a part of Sicily that, thanks to its agricultural vocation, didn't guarantee too much money, but it did free people from need. Here, we've always been far away from the terrible vices of this island."

Francesca continues: "Until 1985, two vineyards were prevalently cultivated in this area, Trebbiano and Catarratto. When the Planetas' experimental field got started up to thirty-five varieties were cultivated, both autochthonous and international."

Alessio "Settesoli is to Menfi as Fiat is to Turin. The wine expert at the time was a Piedmontese from Alba, Torrengo, and in Menfi the enologist was like the parish priest, the mayor and the pharmacist all rolled into one. We were still part of the cooperative but we were starting to take our distance. Here's a figure for you: we had 90 hectares of artichokes. That's how many we had!"

At this very moment some salad is brought to the table and our interest turns from wine to oil. The Planetas make an excellent extra-virgin olive oil. But I should really write another book only about olive oil, because oil is like wine, it joins the land with the sky.

Alessio "We had some land right by the sea. You can imagine how tempted we were to transform that land into terraced housing, but instead we planted 100 hectares of olive trees with the olive-press right in the middle, and made our oil there." Here's an example of courage: giving up the chance to make some quick and easy money to invest in the future instead. I'm really curious about Sicilian oil, vegetables, citrus fruit, but I can't digress. "What's your business revenue today?"

Alessio "13 million euros."

Oscar "That's a lot. You're good, considering that you started from scratch."

Alessio "We were good at launching lots of projects, innovating."

Oscar "Do you earn money?"

Francesca "Yes, but we plow it back."

Oscar "You don't pay dividends?"

Francesca "The least amount possible so that we can pay our salaries, but we invest all the rest. Our partners, our aunts and uncles all lead simple lives. The real privilege is being able to live here, in this heaven on Earth! Living here gives you everything you need. Life is less expensive and you can enjoy much greater values."

Oscar "How did the first half of the year go?"

Alessio "In Italy we're even with last year, which is already a miracle. Outside of Italy we've grown 30%, but I don't think we'll be able to keep it up all year long."

I listen carefully as I taste the oils they've put on the table for me. They're really good. The flavor is that of unripe tomatoes. I prefer one of them in particular, Ulmo. It tastes like a beefsteak tomato that's been seasoned. But, true to my roots, the story they're telling draws all my attention.

Alessio "In 1989 our old enologist left us because he decided to go back to where he came from, which is where you come from. At the time Diego was traveling around Australia, and in Australia he met an amazing enologist, whom he persuaded to come back to Italy. His name was Carlo Corino, and he was a native of, you're not going to believe this, Alba."

Oscar "Him too! Discovered in Australia! Fabulous. We Albesi are everywhere. So then what happened?"

Alessio "Corino had a really interesting story to tell. He had traveled and worked all over the world, first in Ethiopia, then in Australia. Born in 1940, from the same generation as Gaja, Antinori and Diego, he had just the right experience for Planeta, because he combined the typical Piedmontese approach and respect for wine, with his experience in Australia, in the Southern hemisphere. Among other things, his father, Mariano, had dedicated his whole life to translating Bocci's *Natural History of Wine* from the Latin."

Oscar "I can hardly believe that Planeta's success, and I'm talking about one of Italy's most successful wineries, was possible thanks to the intervention of two, not one, but two natives of Alba! I feel so proud!"

Guys, What If We Were to Buy a Winery in Noto?

At this point, as they continue to take turns, the two cousins tell us about the reasons for their success: "We've handled the generational transition while maintaining the right relationship between us, with everyone respecting everyone else's role."

Oscar "Your family sounds perfect. It's almost hard to believe. How do you get results like these? Is it by focusing on the children's education, or is it only thanks to a natural respect for family ties?"

Alessio "This is what we do: we get together and present our decisions to all the shareholding relatives. Like when we bought land in Noto. We asked whether it was all right to do so, and they answered: 'Is there a project? Then it's all right!'"

Speed and trust. I like it.

Oscar "Let's go on with the story."

Francesca "The first cellar was born, for which, in 1995, we invested an amount that was equal to the winery's entire revenue. But we were paid back for our courage. And then there was the issue of choosing a name. Planeta, fine, but with or without the aristocratic title? Without!"

Oscar "Very good. Informal but authoritative. The choice you made is the result of your way of understanding life and your relationship with others. A decision of this kind, made by Sicilians, is unusual. Your excessive pride usually penalizes you. Waiving the coat of arms on the label is a sign of measured pride. Did you all agree, or was it something your father forced you to do?" I turn to Francesca.

Francesca "We all agreed. I was the first to agree. I was twenty, and I couldn't wait to take care of the PR. I didn't give a damn about the coat of arms. I wanted to talk about the wine."

Oscar "Why did you choose to focus on wine and not some other food product?"

Alessio "Chicca, can I answer that question? Because wine had forever been coursing through the family's veins. It was the backbone of our activity, even though it was being sold in casks at the time, without a label."

When You Don't Have Any Debts There's No Stimulus to Grow

They tell us the story about the funding of the investment. Francesca had a great idea (by the way, from this point on in our conversation, Alessio starts calling his cousin by her nickname, "Chicca"). While she was in Turin for an internship—she was twenty-two at the time—she contacted the person in charge of Continente (the Garosci group's wholesale distribution), and together with him and Alessio they organized direct sales, from the field to the store, of Sicilian citrus fruits with the Planeta brand. The project was so successful it lasted four years.

Oscar "So before being wine, Planeta was oranges. Are you telling me that you managed to 'squeeze' the liquidity you needed for your great new winery from your oranges?"

Francesca "Yes. I have to say that we proved to be enterprising. Of course, the oranges weren't enough, but it's thanks to them that we were able to have fewer debts."

That must have been a lot of oranges. Tons and tons of them. We're talking about 1993, I was thirty-nine and working in the Turin area. I must have eaten some of those oranges myself. This is the third time Piedmont has played an important role in the history of the Planetas.

We talk about figures now. The two cousins don't hesitate, rattling them off. In 1996, 100,000 bottles; in 1997, 120,000 and so on, on up to 2012 with 2 million and 200,000 bottles, 45% in Italy and 55% abroad.

Francesca "The company started popping, just like the cork in a bottle of Champagne! In 1998 the Gambero Rosso awarded us the Winery of the Year prize."

I reckon that if you grow 20% every year for sixteen years in a row, that means you go from 100,000 to 2 million. The growth probably wasn't that even but that's the right average.

Oscar "What roles do the two of you fill?"

Alessio "I'm working as an enologist now, because in the meantime Corino was only doing some consulting for us. He'd left us and had gone to live in Tuscany."

Francesca "I traveled around to sell the wine, at a time when Sicilian wine didn't have a good image at all. I was forced to tell people that there was more Merlot than Nero d'Avola in our wine, because there was no demand for Nero d'Avola at the time. You know, those white lies you have to tell for everyone's good!"

You Wouldn't See Fingernails Like These on One of Those Snobs from Milan

Alessio "We also decided to not remain confined to the eastern part of Sicily, and from 1996 we started to expand: first Vittoria, then Noto in 1998, then Mount Etna in 2006, and, lastly, Milazzo in 2010."

Oscar "Do you buy vineyards?"

Francesca "No, we don't. We buy land. We're jealous about our work. We like to do all of it ourselves. We enjoy plunging our hands into the soil and digging. Look at my fingernails! You wouldn't see fingernails like these on one of those snobs from Milan!"

It feels great to be sitting under the pergola. We've already finished drinking two bottles of Planeta, including a red Etna wine that's so good it made my ears twitch. And now, just to spoil ourselves, we get ready to taste the four wines I brought here for them. It's our last visit, and I swear that as of tomorrow I'm going to go on a detox from all this alcohol—no wine for at least a week. I've been drinking such good wines on this tour of Italy that I want to remember all of them, all of them being memorable, as I said before.

The first one is Pietracalda, a Fiano produced by Feudi di San Gregorio, 100% Fiano. I tell them about my reasons for choosing these particular wines, and I explain how I'm completely against blind tasting. You have to know what you're drinking, because even while you're tasting the wine you need to be able to valorize the intangible values that the producer knows how to blend in with his wines.

Alessio is a great admirer of this vine, which is also cultivated in Sicily, and by their winery, too. He says it's an important vine because it's going to spread to other parts of the world over the next twenty years. Yet the yield is completely different depending on whether it's cultivated in the clayey soil near the sea, or among volcanic rocks, such as in Campania. Francesca says she's a die-hard white wine lover, and you can tell she tastes this wine with great expertise. As we wait for Shigeru's verdict I ask them to tell me about the vineyards of Vittoria and Noto, in search of autochthonous vinestocks.

Before Buying a Piece of Land We Go See It at Least Fifty Times

Alessio "Although we're innovators in Menfi, we're traditionalists everywhere else, only local vines. In Vittoria we only cultivate Cerasuolo from Vittoria, the only Sicilian DOCG from that territory. That's where we bought our first piece of land away from home, then we planted the vines and gradually began making wine. After Vittoria, it was Noto, the southernmost corner of Sicily, which is where Nero d'Avola originally comes from."

Francesca "The exact opposite of what I was asking the company to do. No one wanted Nero d'Avola. I wanted Chardonnay and Merlot and they were planting Nero d'Avola. But in the end it worked out perfectly!"

Oscar "You'd understood that Italian biodiversity would eventually pay off!"

Alessio "Actually, we went in search of the great continent of wine that Sicily has always been. Noto was a carpet of vineyards until the

1960s, after which viticulture disappeared because cooperatives were never developed. Noto is still the only place in Italy where you can find authentic *palmenti*, cellars where agriculturers can take their own grapes to be pressed, and then pick up the must after a few hours, sometimes a whole night long, of waiting. That's a Sicilian tradition."

Oscar "Are the two of you aware of the fact that you're responsible for the spread of Nero d'Avola? Those of us who make Barolo are furious because nowadays so many people, when they go to a restaurant, order Nero d'Avola. It's become a fad. And it's all Planeta's fault!"

Alessio and **Francesca** "You mean we deserve credit for it! Besides that, there's no comparing with the average price of your Barolo! Nero d'Avola is more popular, more democratic." Just listen to these Sicilian aristocrats heckling *me*, the son of a Partisan!

Shigeru's ready for us, so the friendly bickering about our origins ends right away with no one getting hurt.

Shigeru "The first thing I'd like to say is that this is a 2011 wine and that it's made near Naples, but in a place where the climate isn't Mediterranean, it's actually more of a mountain climate. The color is an intense straw yellow. The aroma is chamomile, apricot, ripe pear, while the taste is dry, sapid, fresh and well balanced. A Fiano such as this can easily be paired with grilled shellfish, or pan-fried porcini mushrooms served with *salsa verde*, or else with fresh buffalo mozzarella, olive oil and white pepper. Anyone can enjoy this Fiano. It can even be drunk on the beach, at least, seeing how hot it is, that's what comes to mind today."

Oscar "The next wine is from Friuli and it's produced by my American partner, Joe Bastianich. He produces it on the eastern hills of Friuli." Saying Joe Bastianich's name brings out Francesca's fatal attraction for Joe. I needle her: "You're jealous because he's a TV star now and has less time for his friends."

She laughs, but Alessio takes her side again, vigorously defending her from my light-hearted teasing. I simply can't put a dent in this harmony between them.

Shigeru "This wine is also made from a single grape variety, Friulano. It's called Plus and it's from 2008. It's 14 degrees proof, meditation wine, I'd say. The color is a strong golden yellow. The aroma is ripe fruit and baked apple, citrus fruits and honey. It has a full, structured taste, but it's also elegant and subtle. It's a strong wine. I'd pair it with Milanese risotto. In Japanese cuisine it would be ideal with black pork *shiabu-shiabu* with sesame seed sauce. But it's also perfect without food, as an after dinner wine."

Oscar "There's a stroke of genius behind this wine, which you haven't told us about."

Shigeru "Ah, yes, I apologize."—He's so honest, so Japanese I'm tempted to say, he looks ready to do hara-kiri—. "A portion of the grapes are sun-dried: the producer has invented a white wine made using a process similar to the one used for Amarone. Bastianich is the only one who makes it like this!"

We eat, drink, become friends, but sometimes the conversation is slow. Maybe we just have too many things to tell each other. I'd like these young people to tell me why they were so eager to expand across the territory, in Sicily. And they're trying to help me understand the meaning behind their quest for adventure.

Alessio "What I really like is to plan things."

Francesca "Diversification is a good thing. Making wine in the territory but in a way that no one wine will maul another one!" I can tell that the two of them really want to expand, so I instinctively try to cast some doubts on their ambitions.

Oscar "What do you think of felicitous downsizing?"

But as I'm saying this I realize that it's the wrong question in the wrong place. In fact, no one answers. Their silence is the answer. Here a business can grow, there's land that has never been cultivated, there are charming landscapes that still have too little tourism, resources that are generally left untapped. It's not time to talk about downsizing yet. We should really be talking about conscious, healthy growth... And anyway everyone knows that this whole concept of felicitous downsizing is bunk. It can't exist. Downsizing is always infelicitous because in this society it almost always affects the less well-off. But now Alessio speaks up and says something really important that puts some order in our conversation.

Alessio "We're trying to redeem this land! We have to and we can. For us this would be true growth."

It's because of this optimistic desire to do something that the Planetas take the whole island into consideration, build vineyards and cellars everywhere, and go back to valorizing autochthonous vines: in Vittoria it's Cerasuolo, in Noto Nero d'Avola, on Mount Etna the red and white wines of Etna, in Milazzo, the most recent of their projects and still unfinished, Marmertino, the wine drunk by Julius Caesar. They, too, are "in flight." They've taken the longer route, pedaling their way toward Vittoria, clambering up the hills of Noto, and continuing to pedal hard up the steep slopes of Mount Etna, ready for a quick descent that will take them to Milazzo.

Good Wine Is Made in Beautiful Places

While we're talking about Mount Etna, Francesca amazes us with a fabulously simple line.
"Good wine is made in beautiful places."
They're inspired by the *genius loci* of the Latins, the pride of belonging to this land, the desire to be entrepreneurs, to innovate, to go down in history. But also by their quest for beauty: landscapes, vineyards, labels, capsules, bottles, crates. And the wine that's inside them, which also has to be beautiful. She's right: good wine really is made in beautiful places! I think so too, and I can see this in Langa. Incidentally, this Etna red is a lot like Nebbiolo. They served it with the pasta. Very good.
When we got to the salad I said people should come to Sicily if only to sink their teeth into a tomato, at which point Francesca started singing the praises of a particular kind of tomato the Planetas grow in Vittoria.
Francesca "These tomatoes are called Kamarino. They're small, but not as small as Pachino. Sweet, but tasty, too. So delicious, and besides that there are no chemical additives."
She didn't have any with her right there, but she was going to call someone to have a few of them brought over so that we could try them. And now I can't stop thinking about those tomatoes... which seem to be taking ages to get here.
Everyone knows how voracious I am when it comes to food. But when people go on and on about a particular raw ingredient an unstoppable urge comes over me and I just have to taste it. It's much more than voracity, it's what in Italy they call "gola," gluttony. It's

one of the seven capital sins, but I don't agree with that. As I watch Francesca, phone in hand, who is now doing all she can to solve the problem, I decide to kill time as I wait for the tomatoes to arrive by doing another thing I really love: crunching numbers.

Oscar "All right then, give me a few figures so that I can get a better idea about the Planeta universe but give them to me with your hearts more than your heads or wallets." I couldn't have made the two cousins happier. Alessio fires away and Francesca suddenly stops talking on the phone to join him, taking turns with her partner-cousin. Now I'm worried I'll never get those tomatoes.

Alessio and **Francesca** "Fifteen cousins, 120 collaborators, 370 hectares of vineyards, six wineries, five cellars, 2 million and 200,000 bottles, 55% sold outside of Italy, seventy countries. Ten days of vacation per year—but when you live in a place like this you're always on vacation, I think to myself mischievously. Sixty-five thousand kilometers a year of driving for each of them. A hundred days spent abroad each year for sales."

Shigeru seems astonished by all these numbers. Simona is writing them all down frantically for fear of forgetting something, and I'm lapping it all up. For me numbers are harmony. And these numbers, delivered to us this way, are music to my ears. I was so enthralled by all the numbers that I hadn't even realized the tomatoes had finally made their appearance.

Oscar "Great numbers. Besides the actual values, I liked the order you gave them to us in, and the speed, too. This means you really know your numbers." And then I do my usual song and dance routine about how important it is to know your numbers by heart, about your head and your heart, and the supremacy of mathematics... yadda yadda yadda. But they're listening carefully. They laugh when I tell them that Walter Massa even added to his list the number of banks he has borrowed money from.

Oscar "So are you going to let me taste these tomatoes, or am I supposed to just imagine the flavor?"

Francesca "Whatever you want, Oscar. You've been going on and on about these tomatoes for an hour, and now that they're here it looks like you couldn't give a damn."

The basket, filled with these red marvels, is sitting in the middle of the table where someone set it down. I don't say anything. I pick one of them up and take a bite, the way I would if it were an apple. No salt, no olive oil. I eat two of them just as they are, raw and just the way their mother (Sicily) made them.

Oscar "They're the best I've ever tasted!"

Lella (Costa) says I always say that, whatever it is I'm talking about. But, joking aside, these Kamarinos are just amazing: sweet, you can taste the sun inside them, but also exquisitely savory, you can taste the good soil they were grown in near the sea.

Oscar "Shigeru, what do you suggest I drink with these tomatoes?"

Shigeru "Bric du Luv, 2007 Barbera d'Alba made by your friend Beppe Caviola."

What luck, I think to myself. I know this Barbera like the back of my hand. This is way up there in terms of quality. Beppe Caviola, besides producing wine, is my consultant for my cellars. He's phenomenal.

Shigeru "The color is ruby red with purplish hues. The nose is violet, prune, black currant and red currant. The taste is rich, embracing, with just the right amount of acidity. This wine is ideal with *bagna cauda* and Japanese potatoes. It's perfect with roast pork cooked with olive oil and soy sauce. And it's also ideal with all aged cheeses, such as Tuscan pecorino or hard Bra."

Oscar "And with Kamarino tomatoes grown by the Planetas. You forgot to say that, you should try one."

I go back to the numbers. "How many harvests have the two of you done?"

Alessio "Twenty-three harvests since 1991. But it lasts a hundred days here, from early August to late October."

Francesca "I've done nineteen. Together that's forty-two."

Oscar "Just like Angelo Gaja, together you're equal to him. Guys, you're living in a fabulous place. I'm in love with Sicily: I love it so much, but when I think about it I get angry. You're an independent Region (I believe all of Italy's independent Regions should be abolished), you have 30,000 forestry workers, the public debt is way out of control, *clientelismo*, handing out jobs in return for votes..." I stick the knife in.

Alessio "Our adventure started during Sicily's worst years. And since then you might say that the development of viticulture and the wine market is the only positive thing that's happened around here: a breath of fresh air for our island's image."

Oscar "What do you think of the President of the Sicily, Crocetta? Will Sicily manage to make it out of this situation?"

Francesca "We like Crocetta. Before he became president he was the mayor of Gela and really changed that city's image."

Alessio "In Sicily progress comes in fits and starts. Most of Crocetta's councilors are good people. Sicily is going to make it."

Oscar "I think so, too!"

In the meantime, Shigeru has been busy pouring us another glass of red wine. He's already tasted it, and now he's looking at us to try to figure out the right time for him to speak up. I give him a chance to, moving from Beppe's Barbera to… "Shigeru, what is this? Are you serving us French wine now?"

Shigeru "Yes! I mean, no. I apologize, what I wanted to say was that this wine is 100% Merlot. But it's produced by Castello di Ama, one of the finest Tuscan wineries. It's called L'Apparita, 2006 vintage. The color is intense ruby red. The aroma is cherry, undergrowth and there are notes of coffee, cocoa and bitter chocolate. It has a rich, full, warm taste. This Merlot is one of the best examples of what this vine can produce, and it comes from a cru that's a jewel. I've been there. It's ideal with a Kobe-beef steak seasoned with green peppercorn sauce, or else with Parmigiano Reggiano aged at least sixty months."

Oscar "I've been to Marco and Lorenza Pallante's place at Castello di Ama, too, speaking of beautiful places and good wine. They're art lovers, too. Their cellar is practically an art gallery, a concentration of beautiful things, landscape, good wine and art. I'd never seen anything like it before."

Etna Rosso for Eataly? We Can Do It

If Sicily can make it then I want to be a part of it! I love all Sicilian wines, but I'm especially attracted to Etna Rosso, which tastes like Nebbiolo. I fell in love with it, although I was already well disposed to it.

Oscar "Let's make an Etna Rosso together, distributed through Eataly, I'm up for any solution. But what I'd like best is to have a vineyard and a cellar with all of us together. You make it, I distribute it. Doesn't that sound like something that might appeal to all of us? And I'd also like to find some new distribution channels for the wine. I've already started selling it in bookstores: beautiful world, beautiful people! To make it come alive, you have to liven up the shop, increase the number of clients, wine is a good go-between. I'm sure that together we can find the best solution for all of us. And on top of that, I'm going to tell you a secret. Gaja, yes, that's right, the legendary Angelo, admitted to me that he'd be willing to do something together. 'I'm waiting for you to make me a business proposition,' he said to me. We could pull him into it, if you want. Having Angelo on our side would be a huge added value."

Alessio "If you really want to, we're in! Word of honor!" Francesca smiles, to show that she accepts the idea... When they heard Gaja's name their eyes lit up.

It's time to taste the last wine. Francesca and Alessio have chosen their 2009 Santa Cecilia, a Nero d'Avola from a single grape variety that they're so proud of. They tell me it's their best wine. I thought Francesca was going to have me taste one of her white wines. When we first arrived, Simona asked her the name of the shrubbery with yellow flowers that encircles Lake Arancio. "Alastro, just like our wine!" she had said. And then she told us about how she loves white wine. So I expected a white wine, and instead they chose something more traditional, putting their stakes on their thoroughbred.

Shigeru takes a few more minutes to finish off his own personal tasting. So I use that time to think about the great fondness these cousins nurture for each other; this company is characterized by a strong, sincere family relationship. I say what I'm thinking out loud, adding that: "I'm not saying this out of romanticism, but because it really is something that has to do with economics. The creation of harmony is the key to every company's success. Successful companies create jobs. Harmony is a game of multiple equilibriums: the right combination of people, the right dose of creativity and organization, the right research into innovation without overlooking traditions, and the right attention to earnings but without losing sight of ethical values."

Francesca "We love each other!"

Oscar "Right, we can see it, and we can even taste the fact that you love each other in your wines. So I'd add to that fabulous thing you said before that good wine is made by people who love each other."

Alessio "I'd like to know what Mr. Hayashi thinks about our Nero d'Avola..."

Shigeru "Yes, I'm ready now. The color is intense ruby red with purplish hues. The nose is prune, black cherry, citrus fruits and licorice. It has a structured, strong, as well as velvety taste. It's a balanced, pleasant wine with a very long finish. It seems younger than it is. I'd suggest pairing it with meat couscous, grilled lamb served with Japanese mustard, or else tiny slices of tender beef with soy sauce. Nero d'Avola is an exceptional grape variety, one of the best red grapes in Italy!"

Oscar "Let's not exaggerate now!... A great grape variety—I'm imitating him—some things should only be said about Nebbiolo!"

I manage to avoid getting hit on the head with a Kamarino. Francesca picks one up and pretends to throw one at me... but she's laughing. Alessio, as usual, is more self-controlled.

Alessio "As for me, as you can probably guess, I agree with Shigeru. I'm going to give you a bottle of this 2009 vintage. Forget about it in the cellar for about five or six years and then drink it. Remember to call me in 2019 and tell me what you think."

From One Heaven to Another

I'll call you before then, Alessio, you can bet on it. I'm not going to let this idea about making Etna wines slip away. This is what I'm thinking, although I don't say it out loud. I like the idea that a new business can be born from this trip for the book.

And so our journey comes to an end: we started out in the heaven of Valle d'Aosta, and end here in this Sicilian Eden, after having traveled through other heavens, eight Italian regions, one marvel after another. There are lots of things that could be said by way of conclusion. But one above all fills my mind; my gratitude for the most important partner that we Italians, all of us, have: the territory.

What I mean by this is the landscape, the nature, the soil, the sea, the art, the history, the civilizations that have evolved here in this country. A partner that has diversified its investments well. Right now this partner can't be too satisfied with what we have given back to it. In some cases we've poisoned and made our landscape ugly, we've abandoned our museums, our churches, our castles, we've left precious land uncultivated, we've forgotten our culinary traditions and haven't always known how to valorize them, and, our capacity to welcome tourists doesn't come anywhere close to what it should be with the great beauty we have to offer. We need good politics to figure things out so these failings can be remedied, because this partner of ours would be willing to let us work on our heritage asking only for the intrinsic growth of this country in return.

But politics alone isn't enough. Actually, I'd like it not to be too invasive. All it needs to do is set up the conditions whereby individual potential can be released. We're the ones that have to roll up our sleeves. We entrepreneurs, and workers everywhere. We need to stop complaining, waiting for someone to save us, crying out "it's all the government's fault!" All of us, myself included, have to put more effort into our work, more courage. And this will happen, I'm sure of it. Our partner, the territory, will find the right way to spur us on. In the meantime, we don't have to start all over again. This trip has shown me that there are people with plenty of courage. People who walk forward with their heads held high, but that every now and again turn around so they remember where we have all come from.

Notes for Wines Tasted with Francesca and Alessio Planeta
Shigeru Hayashi

Fiano di Avellino Pietracalda 2011 Feudi di San Gregorio
Type white wine
Grapes 100% Fiano
Vinification and fining fermentation at controlled temperature,
fining for 4–5 months in steel on its own yeasts
Production area Campania

Intense straw color. The aroma expresses chamomile, apricot, ripe
pear and wild herbs (chamomile). Pleasant minerality. Dry, sapid,
fresh and well-balanced taste.

It can be paired with hot fish appetizers, for example, grilled
shellfish. I see it as going well with porcini mushrooms cooked
on a griddle with *salsa verde*. Try it with buffalo mozzarella,
olive oil and white pepper.

What a beautiful wine and what a beautiful story! The Ancient
Romans were already familiar with it, in fact, Fiano comes from the
word "apianum," that is, "bees," because it's a sweet type of grape
that these insects really like!
We're forty minutes away from Naples but it feels like we're
in the mountains. The Mediterranean climate is far from here
and the white wines are very acidic: almost like the ones made
in Alto Adige!

Plus Bastianich 2008
Type white wine
Grapes 100% Friulano
Vinification and fining 10% of the bunches are submitted
to a period of drying in order to concentrate the notes of fruit
and the aromas
Production area Friuli Venezia Giulia

Bright golden yellow color. The aroma expresses ripe fruit and
baked apple, citrus fruit and honey. Nice almond note on the
finish. The taste is full, structured, powerful but elegant and subtle,
too. Long aftertaste.

To be served with Milanese risotto with beef marrow. I'd drink it
while eating black pork *shiabu-shiabu* seasoned with sesame seed
sauce. But it's also perfect with Zibello culatello and hard cheese,
or else on an empty stomach.

A spectacular Tocai (even if we're not allowed to use that name for
it). Joe had the brilliant idea of drying a part of the grapes: by doing
so, he invented "white Amarone"! It's the only white meditation
wine I know of.

Barbera d'Alba Bric du Luv 2007 Ca' Viola
Type red wine
Grapes 100% Barbera
Vinification and fining 15–18 days of maceration at controlled
temperature, 16–17 months in barriques
Production area Piedmont

Ruby red color with purplish hues. The immediate aroma is violet,
prune, black currant and red currant. I can also smell a hint of
white chocolate on the finish. The taste is rich, embracing, with just
the right amount of acidity, round, persistent.

Pair with Piedmontese *bagna cauda* (hot olive oil, butter, garlic and anchovies dip) and Japanese potatoes. Perfect with roast pork cooked in olive oil and soy sauce. Aged cheese like Tuscan pecorino.

Beppe Caviola is one of Italy's best and most famous enologists (he's well known in Japan, too) and he always says that being an enologist has helped him to make his best wines! Bric du Luv is a "contemporary" Barbera: direct, mellow, refined.

L'Apparita 2006 Castello di Ama
Type red wine
Grapes 100% Merlot
Vinification and fining 4 weeks in contact with the skins, 18 months of fining in barriques that are half new, half second passage
Production area Tuscany

Intense ruby red color. The aroma is of cherries, hints of undergrowth, wild cherry, notes of coffee, cocoa and bitter chocolate. The taste is rich, full, warm. Embracing aftertaste.

Pair with mixed fried meat and porcini mushrooms. It would be a perfect match with a Kobe-beef steak and green peppercorn sauce. Or else serve it with Parmigiano Reggiano aged for at least 60 months.

This is the most famous, popular (and expensive) Merlot in Italy. A gem for those who love this great vineyard. Castello di Ama wanted to tell the world that Tuscany doesn't just mean Chianti, and from the heart of Chianti he succeeded in making himself heard.

Noto Santa Cecilia 2009 Planeta
Type red wine
Grapes 100% Nero d'Avola
Vinification and fining 12 days in contact with the skins, 14 months
in second and third passage *Allier barriques*
Production area Sicily

Intense ruby red color with purplish hues. Prune, black cherry,
citrus fruit, licorice and graphite aroma. The taste is structured,
strong, but also velvety and very enjoyable. Fresh tannins and long
finish.

Pair it with meat couscous, with grilled lamb and Japanese mustard,
or with tender slices of beef dressed with soy sauce. Also perfect
with medium-aged cheese.

A great Sicilian red wine! The whole soul of Nero d'Avola is right
here in this unforgettable wine. It tastes of the earth, the sea,
history. I'd say that together with Nebbiolo and Sangiovese,
Nero d'Avola is Italy's greatest black grape.

Summary

I have always felt an unbridled love for summaries. Summing things up has by now almost become a weakness of mine. I already confessed in the previous chapters that when I was a student I would make feverish last-minute use of the quick study guides known as "Bignami," the Italian version of Cliff Notes, in every possible subject. I have to admit that I sometimes studied for oral and written exams just by using those legendary booklets. And my grades were actually pretty good.

At the end of every meeting, I can't help taking a blank sheet of paper and writing down a summary. The things we've decided, under the title, naturally, and in order of priority. This is a crucial feature in a good summary: order of priority, chronological order, or some other logical order, whose purpose is to help me understand, remember and then carry out the things that we resolved to do. The summary has to be short and simple. So this summary as well, which I can't save you from (but, please, promise not to read it before the rest of the book!), will have to have all the features of a useful summary: brevity, simplicity and order. I've thought of ten items, but since I don't want to seem presumptuous, I've numbered them from one to nine... and turned the last number into a zero.

1. Wine. It's even more important to me today than when I first started out. It has become crucial. And I'm now sure that wine is crucial to Italy's future, identity and success.

2. Courage. These producers are beautiful people, who feel the duty to work for the good of Italy. They're generous, they have

dreams for the future. They've understood the mysterious rules of the process that leads to beauty and can help bring about a New Italian Renaissance. They've told us stories about courage, which they put to good use as each of them took their first steps however different they may have been. Stories that can be of use to us and help us to become more courageous. Courage can be infectious.

3. The land. There's our real partner. We have had the luck to be born in the most beautiful place in the world. Now we need to be forgiven for our luck. We owe our partner, the land, respect. Let's listen to what the land tells us. Let's be proud of it, let's tell it to the world.

4. Pride. I've come across an involving kind of pride. It is pride born from the values of civilization and history that have influenced us! The right amount of pride offers the capacity to understand the path that needs to be taken, our heads held high, bolstered by our country's beauty, toward the future.

5. Madness. I've discovered a poetics that might appear to be madness, but is poetry instead. Let's call it sheer madness. The truth of the matter is that this very "open" vision of the rudimentary process that leads to the creation of wine is the offspring of historical roots and a sound humanistic culture, and it also involves an excellent knowledge of numbers. An apparently twofold identity that's loved by the world.

6. Generations. Daughters and sons who become mothers and fathers and then grandparents. In the meantime the quality of the wine grows. Relationships, some good, some bad, between generations that were born and grew up in different scenarios, whose aim is to create the perfect wine... which will always come with the next harvest. This, too, will be the offspring of successive generations. 2008 is the child of 1982, which in turn is the child of 1961.

7. Politics. Master winemakers are tuned in to politics and are fully aware of already making political moves by creating a product that represents the national identity, and by traveling around the world to talk about it and to sell it. Some of them are ready, in my opinion, to turn their skills into an experience available to the whole territory, not to their vineyards alone.

8. The past. There can be no future without a deep-seated knowledge of and a healthy respect for the past. The past is an immense

heritage of plain ideas put into practice, to be made available to the future.

9. The future. There's optimism, there's hope. There's the awareness that the future is the world. Seven billion human beings evermore ready to enjoy Italy's unique beauty. Quality wine producers are a model for the future.

... But first and foremost:

0. Love. There's love. There's a lot of love in people who make quality wine. It's a passionate love for the land, for fathers and mothers... and for their children. A love so great I can't help saying: "Wine, I love you."

The Things Said in This Book
Memorabilia

"I Became a Wine Expert While Looking at Myself in the Mirror."
(Cit. Costantino Charrère), p. 41

"Doing, Knowing How to Do, Knowing How to Get Someone Else
to Do Something, Making Something Known."
(Cit. Clotilde Rei Gaja), p. 61

"He Who Knows How to Drink, Knows How to Live."
(Cit. Angelo Gaja), p. 67

"At the Heart of Quality Lies Scarcity."
(Cit. Beppe Rinaldi), p. 77

"Wine Is the Balancing Point above the Madness."
(Cit. Walter Massa), p. 104

"The Land Is the Only Asset That Can't Increase in Quantity."
(Cit. Marilisa Allegrini), p. 136

"Nature Gives Us Everything, Every Now and Again
It Has the Right to Take Something Back."
(Cit. Josko Gravner), p. 166

"As Long as I'm Enjoying Myself I'll Keep on Working."
(Cit. Piero Antinori), p. 194

"My Dream Is to Find Another Ribot!"
(Cit. Niccolò Incisa della Rocchetta), p. 223

"Thinking Local, Acting Global."
(Cit. Ampelio Bucci), p. 235

"That Taste We've Become Accustomed to Is Our *Madeleine*."
(Cit. Teresa Severini), p. 262

"Better to Wear Your Coat Inside Out than Take Money
Away from the Company."
(Cit. Chiara Lungarotti), p. 264

"My Mother Taught Me to Smile."
(Cit. José Rallo), p. 283

"Let's Try to Redeem Our Land."
(Cit. Alessio Planeta), p. 298

"Good Wine Is Made in Beautiful Places."
(Cit. Francesca Planeta), p. 310

Lastly, Here Are
Six People Who Help Me Have More Courage

"To suffer from courage is the most beautiful disease of all."
Renato Zero

"I'll take you away with me.
We'll stand this world upon its head."
Lorenzo Jovanotti

"So few of us make love, put our hearts into it. I can see you're
there and for the rest of my life I want you."
Gianna Nannini

"You need the courage to say that certain ideological criteria
have to be put aside."
Matteo Renzi

"There was a man who always walked ahead in a straight and
determined way, but every now and again he would turn his head
around to look behind him. When he was asked why, he replied:
'If I don't look back, I won't be heading in the right direction.'"
Tonino Guerra

"What will save us will never be what we have jealously guarded
from the ravages of time, but what we have allowed to change,
so that in a new era it may become itself once more."
Alessandro Baricco

The Wines (and Beers) Tasted

Ribolla Gialla Anfora 2006 Gravner, p. 180

Riviera Ligure di Ponente Braie 2011 Durin, p. 294

Roero Arneis Arnus 2011 Castello di Santa Vittoria, p. 273

Rosso di Clausura 2009 Certosa di Belriguardo, p. 274

Rosso di Torgiano Rubesco 2009 Lungarotti, p. 275

Roycello Fiano 2010 Tormaresca, p. 122

Sagrantino di Montefalco 25 Anni 1999 Arnaldo Caprai, p. 148

Solaia 2009 Marchesi Antinori, p. 205

Sterpi 2009 Vigneti Massa, p. 228

Tignanello 2009 Marchesi Antinori, p. 74

Torgiano Rosso Rubesco Vigna Monticchio Riserva 2005
   Lungarotti, p. 54

Trento Brut Perlé 2006 Ferrari, p. 295

Valle d'Aosta Chardonnay Cuvée Bois 2009 Les Crêtes, p. 73

Valle d'Aosta Fumin 2008 Les Crêtes, p. 55

Verdicchio dei Castelli di Jesi Classico Superiore 2011
   Fulvia Tombolini, p. 202

Verdicchio dei Castelli di Jesi Classico Villa Bucci Riserva 2004,
   p. 252

Verdicchio dei Castelli di Jesi Classico Villa Bucci Riserva 2008,
   p. 295

Vermentino di Sardegna Opale 2011 Mesa, p. 52

Viognier 2011 Calatrasi e Micciché, p. 147

Translator's Notes

Silvio Berlusconi (1936) is an Italian politician, entrepreneur, media tycoon, who served three times as Prime Minister of Italy, from 1994 to 1995, 2001 to 2006 and 2008 to 2011. (p. 18)

The line "where the River Piave murmured" (il Piave mormorò) is taken from an Italian patriotic song written after the Battle of the Piave River in 1918. (p. 18)

The Lega Nord (Northern League for the Independence of Padania) is a federalist and regionalist Italian political party founded in 1991 that especially strives for fiscal federalism and greater regional autonomy, especially for the northern regions. (p. 18)

Cesare Pavese (1908–1950) was a major Italian poet, novelist and translator (among others, he translated *Moby Dick* and *A Portrait of the Artist as a Young Man* into Italian) from Turin. (p. 19)

La Stampa is an Italian daily newspaper published in Turin. (p. 19)

Domenico Modugno (1928–1994), Italian singer-songwriter, wrote many songs, including one that went *Siamo sempre in tre, tre briganti e tre somari*. However, he is probably most famous for his 1958 song *Volare*, translated into many languages, including English, and sung by such artists as Dean Martin, David Bowie, and many others. (p. 28)

ISEF (Istituto Superiore di Educazione Fisica), a college-level institution that trained physical education teachers in Italy. (p. 32)

FIVI (Federazione Italiana Vignaioli Indipendenti), Italian Federation of Independent Winemakers. (p. 35)

Carlo Petrini (known as Carlin) (1949), popular Piedmontese
   founder of the International Slow Food Movement and journalist.
   (p. 35)
"Scandalo del metanolo," methanol wine adulteration scandal that
   broke out in March 1986 in Italy, when a series of deaths were
   said to have been caused by methanol poisoning. (p. 50)
Enzo Biagi (1920–2007), popular Italian journalist, writer and TV
   personality. (p. 58)
Giovanni Soldini (1966), world-renowned Italian sailor. (p. 59)
Cavaliere del Lavoro della Repubblica, Order of Merit for Labor:
   this is the highest honor that the Italian President awards each
   year to twenty-five entrepreneurs who have distinguished
   themselves most in their field of business. (p. 68)
Pier Luigi Bersani (1951), Italian politician, leader of the Italian
   Democratic Party from 2009 to 2013. (p. 71)
Giuseppe Piero Grillo, known as Beppe (1948), Italian comedian,
   political activitist, blogger, and founder of the political Five Star
   Movement in 2009. (p. 71)
Beppe Fenoglio (1922–1963), Italian novelist and playwright from
   Alba (Piedmont). (p. 77)
Pier Paolo Pasolini (1922–1975), Italian film director, poet, writer
   and intellectual. (p. 79)
Giorgio Gaber (1939–2003), popular Italian singer-songwriter,
   actor and playwright. The song *Quando è moda è moda*
   is a critique of contemporary society. (p. 79)
Tonino Guerra (1920–2012), Italian concentration camp
   survivor, poet, writer and screenwriter. (p. 96)
Giuseppe Pellizza da Volpedo (1868–1907), Piedmontese
   Neo-Impressionist painter. (p. 104)
Vasco Rossi (1952), Italian singer-songwriter. A "dangerous life"
   is just one of the catchphrases of his songs. The song *Sally* goes:
   "Perché la vita è un brivido che vola via, è tutto un equilibrio
   sopra la follia." (p. 113)
Matteo Renzi (1975), Mayor of Florence since 2009, leader
   of the Italian Democratic Party since 2013. (p. 117)
Comunione e Liberazione, secular ecclesial movement within
   the Catholic Church; "Ciellini" is the nickname given to its
   members. (p. 135)

Bettino Craxi (1934–2000), leader of the Italian Socialist Party from 1976 to 1993, Italian Prime Minister in the 1980s. (p. 165)

Ugo Tognazzi (1922–1990), popular Italian film, TV, and theater actor, director, and screenwriter. (p. 182)

Mario Monti (1943) is an Italian economist who served as the Prime Minister of Italy from 2011 to 2013, leading a government of technocrats in the wake of the Italian debt crisis. (p. 195)

"Dal letame nascono i fior" were the words sung by Fabrizio De André, one of Italy's top singer-songwriters, also famous for releasing an album inspired by American poet Edgar Lee Masters' *Spoon River Anthology.* (p. 201)

Giosuè Carducci (1835–1907), major Italian poet, and the first Italian to win the Nobel Prize for Literature (1906). The lines are from the poem *Davanti a San Guido* and read: "Cipressi che a Bolgheri alti e schietti van da San Guido in duplice filar…" (p. 206)

Il Gattopardo, a novel (English translation: *The Leopard*) set in Sicily written by Giuseppe Tomasi di Lampedusa. In 1963 the novel was made into an award-winning film directed by Luchino Visconti, starring Burt Lancaster, Claudia Cardinale and Alain Delon, among others. (p. 279)

Stefano Bollani (1972), top Italian jazz pianist. (p. 290)

These producers are beautiful people, who feel the duty to act for the good of Italy. They're generous, they have dreams for the future. They've understood the mysterious rules of the process that leads to beauty and can help bring about a New Italian Renaissance. They've told us stories about courage, which they put to good use as they each took their first steps however different they may have been. Stories that can be of use to us and help us to become more courageous. Courage can be infectious.

Costantino Charrère
The "Rich" Son of a Poor Culture

Costantino Charrère
as he points "heaven" out to me.

Angelo Gaja
Quality Personified

Angelo Gaja at the University of Food Science in Pollenzo:
"Agriculturers are proud of their work."

Beppe Rinaldi
Blessed among Women

Beppe Rinaldi in his yard:
"Barriques are just not a part of the Langhe."

Walter Massa
Smiling Eyes, Embracing Arms

Walter Massa in his kitchen.
We were on our sixth wine by then.

Marilisa Allegrini
When I Was Eighteen I Told My Father
He Couldn't Depend on Me

Marilisa Allegrini is seated between us,
in the "Mascheroni" Room of Villa della Torre:
"The world of Italian wine is beautiful."

Josko Gravner
Little Is Good: My Father Was Right

Josko Gravner in the tasting room of his wine cellar:
"This is a place where many wars have been waged."

Piero Antinori
I Was Lucky to Experience the Forty-Five Most Beautiful Years in the History of Wine

Piero Antinori standing between us,
in his new cellar in Bargino:
"There's a whole world around us."

Niccolò Incisa della Rocchetta
I Live in the Hope of Finding Another Ribot

Niccolò Incisa della Rocchetta
in the large reception hall of his wine cellar in Bolgheri.
I managed to get the father of Sassicaia to drink Lambrusco.

Ampelio Bucci
A Man as Gentle as His Hills

Ampelio Bucci in the Pongelli estate of Ostra Vetere:
"You have to be crazy like me to buy old vineyards."

Teresa and Chiara
The Miracle of Complementariness

Teresa Severini and Chiara Lungarotti
in the tasting room of their wine cellar in Torgiano:
"We have the same mother, so we're half-sisters."

José Rallo
Wine Song

José Rallo sings in the barriquerie
of her Marsala wine cellar:
"My singing has helped me to improve."

Ferdinando-Bacchus

"Young Ferdinando, José's son,
a picture taken before his first birthday, cradled
in a sea of freshly picked Nero d'Avola grapes.
As naked as the day he was born. A great picture
with such a great idea behind it that I asked José to send me a copy.
I'd like to use it because it depicts a symbolic idea: 'vita,' life,
and 'vite,' the vine, all in one" (cit. p. 282). Photo L. Pomara.

Francesca and Alessio Planeta
Good Wine Is Made in Beautiful Places

Francesca and Alessio Planeta in the Ulmo estate,
in Sambuca, Sicily: "Would you like some pasta?"

There's a lot of love in people who make good quality wine.
It's a strong love for the land, for fathers, for mothers... children.
A love so great that I can't help but say: "Wine, I love you."

Oscar Farinetti at Antinori's estate, with the glasses empty before him.

Shigeru Hayashi at the Planeta estate, attentive and focused
in exquisitely Japanese style.

Simona Milvo photographed by Franco Borrelli
at Eataly in Turin. It's morning, the children's food education
course is about to start.